Hunab Ku

Hunab Ku

⊷77⊶
Sacred Symbols for Balancing Body and Spirit

Karen Speerstra & Joel Speerstra

THE CROSSING PRESS
Berkeley | Toronto

Copyright © 2005 by Karen Speerstra and Joel Speerstra

All rights reserved. No part of this book may be reproduced in any form, except brief excerpts for the purpose of review, without written permission of the publisher.

The Crossing Press
A Division of Ten Speed Press
P.O. Box 7123
Berkeley, California 94707
www.tenspeed.com

Distributed in Australia by Simon & Schuster Australia, in Canada by Ten Speed Press Canada, in New Zealand by Southern Publishers Group, in South Africa by Real Books, and in the United Kingdom and Europe by Airlift Book Company.

Cover design by Nancy Austin
Interior design by Jeff Puda

Library of Congress Cataloging-in-Publication Data
Speersta, Karen.
  Hunab Ku : 77 sacred symbols for balancing body and spirit / Karen Speerstra and Joel Speerstra.
             p. cm.
  Includes bibliographical references and index.
  ISBN-10: 1-58091-168-4
  ISBN-13: 978-1-58091-168-9
  1. Divination. 2. Numerology. 3. Signs and symbols. 4. Chakras. 5. Maya cosmology. I. Speerstra, Joel. II. Title.
  BF1761.S64 2005
  133.3'3—dc22
             2004026850

First printing, 2005
Printed in Singapore

1 2 3 4 5 6 7 8 9 10 — 09 08 07 06 05

CONTENTS

✸

Acknowledgments / viii
Introduction / x

✸

Part I: RED / 1

1 **Great Bear** (*Solitude*)
2 **Ram** (*Risk*)
3 **Scorpion** (*Conflict*)
4 **Father** (*Logic*)
5 **Earth** (*Matter*)
6 **Womb** (*Gestation*)
7 **Serpent** (*Awakening*)
8 **Weaver-Warrior** (*Survival*)
9 **Labyrinth** (*Initiation*)
10 **Peacock** (*Insight*)
11 **Ouroboros** (*Unconsciousness*)

Part II: ORANGE / 45

12 **Sun** (*Success*)
13 **Venus** (*Fertility*)
14 **Lioness** (*Protector*)
15 **Mother** (*Intuition*)
16 **Water** (*Movement*)
17 **Child** (*Birth*)
18 **Meander** (*Reversal*)
19 **Player** (*Sensuality*)
20 **Mountain** (*Revelation*)
21 **Hummingbird** (*Vitality*)
22 **Giant** (*Control*)

Part III: YELLOW / 89

23 **Star** (*Inspiration*)
24 **Twins** (*Androgyny*)
25 **Virgin** (*Perfectionism*)
26 **Artist** (*Creativity*)
27 **Fire** (*Energy*)
28 **Youth** (*Growth*)
29 **Triangle** (*Harmony*)
30 **Trickster** (*Confusion*)
31 **Wheel** (*Change*)
32 **Dove** (*Peace*)
33 **Dragon** (*Fear*)

Part IV: GREEN / 133

34 **Constellation** (*Community*)
35 **Centaur** (*Action*)
36 **Dolphin** (*Addiction*)
37 **Healer** (*Wholeness*)
38 **Air** (*Breath*)
39/39 **Hunab Ku** (*Lover/Relationships*)
38 **Cross** (*Connection*)
37 **Bard** (*Song*)
36 **Bridge** (*Passage*)
35 **Eagle** (*Courage*)
34 **Phoenix** (*Hope*)

Part V: BLUE / 177

33 **Saturn** (*Blockage*)
32 **Water Bearer** (*Service*)
31 **Goat** (*Practicality*)
30 **Teacher** (*Knowledge*)
29 **Sound** (*Vibration*)
28 **Adult** (*Work*)
27 **Ankh** (*Life*)

26 **Magician** (*Power*)
25 **Boat** (*Journey*)
24 **Pelican** (*Sacrifice*)
23 **Winged Dog** (*Guardian*)

Part VI: INDIGO / 221

22 **Moon** (*Dreams*)
21 **Bull** (*Strength*)
20 **Balance** (*Choice*)
19 **Counselor** (*Nurturing*)
18 **Light** (*Imagination*)
17 **Wise Old One** (*Rest*)
16 **Square** (*Opening*)
15 **Shaman** (*Ecstasy*)
14 **Chalice** (*Quest*)
13 **Vulture** (*Death*)
12 **Sphinx** (*Time*)

Part VII: VIOLET / 265

11 **Universe** (*Consciousness*)
10 **Honeybee** (*Emotions*)
9 **Scarab** (*Manifestation*)
8 **Mystic** (*Wonder*)
7 **Vision** (*Understanding*)
6 **Released Soul** (*Rebirth*)
5 **Double Spiral** (*Infinity*)
4 **Angel Guide** (*Message*)
3 **Crown** (*Reward*)
2 **Owl** (*Wisdom*)
1 **Unicorn** (*Unity*)

Symbol Readings / 309
Bibliography / 318
Index / 326

ACKNOWLEDGMENTS

One colorfully painted scene on a Late Classic Mayan vase shows several seated scribes surrounded by baskets of codices. The writers, with bundles of quetzal-feathered pens sticking out of their hair, are holding up pottery cups and "tipping a few." This depicted ceremony was called "cleansing of the books."

We feel that's what The Crossing Press did. They took our art and our manuscript and thanks to Jo Ann Deck's keen eye and early enthusiasm as the publisher, and Brie Mazurek's kind and careful editorial management of all aspects of our book's life, this is the handsome result. Furthermore, we are indebted to Shirley Coe, our diligent copyeditor, who asked dozens of the right questions and painstakingly waded through layers of detail on every page, and quite literally, like the early Mayans, "cleansed" it. We are also very grateful to the cover designer, Nancy Austin, and to Jeff Puda, who masterfully crafted the pages of this *hun*—this book—which we have held in our minds for roughly thirteen years, from inception to fulfillment, and now, together, we can hold in our hands. We raise our cups to you all.

Those early Mayan writers, or *ah ts'ib*, were also called *ah ku'u hun*, "keepers of the holy books." We thank these esteemed calligraphers, who brushed red hematite paint onto bark paper and made careful gridlines for their intricate drawings. Without them, the Hunab Ku design would have disappeared. And we thank all the other ancient artists, sculptors, builders, and keepers of the seventy-seven sacred symbols that found their way into *Hunab Ku*.

We traded Mayan quill pens and conch-shell inkpots for drawing pens and Photoshop. Together, we worked and reworked this "codex," often scrubbing the pages as talc-clean as did those early *ah ts'ib*. And, like them, we also reveled in the precious collaborative hours we spent together creating *Hunab Ku*.

To every author listed in our bibliography, we thank you for your research and for your own ingenious *hun*-making. Our special admiration and thanks go to José Argüelles and Carl Johan Calleman, for sharing with us their insights regarding the Mayan calendar and culture. To them, we say "Bravo!"

Hunab Ku

Our deepest gratitude goes to a diminutive, bright-eyed Lithuanian woman named Marija Gimbutas, who, before she died, graciously gave us her permission to recopy any of her art, asking, "Will the illustrations be used for healing?" "That is our fondest hope," we assured her. "Then, draw them!" she smiled. Gimbutas was eager to inspire everyone with the goddess culture of prehistoric Europe.

We have shared these images with many friends over the years; some of them, like Laura, read and helped edit portions of the manuscript. Some, like Julia, helped with scanning and digitizing the art. Some just played with the images. So, we thank you: Laura Baring-Gould, Julia Blackbourn, Janet Ryan, John and Nancy Whiteman, Sharon Bauer, and, of course, all the Sophias for their wisdom and tender support. And, we offer a special prayer of thanksgiving to our extraordinary friend John, who, when we were discouraged, said, "Go back to the tree when the fruit is ripe."

And finally, our thanks to Nathan Speerstra and John Speerstra, the other two members of our family, who have encouraged us, nurtured us, listened to us, read our multiple drafts, and waited, expectantly, as *Hunab Ku* took shape and was born. Every *ah ts'ib* deserves that kind of enthusiastic and unconditional loving support.

ACKNOWLEDGMENTS

INTRODUCTION

Mayan Mentors

The Maya people of Central America left large footprints behind, including lingering impressions of the universe for us to ponder. Their name most likely came from Mayab, the Yucatán Peninsula on which they settled. But it seems no small coincidence of language that the Eastern word *maya* brings to mind *mother, matrix, magic, mind, measure*. And, of course, *mystery*. They abandoned their dozen or so magnificent cities around 830 CE. Tikal, alone, covered twenty-three square miles and had a population of about 500,000. Rome's perimeter boundaries at the time measured only eight miles. The Maya people left their network of irrigation canals lined with raised gardens and walked down white stone roads to disappear into the rain forest. Where had they come from? Why did they leave?

In the 1550s, Spanish galleons slipped into Central American bays and coves; the newcomers noted vine-covered pyramids stepping up two hundred feet into the air and jaguars prowling abandoned temple courtyards. The people who greeted the strange eastern ships knew of their own ancestors from the carved stones, stories, and books they had left behind. The great stone stairway in Copan, for instance, with its twelve hundred glyphs, dedicated in 755 CE, still stands as a strong, quiet reminder of their mythology.

Five or six million Maya live in Mexico and Central America today, speaking thirty-one distinct languages. Surviving Quichés, largest of the several dozen Mayan nationalities, still worship at these ruins and keep safe the ancient calendar their ancestors left.

It didn't take long for those sixteenth-century Spaniards to ferret out and begin to translate the clever riddle- and pun-filled books. Their hinged gesso-covered pages proudly displayed brightly painted ideograms—a picture language, similar in some respects to Egyptian and Chinese. When unfolded, some of these codices, with their cat-skin covers, extended twenty feet. After they were proclaimed heretical and dangerous, the Mayan books were tossed onto bonfires; only three documents are left, and

Hunab Ku

some of those are copies of copies. All of the surviving Mayan languages spoken today come from two languages these ancient texts were written in: Yucatecan and Cholan.

Enough glyphs remain intact for us to unravel the Mayan's sophisticated solar and Venus calendars capable of counting time precisely over millions, even billions, of years. They invented the concept of zero, an eye-shaped glyph, and created an ingenious binary math system, based on the prime number 13, using dots and dashes.

Calendars and Cycles

These ancient people believed that time flowed in measurable, repeatable cycles, and they plotted their cosmic calendars, without the aid of telescopes, by watching the night sky. They felt the pulse of planets and charted the paths of the earth, the moon, the sun, and the planets over time. Past and future echoed in their sacred calendars. The sun marked their year (*tun*) of 18 months, each with 20 days, creating a year of 365 days. Five of those days were dark, and carried no "god names."

Besides measuring time, as we do, in solar years, they also counted time by watching Earth's sister planet, Venus. It takes Venus 584 days to circle the Earth. They linked their Venus calendar to their Sun calendar by knowing that five Venus cycles equaled eight Earth Sun years. The Dresden Codex (one of the three surviving Mayan codices) tells us of the Venus almanac and the Long Count. We don't seek to explain these intricately meshed calendars and layered sacred rounds in complete detail, but rather introduce you to the Mayan ways of measuring time. The Maya cleverly placed their days and months into groups of thirteen, so a calendar wheel revolved every 260 years, to form a *katun* (13 times 20). For every 400 years of 360 days, they marked one more *baktun* or 144,000 days. Thirteen *baktun* cycles form their great cycle of 5,125 years. After each of these great cycles, it is as if the universe takes a deep breath and begins again. With these devices, Mayans measured time for millions of years backward as well as into the future! The Maya predicted their civilization would last about 1,900 years. They were right.

Many people, including José Argüelles in his well-read *The Mayan Factor*, have written about Mayan predictions based on their ancient calendars. In *The Mayan Calendar and* the *Transformation of Consciousness*, Carl Johan Calleman claims the calendar "carries a universal truth that is probably a much more urgent topic for study in today's global community than it ever was to the Maya." It provides us, he says, "with knowledge of the energies that guide evolution." At the end of each of these great cycles, the world, they said, is destroyed and reborn by the great force of the Hunab Ku, the *One Giver of Movement and Measure.*

What Is the Hunab Ku?

The Maya believed in harmonic resonance. Their Hunab Ku glyph, a perfectly balanced yin-yang figure, was centered in their model of space and time, or "Loom of Maya." All of life's cycles and passages are woven on this heavenly loom. Through time's interweavings, we are ushered through passages and between cycles of world systems. The Hunab Ku represents the galactic core—the opening for knowledge and understanding pouring down, at specific times, onto the earth. The Hunab Ku or Hun Ahau, the One Lord, is the god that ushers us all through passages between worlds. Calleman likens the Hunab Ku to the Universal World Tree and translates it as "One Source of Limits and Energy."

We are about to move into what the Mayans called the *Age of Itza—Age of Consciousness.* In other words, we're in the process of waking up! We sometimes call this crossover time the Age of Aquarius. The movement into our coming cycle begins, according to some interpretations of the ancient Maya Long Count calendar, on December 21, 2012. That winter solstice will mark the time on our planet when the gateway to the galaxies, the great mover, the Hunab Ku, pulses and fills us with intelligent energy. Aluna Joy Yaxk'in, who works with Mayan teachings (www.kachina.net/-alunajoy), says the Hunab Ku "will flash like lightning and pierce the shadows." It will be a time of great awakening and creativity. We will, at this time between the Mayan *baktuns*, experience a new unfolding of balance and understanding. (See **Hunab Ku 39**/39.)

Does the Mayan cosmology hold real truth for our time? Many people around the world watch as this day draws closer, some with fear and some with joy. Even if the Mayan calendar count is right, it will not likely be "one date" on which everything changes. Our earth does not have one colossal reset button. While we most likely will not find ourselves in an apocalyptic movie with a big-bang ending, we are already on a spiraling pathway that carries us all forward. We are being carried on an updraft of cosmic winds, "winds beyond human manipulation and invulnerable to weaponry," according to Calleman.

As did the Mayans, we also yearn for harmony and resonance in our lives. All too often we search in vain for it among our material toys. But we can make other choices. Generations of wisdom are available to assist us, recorded in every ancient culture on our planet, marking many previous journeys through the Hunab Ku to the beginning of a new age.

Seventy-Seven Ancient Archetypal Images

Archetypes are those *big ideas,* as Carl Jung, the Swiss psychotherapist, explained them, capable of exploding us into different dimensions of understanding. No matter what our own personal backgrounds, we all share these universal concepts. Jung believed they arose from the collective unconscious. They can heal us and restore balance in our lives. They can energize our creativity, and, if we allow them entrance, they can move us deeply. Particularly when we pose meaningful questions, we are able to access our own forgotten wisdom in thought-provoking ways. Archetypes tell stories and invite us to journey inward.

We have carefully selected, redrawn, and organized seventy-seven images into seven color palettes, each reflecting one of our body's seven energy centers. Within each of these palettes, or book parts, you will find eleven big ideas or archetypes associated with that chakra, or energy center. The earth has a subtle energy system with lines of energy crisscrossing its surface, just as our own bodies do. Over the years, people have performed earthly acupuncture on our planet by marking certain places with stones and structures and honoring them through ritual and meditation. Later groups of people co-opted them for their own sacred spaces. Holy wells, stones, and mounds became platforms, and platforms in turn became cathedrals, temples, and mosques. People continue to journey to these places from Egypt to the Yucatán and all over our planet to

INTRODUCTION

become reinvigorated. By our intentional presence at these sacred spots, we honor the earth, and who knows how far the consequences are felt.

Many of the descendents of the First Peoples on earth still honor, as do the Mayan Quichés, special earth places with their presence and their ongoing prayers. Some of our earth's sacred places are mountains: Delphi at Mt. Parnassus, Shasta, Fujiyama, and Everest, which the local Tibetans called "Goddess, Mother of the World." Some are moving rivers: the Ganges, and the Meander in Ephesus. Others are islands: Easter, Crete, and Hawaii. Some are simply lines, such as the Nazca Lines drawn in the Peruvian desert, or petroglyphs, etched on large rock faces. We continue to be drawn to standing stones: Stonehenge, Avebury, Karnak. And to the holy rocks of Petra, Jerusalem, Mecca, and Ayers as well as the piled rocks of pyramids, ziggurats, and temples. We are even attracted to smaller rocks placed in prayer circles and medicine wheels or piled in cairns for all to see. Many mounds still mark sacred earth: Newgrange in Ireland, Silbury Hill in England, and the Great Bear Mounds of the Mississippi River Valley. Whatever our religious leanings, we all hold these places sacred. They were built by our ancestors, and their names anchor them to our cultures: Chartres, The Temple of Heaven, Chichén Itzá, the Serpent Mound, Hagia Sophia, Jerusalem's Mount, Compostela. Like iron filings, we are drawn to magnetic places known for old initiation rites. We gather there, straining to hear the old stories. If only for a short time, we feel as if we have come *home*.

In *Hunab Ku*, you'll find seventy-seven images of *home*—multiple ways to view our earth and ourselves. These images, like the Hunab Ku itself, measure and move us and encourage us to embark upon our own sacred journey. The Hunab Ku lies at the very center of these images, reminding us to balance our intentions, to center our understandings, and to become more conscious of what ancient wisdom continues to teach all of us today.

The images in this book offer a virtual pilgrimage to our ancient "homescapes." The labyrinth on the floor of the Chartres cathedral, positioned on an old sacred Druid university, was used during the Middle Ages as a virtual pilgrimage (see **Mystic** 8). Not everyone was able to actually pilgrimage to Jerusalem, the city that lay at the center of every ancient map of the world. So people walked to the center of labyrinths instead.

Hunab Ku

Think of this book, then, as a virtual walking meditation to ancient sacred sites. You need not be physically present at these seventy-seven places to unlock their wisdom.

At a time when our planet cries for healing, the images in *Hunab Ku* invite us to delve deeply into these old visual metaphors gathered from honored sites, valued artifacts, and earthworks. Some of our planet's First Peoples created these seventy-seven sacred shapes to reflect, like mirrors, patterns deeply embedded within each of us. They no doubt hoped the shapes would last long enough to tell their symbolic stories to future generations willing to listen. These images tug at us, and some make us deeply nervous, for reasons we would just as soon sublimate.

Through the years, many ancient structures and images have been destroyed. Just as Diego de Landa once viewed the vast libraries of Mayan books as works of the devil, people often take the holy work of others to be heretical icons. We've watched, in fear or complacency, as Taliban gunmen destroyed ancient Buddhist statues; we have seen bombs blast apart holy Iraqi sites. And we hear the threats of fundamentalists in Egypt who want to dismantle the pyramids, stone by stone. Rubble builds up; dust settles. But for some reason, the images you find here have remained. Why? Perhaps, to call us back to cherished ideas.

Hunab Ku invites you to "read" these shapes in order to learn more about who we are and what our future choices might be, for each image can be viewed as a milestone marking our individual and collective human journey. Some images call us back as far as thirty thousand years.

While it might sometimes feel as if we're on this journey alone, we do, in fact, have many helpers. We have sacred texts. The Popul Vuh. Chilam Balam. The Torah. The Bible. The Koran. The Upanishads. We have music. We have ancient structures and treasured images. Some of these voices may speak in subtle ways, easily missed or misunderstood. But on more careful scrutiny, we learn to use our intuitive senses, our inner ears, our enhanced vision. It is as if we are separated by a gauzy theater scrim from our helpers. But they continue to speak to us through synchronicities, through meditation, and through dreams. As you ponder these images from the past, allow their multiple interpretations to deepen your understanding of what you already know and desperately need to remember.

INTRODUCTION

How Do I Read This Book?

These images can be understood on many levels. Therefore, they may be accessed in various ways, offering multiple insights at different times. You might choose to read the book conventionally, as a mini ancient art history tour, from beginning to end. That is one valuable and rational process. Or you might choose to open to one page at random, and meditate on it. Or you can read all the "Red" entries one day and all the "Orange" entries the next, working your way through all the colors and thus through the seven chakras.

You will notice that the images are numbered 1 through 39 and then back again to 1. Two sets of numbers begin at either end and move toward the center: **Hunab Ku 39/**39. The first set of numbers, indicating body images, moves up from **1**, beginning with the complete physical separation of **Solitude**, and journeys toward the central image of **39: Lover/Relationships**. This Hunab Ku image marks our central union with one another. It joins the body and the spirit images. Then the spirit image numbers move from 39 back again to 1, eventually reaching the ultimate **Unity** of all things.

Argüelles called the Hunab Ku the "eye of the hurricane." While it may feel at times as if we could be blown away, we actually are grounded and anchored by time-honored archetypes.

So, as you can see, this unconventional book is a codex in its own right. It's a labyrinth, of sorts. As you enter the labyrinth, you move down a path, to the center, to the **Hunab Ku**, number 39/39, by first passing through numbers **1** through **38**. Then, if you choose, you can move back out to the world again, by passing through numbers 38 through 1, collecting insights as you spiral your way to the end.

You will find a number of cave art illustrations included. A recent theory proposed about cave art postulates that they were, in fact, moving pictures. If a torch is passed along some of them, it seems as if the animals are running and hunters are actually throwing spears. Flipping the pages of *Hunab Ku* can create a movement of images—dance steps, in various combinations. We selected these images because they seemed to invite us to enter a sacred space to play. So flip the pages; open the book at random.

Hunab Ku

Follow your intuition. There are many ways to gather and order these images. As you play with this book, you will discover them.

You might pretend *Hunab Ku* is an ancient oracle and ask it a specific question. By posing big powerful open-ended questions, the images afford you numerous opportunities to hear profound "answers." Hold a question in your mind and, without looking, let your finger land on a number on page 308 of this book. Look up that number; explore the image. Match the body and spirit numbers and read them together. Or if you are comfortable with a pendulum, you might dowse that image to invite numbers of images to speak to your questions.

But, How Do I Read the Signs?

Jung said, "Events can, so to speak, bunch together in time and space, not because one is causing the other, but because their meanings are linked." When synchronicity happens, an archetype springs to life. One of Carl Jung's classic synchronicity stories revolved around a patient's dream about a scarab, an ancient Egyptian symbol for resurrection and rebirth (**Scarab** 9). Just as she was describing her dream, in which someone had given her a golden scarab pin, they both heard a sound at the window. Jung opened the window, and in flew a real golden-green scarab, a beetle that had waited to join them at just the right moment. Our rational minds simply cannot explain these profound coincidences. How do you explain needing some bit of information and turning around, only to find it in an unexpected place? How do you explain thinking of someone and having them call you at that very minute? How do you explain the right book falling off the library or bookstore shelf into your outstretched hand? Certainly not with logic. Your rational mind, your ego, questions all of this, but your soul knows the world is all ordered just the way it should be.

These seventy-seven images open doors, create bridges, and shed light on what is already within you, waiting to emerge. Jung called this inner wisdom *numinosity*. The Latin word *numen* means "divine power." A spiritual, holy, or divine presence is *numinous*. It invokes the eternal, the intangible, the ethereal. You will begin to sense a

INTRODUCTION

divine presence in each of these seven color fields as you work and play with them. Perhaps you will discover the most numinous images to be those falling within the blue, indigo, and violet ranges. Those colors call you to connect to your spiritual side, just as the lower chakra colors of red, orange, and yellow encourage you to connect with your body and its more primitive psychic energies. But whether body images or spirit images, each summons you to a new understanding.

"True maturation on the spiritual path requires that we discover the depth of our wounds," says Jack Kornfield in his book *A Path with Heart*. "What we find as we listen to the songs of our rage, or fear, loneliness or longing, is that they do not stay forever. Rage turns into sorrow, sorrow turns into tears; tears may fall for a long time, but then the sun comes out." Each of these seventy-seven archetypal images begs to be integrated into our sun-filled, conscious minds. There is an invisible web connecting all things. Now and then we get a quick glimpse of some of the strands, but usually the web remains well hidden. Imagine each of these images attached to a giant web. When one jiggles, it affects all the others. Reading the images in patterns can re-create snapshots from a larger, radiating web. We begin to sense a transparency that gradually opens and allows us to understand life in new ways. We begin to question some of our old beliefs. Why, for instance, do we stay away from the number 13 when the Mayans honored that number as sacred? We say the number is "unlucky" and build hotels with no thirteenth floor. In this archetypal system, we have the number 13 twice: Venus and Vulture. Venus calls us to fertility, and Vulture reminds us of death. Both are necessary for life. There are three death images in *Hunab Ku*, and each invites us to consider what "end times" might mean for us. None are to be avoided or feared. You will find insights into the natural endings of things in **Wise Old One** 17, **Vulture** 13, and **Released Soul** 6. Each calls you to face your shadows and look into the dark. They are as important to your health as are the birthing images you will also find here.

While single images can answer many specific questions and offer various insights, you will find that by gathering the images in combinations, they will form more complex webs of meaning—all intended just for you. Right now. Once you've acquainted yourself with the symbols, you can turn to the end of the book, where we have outlined several readings you can try for insight work, chakra healing, courage, or guidance.

Hunab Ku

These are only a starting point. You will discover many other ways to read these images. Whatever method you choose, remember that the Hunab Ku, the One Giver of Movement and Measure, waits at the center, at the heart, blessing your movements and your measurements. As we come to the realization that we are all one, and that our nations interconnect as one earth body, we search for ways to deepen that understanding. It is our hope that *Hunab Ku* may be one of them.

Hunab Ku's matrix of ideas, ancient art, and archetypes forms an interactive system for learning, healing, and meditation. We designed it over many years to thoughtfully intersect with other ancient systems and ways of understanding our bodies, minds, and spirits, and the longer you work with this book, the more layers of organization you may discover. It is a gift from the people we were to the people we are becoming. This collection of images and accompanying words remind us of what we already know. This book is not designed to scare anyone into an apocalyptic fever, but to provide a simple tool for staying balanced while we enjoy our front row seats for the coming Hunab Ku. We can choose to pass through this great moment together, not mired in confusion and fear, but filled with grace and love.

The 77 Sacred Symbols

Effigy bear mound, 900 CE, McGregor, Iowa, United States

1

Great Bear

THE ANCIENT PEOPLE OF NORTH AMERICA PILED UP THE EARTH IN VARIOUS shapes—as lizards, birds, snakes, turtles, panthers, and bears, as well as humans. Many of these effigy mounds can still be found in the Ohio and Mississippi River valleys. Other earth shapes mark unplowed and undisturbed areas in New York and Florida, the Dakotas, and parts of Texas. The bear shape pictured here, along with dozens of others like it, has been preserved at the Effigy Mounds National Monument overlooking the Mississippi River near McGregor, Iowa. Earth mounds were formed across North America from 300 BCE to the coming of the Europeans. The effigy mounds culture created bear mounds from 650 CE to 1200 CE, but little else is known about them.

Why did they build these huge earth sculptures? Excavations of some of the mounds indicate no evidence of burials at all. And when the remains of humans *are* found, they have been placed at the spot where the heart of the bear would lie. Perhaps a special holy person was laid to rest in these instances. The mounds may have been clan totems or signatures of families. They likely were ritual sites, gathering places to mark important seasonal celebrations. The people who worked the earth into these sculptures may have been related to the Hopewell people and the later Temple Mound people who (much like the Toltecs and Aztecs of Mexico) built mounds farther downriver, and crowned them with temples, some one thousand by seven hundred feet at the base. The Ohio Serpent Mound (**Serpent 7**) curls across the landscape for nearly a quarter of a mile. The bear mound pictured here is so large it can be viewed effectively only from the air. Artifacts found near these bear mounds indicate that the people who built them traded up and down the river and valued beauty in many forms: glazed pottery, intricate tools, obsidian, and jewelry made of copper, gold, and inlaid shells.

PART *i* ~ Red

Solitude

Loneliness is the poverty of self; solitude is the richness of self.

—May Sarton

Meridel LeSueur in *The Mound Builders* says, "The mounds speak a message we are just beginning to read." As we begin to "read" the bear mound, we feel called to a sacred task—to hibernate. To go inside and feel our own inner strength. When we learn to be quiet like a bear, we can enter the great void. There we find nothing and everything. There we find the spirit of Bear's wisdom. There we can empty ourselves of all that is unnecessary and become one with our cave, just as this earthen sculpture became one with the earth children who built it.

Look to the north in the night sky, and you will find seven stars forming the Great She Bear, Ursa. She guards her children with ferocity and gives strength to all below her. This bear shares her power: the power to nurture, the power to protect, and the power to stand against all enemies. Most cultures recognize the bear shape, which includes the Big Dipper, in various ways. Revolving around the pole star, the bear is central to how people north of the equator view the night sky. We look up and feel rooted and held by that familiar image.

Just as the hermit bear returns to life after a long solitary winter's sleep to a budding springtime, so, too, will our lives go on, as we return to familiar paths. Bear reminds us that we are linked to the stars and to one another, but we need solitude and rest before we face action once again. Solitude, as the poet Sarton put it, is, indeed, *the richness of self.* Bear encourages us to dream fearlessly and not to fear the "empty" darkness, for it is filled with life, just as the dark womb is filled with the richness of a new self. Bear reminds us that from the underground life comes again, life capable of reaching up to the stars.

Bear begins our journey to the **Hunab Ku 39**/39 by rooting us in red. Red ocher is often found in earth mounds, as in other early sacred places. This earthy color embodies

Hunab Ku

life and death, birth blood and death blood, sunrise and sunset. Bear, emboldened by red, invites us to give up fear and to honor our bodies as our sacred partners on earth.

Here, in our first energy center or root chakra, we feel our right to be one with the earth. We feel safe: fed and held. And although our adrenal glands are ready to pump us full of adrenaline and prepare us for any flight or fight, we can also relax here, firmly grounded. In Sanskrit this center is called *Muladhara* chakra—root support.

The number 1, which the Mayans depicted as a single dot, represents both **Unity** 1 and **Solitude 1**. We begin our journey to Hunab Ku, and back again, deeply grounded, at ease in the waiting and in the singularity of our personhood.

And yet, there is only One great thing, the only thing:
To live to see in huts and on journeys the great day that dawns,
And the light that fills the world.

—Inuit song

PART i ~ Red

GREAT BEAR

1

Ceramic statue, c. 4500 BCE, Karanovo, Bulgaria

2

Ram

Worldwide, early cultures associated the ram with both the feminine and the masculine god force: virile, fertile, and creative. The ram proved important in the lives of our ancestors, providing fleece for spinning and weaving, as well as meat. Of all animal bones unearthed in the remains of early Neolithic communities, 90 percent were from sheep and goats. It may have been our earliest domesticated animal.

Ram figurines have been found throughout Europe dating back to the seventh millennium BCE. Many carry the chevron and spiral markings of the ceramic container pictured here, which was found in Bulgaria. Archaeologists date this particular one between 5000 and 4500 BCE. It has a snake coil on its front and lines that could be depicting running streams on its sides. Chevrons, snake coils, lozenges, triangles, circles, meander lines, and stripes are all sacred script notations for Goddess markings—motifs that mean regeneration, fertility, and life-giving powers. Marija Gimbutas, renowned author and professor of European archaeology, claimed these yet-to-be-deciphered glyphs and markings were in common use eight thousand years ago, painted on walls and etched into pottery. She and fellow researchers isolated 210 core signs, predating Sumerian writing by about two thousand years.

Ram horn motifs decorated numerous ancient ceramic vessels, as did V shapes, as symbols of abundance and well-being. Perhaps because of its connection to the masculine horned god, later cultures adopted the ram as a sacrifice figure and as a mascot of the gods. Rams, as scapegoats, were sacrificed to Zeus and Athena. The Hebrew God, Yahweh, spared Abraham's son Isaac and substituted a ram, caught by its horns in a thorny thicket.

PART i ~ Red

Risk

The back porch is more secure, but the fun is in jumping the fences.
—Marjorie Holmes

The ram's head, symbol of Aries, announces the beginning of spring. In Egyptian hieroglyphs, ram means "solar heat." To the ancient people of the upper Nile, the ram was a symbol for the supreme deity, Amon—the virile male, the holy phallus, the ram of rams. Throughout early history, a ram's horns signified regeneration. Like the horns of the moon, they stimulate life energies and remind all of Earth's children to listen to their bodies and honor their sexuality.

Ram, as Aries, calls you to be direct. It is a fire sign filled with idealism and enthusiasm. Mars rules Ram; it's small wonder, then, that rams' horns clash and rattle rugged mountain valleys when the drama of rams' aggressive action is played out for the ewes. Counselors who work closely with clients report that Aries personalities often engage in high-risk hobbies or professions. Their courage and competitive natures lead them to take risks.

Risk can be defined as exposing yourself to possible loss or danger. Ram calls you to adventure and daring. Helen Keller said, "Life is a daring adventure or nothing." No one wants to live with "nothing." So we risk—big risks and little risks—seeking challenges and excitement. Of course, every time we get out of bed, we risk danger, but staying in bed also poses its risks. Johann Schiller said, "Who dares nothing, need hope for nothing." What do you dare? For what are you willing to risk everything?

Children are inherent risk takers. Adults often are reluctant to suspend the rules, but children jump just for the sake of jumping, with no thought to the landing. Children smell and taste with no thought to duplicating or saving those sensations. Children know how to create *bricolage*—to pick up anything at hand and turn it into something fun. Children move without analyzing or perfecting or judging their moves. We adults, however, are much more ambivalent. We love and fear risk at the same time.

Hunab Ku

Risk allows us to grow, to fall in love, to dare to become parents. Risk allows us to break belief barriers, to travel new paths.

The Dalai Lama once said, "Take into account that great love and great achievements involve great risk." Invite Ram to inspire your risks. Use your two ram's horns to risk what you truly wish to do. Pythagoras, the ancient philosopher, musician, and mathematician, used the number two to signify matter. Two depicts a move away from unity into duality or opposites. Two invites us to risk relationship.

Red is the color with the longest wavelength and the slowest vibrations. Red stimulates the pituitary gland and releases adrenaline; it elevates the pulse rate and one's blood pressure. Restaurant owners often decorate their dining rooms with red to encourage people to eat faster, thereby allowing for more customers. Note the number of flags sporting red. Red is, indeed, a powerful fire symbol—dynamic, active, and brave. The ruby, said to stimulate the libido, is the jewel for Aries. As the color of life, Egyptians wrote sacred rites and ceremonies in red ink. This red energy center controls your fears. Meditate on red at the base of your spine; calculate your risks and release your fears. Leap for joy!

The company of Gods rejoice at thy rising, the earth is glad when it beholdeth thy rays... thou goest forth each day over heaven and earth, and thou art made strong each day by thy mother Nut. Thou passest over the heights of heaven, thy heart swelleth with joy.

—HYMN TO RA, *The Egyptian Book of the Dead*

Boundary stone, 1100 BCE, Babylon (Iraq)

3

Scorpion

THE SCORPION ARCHER PICTURED HERE IS A RELIEF FROM A PROPERTY MARKER stone in Mesopotamia called "Kudurrus." This scorpion archer appears directly above another scorpion figure, and they share the same detail on tail and body. This boundary stone dates from about 1100 BCE, but the archer was carved for Nebuchadnezzar I, king of Babylon, who ascended the throne in 605 BCE. He was named after a Babylonian god, Nebo, and his name means "defend the boundary."

Like the scorpion, Nebuchadnezzar struck viciously, slaughtering the Egyptians, enslaving the Israelites, and burning Jerusalem's temple. He used slave labor to build his elaborate walls and his magnificent palace and to refurbish the temple of Marduk, the Babylonian creator god. It was this great warrior who built the hanging gardens, one of the seven wonders of the ancient world, so his wife could be reminded of the hills in Iran, her home.

While the scorpion is usually thought of as male, in South America the scorpion is called Mother Scorpion.

Conflict

Remember that you came here realizing the necessity of struggling only with yourself and thank anyone who helps you engage in this struggle.

—George Ivanovich Gurdjieff

"Watch out for my tail! Sometimes my sting is fatal. I crawl to you at night, and you won't know I'm there until it's time to do battle."

Scorpion portrays a battle image. Knowing a challenge may come, you will be better prepared for it; in other words, check your shoe before putting it on. Mars, the red planet, lends you subtle energy for any conflicts on your horizon. In the Middle Ages, some people believed a scarlet cloth would stop a patient's bleeding. Red was used to cure "red." It might be helpful to note that the Kabbalistic meaning of red is severity. Scorpion *is* severe. And very bold.

Pluto, Greek god of the underworld, is Scorpio's companion. The Egyptians also related the scorpion to the underworld and teamed this image up with Selkhet, the goddess who ushered people to the other side. A scorpion stung Horus, the child of Isis. He died, but was brought back to life. Scorpion, like the serpent, shares both dangerous and life-giving qualities with us. It brings tests and initiations.

Darkness must come before dawn, and out of conflict comes resolution. Sometimes Scorpion's swiftness is the best way to approach a test or a trial. You are independent and strong; you will survive. People born under this astrological sign tend to enjoy their intense search for spiritual transformation; they are often gifted at introspection, secretively going into the dark and searching out knowledge. Scorpion reminds you that, while you tend to attract emotional battles, your dynamic nature, your wisdom, and your compassion balance your pride and intensity.

Conflict often comes through egoism; surrender is not viewed as a viable option to conflicting parties. But turning back may bring peace. When we learn the validity of differing perspectives, when we assimilate many points of view, we grow in wisdom,

Hunab Ku

and we not only survive, but thrive from that new understanding. When under stress, the adrenal glands flood the body with adrenaline and cortisol. We sometimes lash out, sending forth pricking words and stinging reactions. If our survival mechanisms continually operate at peak performance, Scorpion's poisonous ferocity can turn itself back onto the sender.

Scorpio, a water sign, represents separation. Coming in late October and early November, it ushers in winter in the Northern Hemisphere, marking the time of quiet and rest. Scorpion reminds us that sometimes the old must be destroyed before the new can come forth. Death must precede birth. What is being transformed in your world right now? What carries shadows for you? From what or from whom are you now ready to separate?

Three is a very dynamic number. The Mayans represented three with three dots, indicating rhythm. Three shows vitality and excitement. Three combines a pair of opposites with another factor. In the scorpion image pictured here, the third factor allows for conflict: two legs plus a poisonous tail or two arms plus a deadly arrow. But, paradoxically, conflict can also be alleviated by a third element. A conflict management technique developed at Harvard encourages the discovery of a "third side," one different from two initially held opposing views. How does "three" come to heal you today?

A weapon, howsoever powerful it may be,

Can always be superseded by a superior one;

But no weapon can, however, be superior to nonviolence and love.

—JAINIST PRAYER FOR PEACE

Mattang navigational tool, c. 650 CE, Polynesia

4

Father

STICKS CAREFULLY BENT AND TIED INTO INTRICATE DESIGNS FORMED EARLY navigational tools used to cross vast ocean expanses. The one pictured here is called the *mattang*. The elders taught young seagoing men how to make and use them. They also taught them how to tell their sacred myths, how to mark the wheeling stars, and how to sing the sea chants that named the winds blowing off various coasts. By holding the *mattang* near the water at the prow of their boats, sailors could match any wave's pattern. Just as the stars overhead follow predictable patterns, so also do waves. By reading the wave patterns with a *mattang*, they could determine where major islands lay and where reef barriers broke the ocean's surface.

When early Polynesian navigators took to their boats, they believed they were re-creating voyages taken by their mythical ancestors who left behind such survival tools as the *mattang*. They read the same wave patterns their ancestors read. Past, for them, became the present, and the present became the future.

Like the male essence, this rigid navigational tool is practical, structured, linear, logical, and analytical. It thrusts a boat forward in what is akin to fertilizing energy. The *mattang* sets the pattern for setting and achieving constructive goals. It is a stabilizing influence for people striking out into uncharted waters.

PART *i* ~ Red

Logic

The old maps are outdated; we require new navigational aids. And the inescapable fact is: you are your own cartographer now.

—Ralph Blum, *The Book of Runes*

Regardless of our gender, each of us has within us a solid measure of the father and grandfather archetype. Each of us kneels at the prow of the boat we steer through life. Life is a journey, and challenges lie ahead. We reach our goals and overcome barrier reefs because the laws that guide us are logical; the way may not always be straight, but others have gone before us, and they can teach us the songs that will show us our path.

We may not always know the precise distance from "island" to "island," but we have been given tools to help us stay the course. The *mattang* teaches us that we are held by a web; all things are interlaced, and each one supports the other.

As we set out, into the wind, sometimes it is prudent, given our life changes, to vary our course. This image, named for the masculine force, encourages us to connect with our own reality in a very practical way, sensing our virility and claiming our authority. The Polynesian people knew about *mana*—our virtue and grace. It is ours to claim, along with vigor and energy.

This image may help you realize that some definite action is needed. Exert your will; develop a practical plan for achievement, but beware of rigidity and inflexible authoritarianism.

The red color emanates from your yang energy. Red stimulates your sensory nerves, enhancing all your senses.

Four is considered a male number. An earth-based number, four represents the four seasons and the four directions or cardinal points. The *mattang* is constructed as a four-armed cross by weaving together sixteen major pieces of four different lengths. The Mayan symbol for the number four is four dots in a row. Like the directional points of the *mattang,* four calls us to take measure.

Hunab Ku

This *mattang* image, tied as it is here to logic, reminds us of the relevance of principles and reasoning. Logic comes from the same stem as *logos* or "reason." For the Greeks, *logos* was the principle that controlled the universe. Aristotle used the term *nous* to refer to the thinking or rational soul. Philo of Alexandria, who lived around 20 BCE to 40 CE, combined Aristotelian, Platonic, and other Greek thinking with Hebrew rituals and traditions. Philo was likely the first to capitalize *Logos* to mean the vehicle carrying the *nous,* or "divine wisdom."

Logic, or the science that deals with the formal principles of reasoning, invites us to ask the questions: Does my conclusion follow valid inferences and premises? Is my reasoning based on a solid foundation? Are my arguments sound? The American mathematician and logician Charles Peirce said, "There is no royal road to logic; and really valuable ideas can only be had at the price of close attention." The *mattang* invites you to closely scrutinize your environment, inner as well as outer.

Ancestral immortals, bring forth from the spirit world the gifts of good health and abundance and manifest these blessings. The prayer has flown ... the restrictions are lifted. Ho'ike a mai ike ola, Amama ... ua noa.

—OLD HAWAIIAN CHANT

PART **i** ~ Red

• *Volcanic stone bowl, c. 1000* BCE, *Costa Rica* •

5

Earth

MADE FROM VOLCANIC STONE, THE ZOOMORPHIC EFFIGY BOWL PICTURED here was found in the Atlantic watershed zone and is now in the Museo Nacional de Costa Rica. It is 3.5 inches high and 10.5 inches long and was crafted between 1550 and 1000 BCE.

Native American legends speak of the earth as the Great Turtle. A California tribe, the Maidu, tells a creation myth in which Turtle dived into Chaos's waters, was gone for six years, and came back with dirt under her nails. A being who dropped from the sky on a rope of feathers rolled the dirt into a ball, and it grew into our planet.

Asian and African legends tell of the earth supported on the back of a giant tortoise. One woman, confronted with the logic of this myth, was asked this question: "Then, what's under the turtle?" She replied, "There are turtles, all the way down." A Hindi myth speaks of Old Tortoise Man, father of all creatures and mate of the Goddess of Water. Greeks thought Hermes created the first lyre from a tortoise shell. Hermes's turtle music echoed universal harmonies of the planetary spheres.

The tortoise carries its protective shield around with it at all times, yet she goes off and trusts the sun to hatch her eggs.

PART i ~ Red

Matter

What if the Universe were indeed the mind of God, operating as a holographic entity so that each part of the macrocosm is a perfect, though perhaps less distinct, mirror image of the whole? This would mean that we are all of the same matter…

—Liz Simpson, *The Healing Energies of Earth*

Matter. Mater. Matrix. Metric. Mother and Measurement. These are all names for our mother, the earth. We have also adopted her name, Gaia, the Deep-Breasted One, from the Greek poet Hesiod. Our planet, we later discovered, is formed by precisely the same compounds that form our own bodies. The scientist-philosopher James Lovelock wrote in the 1970s about the "Gaia theory" of Earth being alive with an ecosystem that, thanks to our greed, has become sick. Native Americans, who have long known the earth as a being, call the North American continent Turtle Island. The poet Gary Snyder published a collection of poems under that title, and in his introduction, he says, "Each living being is a swirl in the flow, a formal turbulence, a 'song.' The land, the planet itself, is also a living being—at another pace." A turtle's pace, perhaps.

Hildegard of Bingen, the German mystic who lived in the twelfth century, wrote, "The earth has a scaffold of stones and trees. In the same way is a person formed. Flesh is the earth, the bones are the trees and stones." Ancient rocks carry Earth's story and also vibrate with life, albeit very, very slowly. Earth's crust is composed, geologists tell us, of only about six different minerals—combined, cooled, having collected bits of animal deposits, pressed, and changed over time.

Earth says that you, too, have a solid core. You are well grounded, stable, and protected in your armored shell. Like amphibious turtles, you live in two worlds—above and below. Inner and outer. Body and spirit.

Hunab Ku

Similar to the volcanic essence that formed this ancient bowl, red moves slowly as if out of Earth's core, radiating heat. Visualize drawing hot red strength up, up from the earth, flowing like rivers of lava throughout your body.

The number five signifies blossoming life. Notice how often flower petals appear in groups of five. The pentacle, a five-pointed star, signified health and life to ancient people. Five lies at the center of the ancient Chinese magic square, or square of Saturn, as others called it (and which formed our early tic-tac-toe game), with numbers that add up to 15 in any vertical, horizontal, or diagonal combination:

8	1	6
3	5	7
4	9	2

The stone turtle pictured here has five discrete parts: a head, a tail, and a stone bowl supported by two panther pillars. "Let me carry you on my strong back," she says. "For hundreds of thousands of years I have nurtured you and held you safe. I will not abandon you."

The Mother of us all,
The oldest of all,
Hard, splendid as rock.
Whatever there is that is of the land
Is she who nourishes it . . .

—HOMERIC HYMN TO THE EARTH, 6500 BCE

PART i ~ Red

EARTH
5

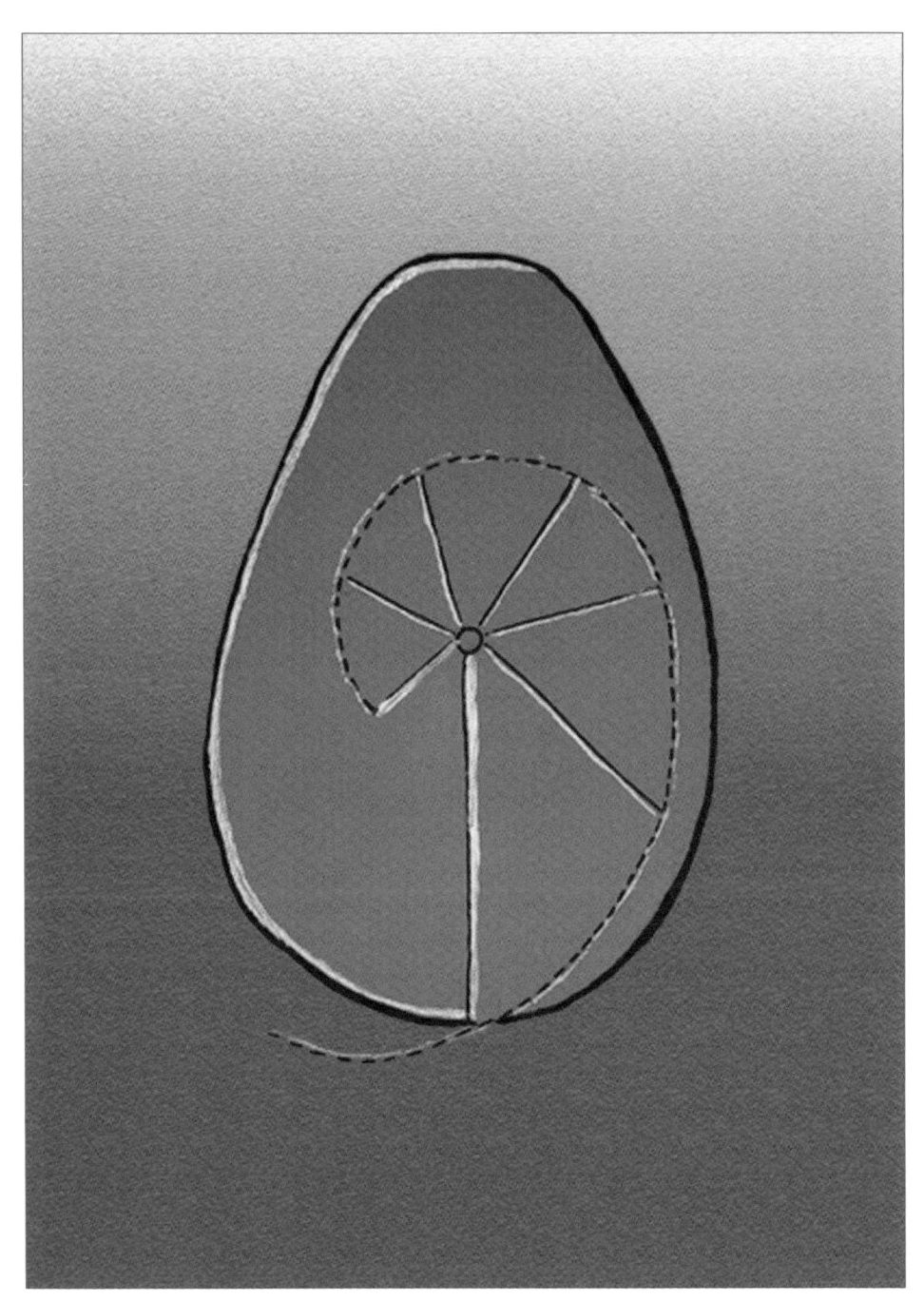

• *World Egg drawing, c. 3000 BCE, Dogon people, Mali, West Africa* •

6

Womb

THE MYTHOLOGICAL AND ASTRONOMICAL KNOWLEDGE PRESERVED AMONG THE Dogon people who once lived in cliff dwellings near the Niger River in the Mali Republic of West Africa has been much documented and discussed. They imagine the cosmos as an egg with a spiraling center: the World Egg. In the beginning of time, the Dogon believe, the World Egg was shaken seven times and divided into twin placentas, fathered by Amma's divine seed: water. The image pictured here, as drawn in sand, shows the orbit of one special star as it seeds creation.

In 1931, the French anthropologist Marcel Griaule began hearing from the Dogon people about a special star. We were not able to photograph it until 1970, but these early Egyptian descendents carried with them astronomical information dating from before 3200 BCE; they knew this little heavy white star orbited around Sirius, the brightest star in the night sky. They called it *Po Tolo*, "deep beginning" or the smallest seed. The Dogon claimed this "egg of the world" contains everything that exists, visible and invisible, including air, earth, fire, metal. It is, as the Dogon people colorfully put it, the "granary for the world." As this image shows, this heavy embryo produced beings whose souls follow the spiraling dotted line out to another star called Sorghum-Female, a woman star. It is represented by a cross and forms one of many glyphs for points in the heavens. Modern astronomers confirm that this second heavy star exists, and they have named it Sirius B, Digitaria. A white dwarf, it is truly massive and super-dense. Scientists estimate one cubic meter of its matter would weigh 20,000 tons. Its gravity is so powerful that it creates a wobble in Sirius A that is responsible for the unique Sirius pulses and flickers in the sky.

Spirals fly off this star, the Dogon say, to form the Milky Way galaxy. Our earth, they are convinced, is just one part of that spinning.

PART ι ~ Red

Gestation

Creativity is like a great receptive womb.

—Lynn Andrews

The womb represents total possibility. Anything can emerge from the womb's precious cocoon. For the embryo within a womb, everything is "self." Rounded in its egg-like perfection, an embryo spins out from a tiny sperm-seeded self, holding all opportunities, all innocence, all life. Round like a zero, an embryo can become nothing or all things.

Egg images, symbols of regeneration and rebirth, appeared in cave paintings in southern France as early as 1200 BCE. The cosmic egg as a womb likely underlies the reasons for such mound structures as Silbury Hill, near Avebury in England, and Newgrange, Knowth, and Dowth, in County Meath, Ireland. All of these gigantic mounds were once covered in white quartz, looking very much like giant eggs; whether they were tombs or wombs we are not sure.

Early followers of Orpheus taught that the Great Goddess, Mother Night, brought forth the World Egg. In it were infinite possibilities. Bird figurines with eggs date back to 18,000 BCE, according to Marija Gimbutas, and connect to what she called "an ornithomorphic Goddess." Serpent eggs once played a major role in Druid mysteries (see also the egg image in **Serpent 7**); they were later replaced with hen's eggs. Easter eggs create today's colorful symbols of new birth, resurrection, and life.

The egg is a symbol of emerging, becoming something new. What might be starting in your life right now? What is awakening? What is thrusting out from the dark into the light? Our nine-month period in the womb teaches us not to fear the dark. We can, at the end of our stay on earth, return once again to the great womb, to wholeness, security, and oneness with all.

The cosmic egg symbol reminds you of your potential. While you may feel tethered by some umbilical cord, you are really free. But birthing is a lifelong process.

Hunab Ku

Six is a number of wholeness. The six-pointed star is created by two triangles, one pointing up and one pointing down. It is sometimes called the Star of David or Solomon's Seal. In India, the hexagram unites the elements of fire and water, the aspects of male and female. The Mayans wrote the number six by placing a dot over a bar. It represented organic balance. Pythagoras called six the perfect number, "the Mother." Many women, especially in northern Africa, still wear a six-petaled flower, "the flower of Aphrodite," to assure a safe pregnancy.

In this Dogon image, six pie-shaped wedges spiral out from the center, depicting great power trapped within stillness. It is a number filled with symmetry and life. *Womb* may be telling you that this is a time to revel in your centeredness, your balance, and your power. Red, a birthing color, comes to thrust you into new dimensions. You have a ready source of nourishment; as if with mighty uterine contractions, your previously dormant creative energy emerges triumphantly.

Abwoon d'bwashmaya, O Birther, Father-Mother of the Cosmos,

you create all that moves in light.

—Aramaic, "The Lord's Prayer"

PART ἰ ~ Red

WOMB

6

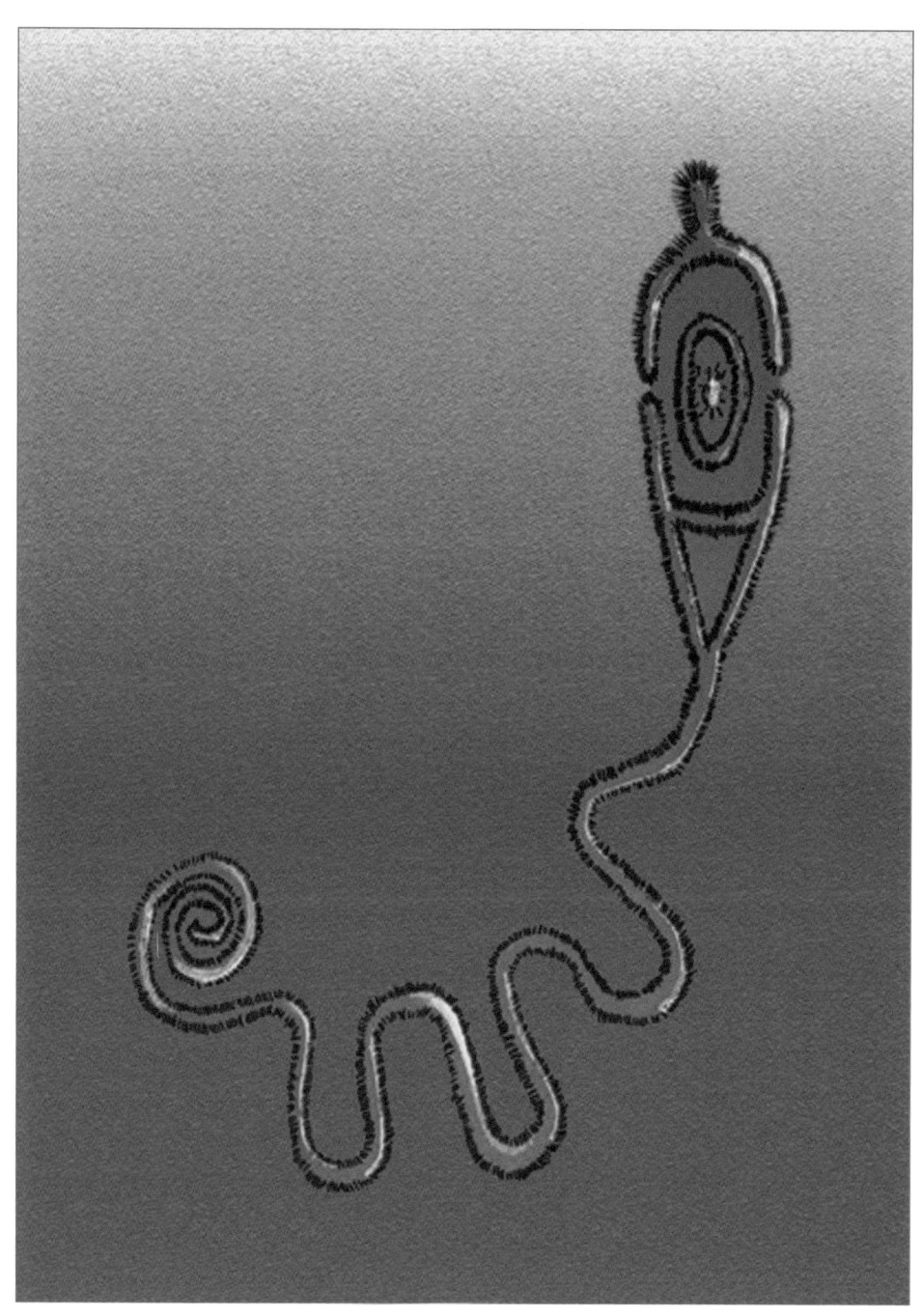

• *Great Serpent Mound, c. 1000 BCE, Locust Grove, Ohio, United States* •

7

Serpent

THE GREAT SERPENT MOUND NEAR LOCUST GROVE, OHIO, SPIRALS ALONG A ridge for fourteen hundred feet. It is twenty feet wide and three to five feet high in places. No one knows the exact date when this Hopewell or Adena earthwork was created, and it may be even older than the generally accepted dates of 1000 BCE to 700 CE.

Some see a serpent's jaws open to encircle an egg-shaped mound that has been called the cosmic egg or the maternal ovum. Others speculate that this is a gigantic fertility symbol: sperm and egg. Or it may be an astrological device. According to the Hopi Snake Clan, the jaws of the snake encircle and protect a village. It faces west to protect traveling clans. The yellow clay snake's body makes seven distinct waves before leading into its tightly coiled tail. The Hopi people, who sometimes dance with rattlesnakes in their mouths, believe that their ancestors created this mound to guard the Eastern Gate. Their name for the serpent is *Tokchi'I*, Guardian of the East. Another people, the Adena, with their high foreheads and ear ornaments, built many conical mounds as well as effigy mounds throughout North America (see **Great Bear 1**). The Adena used red ocher on some of their objects, which have been radiocarbon-dated to 2450 BCE in New York State.

Joseph Campbell connected this Ohioan mound with the Eastern cosmic dragon bearing the sun in its jaws or the Indian serpent of the cosmic sea with the universe on its head. It seems clear that the mound pictured here was a holy place for early Americans, with the serpent and egg forming a sacred stage for prayers, dances, and rituals. In Native American mythologies, the Horned Serpent or Water Monster guards all sources of life arising out of the earth or water.

PART *i* ~ Red

Awakening

It is in the doing with awareness that the learning comes.

—William Horwood, *Duncton Quest*

The serpent image carries deep symbolic meaning and can be found in every culture. The Walbiri and Marinbata Aborigines in Australia paint Rainbow Snake on rocks and hardboards; the Aztecs and the Egyptians painted winged serpents. And from even earlier times, the serpent represented the Mother Goddess, and coiling snakes were kept in her Neolithic temples. One Sumerian goddess was known as the Great Mother Serpent of Heaven, and she was depicted with Milky Way spirals. Isis was often shown as the Serpent Goddess. One of the greatest Central American Mayan temples, Chichén Itzá, is associated with the Snake Clan. Even today, when the descendents of the Mayans weave cloth, many of them first pass their hand over a snake and then place that hand on their own forehead and eyes to absorb its powers. The snake's skin patterns, many cultures say, represent stars in the solar system. It's interesting to note that the Mayan hieroglyph for the constellation of stars known as the Pleiades is a rattle from a snake.

The snake means "awakening wisdom" in many cultures. In Hebrew and Aramaic, the serpent is called "wizard," or wise one. To open the third-eye chakra, to become awake, Egyptian rulers who followed symbology associated with Isis wore an image of the cobra on their brows and called it *Uzait*, "the eye." The snake, most likely because of its ability to shed its skin, also represents eternal life.

Serpent Mound, with its seven undulations, reminds us of underground currents, of our own inner serpentine pathways. As our paths spiral, we seem capable of moving the entire cosmos. There is psychic power in spiraling serpentine lines. In Africa, clairvoyants were described as people with snakes coming out their nostrils. Snake venom contains chemically altering substances. So the serpent image calls us to be awake to things we cannot ordinarily see with our physical eyes. The Great Serpent encircles our

Hunab Ku

world and holds it together, and when earthquakes make us shudder, some folks believe, Serpent is uncoiling.

We become more awake when kundalini, the energy serpent coiled at the base of our spine, begins to move up in seven great waves to the crowns of our heads. This earth energy invites us to open and to grow, to hold our eyes open as serpents must, unblinking. Serpent helps you energize and complete your work. Some see this image as a sperm fertilizing an egg—the ultimate moment of awakening to this world.

The number seven is a combination of male (4) and female (3). The **Ouroboros 11** also combines the male and female principles. The Mayan symbol for seven is two dots over a bar, the pulsation of mystic power. The number seven is associated with wisdom: the Seven Pillars of Wisdom, the seven sisters of Pleiades, Egypt's seven Hathors, and the Arabian seven sages. They call us to wake up and, like the serpent, to wind our ways through life's challenging passages.

Earth our mother, breathe and waken
Leaves are stirring, all things moving
New day coming, life renewing.

—Pawnee Prayer

• *Ceramic spindle whorl, 5000 BCE, Volos, Thessaly, Greece; mace, 100 CE, Costa Rica* •

8

Weaver-Warrior

THE TWO IMAGES PICTURED HERE REPRESENT SURVIVAL AT ITS MOST BASIC social level: a prehistoric drop spindle for making yarn and a ceremonial mace head—creation and destruction.

Women over the ages have tied handfuls of wool to drop spindles to create yarn that could then be knitted or woven. Loom weights and spindle whorls from as early as 5500 BCE were often decorated with sacred writing—meander marks, V shapes, and M shapes—all of which might be attributed to an early feminine divinity. This ceramic spindle whorl assisted women in spinning wool around 5000 BCE. It is about three centimeters in diameter and was discovered at Volos, Thessaly, Greece. According to Marija Gimbutas, these types of inscribed objects were first discovered in 1874 in Transylvania, but they didn't inspire much interest until the early 1960s. This script, according to radiocarbon chronologies, began appearing in Europe some two thousand years before the Sumerians began writing. It coincided with what archaeologists now tell us was a culture complete with an extensive metallurgic industry, sophisticated architecture, a high level of craftsmanship, far-reaching trade relations, and an elaborate system of religious thought and practice.

Fashioned from volcanic stone, the eight-spoked mace head pictured on the right side of the image was discovered in Costa Rica's Atlantic watershed zone. It is about eight inches in diameter and was most likely used as a ceremonial staff decoration rather than as an actual weapon.

PART i ~ Red

Survival

Every good and excellent thing in the world stands moment by moment on the razor-edge of danger and must be fought for.

—Thornton Wilder, *The Skin of Our Teeth*

These two images of weaver and warrior are joined so we might begin to balance both aspects within us. Both are needed for survival. War, regardless of where or when, is horrible. It is sometimes called a necessary evil or a patriotic duty; people who have experienced it speak of its debilitating intensity. However, this razor-edge of danger of which Wilder spoke can stimulate people and can be for men what childbirth often is for women: a threshold, an enlivening initiatory experience. When the power of life and death are felt in one's blood, it can create a terrible ecstasy. Some peoples spend entire lifetimes caught up in war, with very little time to weave anything of comfort or beauty. Warriors often fight for their own lives and the lives of those they love. They must stand up to injustices, protect boundaries, and confront dragons. Weavers, on the other hand, connect and spin parts into a whole, fragments into completeness, threads into sturdy fabric. Weavers heal the frays; weavers bind together rather than tear apart. Weavers duplicate the earth loom through which planets weave their vibrations, weaving with the Creator a fabric of interdependent strands. Each of us is both warrior and weaver. Gender is irrelevant. A warrior-weaver's task is never completed. We are always in the process of being woven and of defending the right to exist, to be ourselves.

In early Scandinavian mythology, three sisters sat by the gnarled underground roots of the World Tree. Urth spun the yarn, Verthandi wove it into cloth, and Skuld, with her clever scissors, snipped the threads free. In ancient Greek times, the three Fates—the Spinner, the Measurer, and the Cutter—handled life's threads and set patterns for people. Later, Athena is credited with bringing weaving arts to her people. In Northern Europe, the Goddess day was Friday (Freya's Day), and no twisting of threads or weaving was to be done on that day, in order to honor her.

Hunab Ku

Navajo women always turn their spindles in a clockwise or sunwise direction. If spun the other way, they believe, the yarn will unravel and the people may get sick. For the Dogon people of Niger in West Africa, spinning is likened to speech. Spinning, weaving, planting, speaking, making love—they are all ways of creating, all examples of sacred speech. Spinning and weaving, like waging war, have far-reaching implications.

When weavers are absent, warriors will prevail. And when only weavers are present, people lack the focus and drive to reach their highest and most courageous selves and protect our rights to weave. Red often symbolizes the will to survive, the urge to go forward.

Jung suggests that the number eight is a complete and strong symbol for one's self. The number eight was sacred to Pythagoreans because it was the number of the equal corners on a cube. When the mace and spindle weight are viewed as one, they form the infinity symbol: the figure eight (See **Double Spiral** 5). In Indian tradition, the two circles stood for sexual union and completeness; they moved clockwise (male, solar, right-handed) and counterclockwise (female, lunar, left-handed). Since neither of these images is above or below, they form a symbol of infinite perfection. Only when beauty and energy are combined do they sustain life. A joining of opposites always depicts the power to create and the power to destroy; both are needed.

Warrior, the wolf's fangs you've crimsoned, the worm-season of the hero comes,
hold high the flashing blades ... launch the rites of the battle song ere the sun sets.
By Egil the word-spinner who said, "In each man's ear Odin's horn sounded,
His word-mead melted every man's heart."

—*Egil's Saga,* PERHAPS BY SNORRI STURLUSON, ICELAND

• *Kiva petroglyph, traditional, southwestern United States* •

9

Labyrinth

THE HOPI PEOPLE REPRESENT MOTHER EARTH BY DRAWING A MAZE OR labyrinth, either circular or rectangular, like the one pictured here. Labyrinths, like this one called *Tápuat* or "mother and child," represent spiritual rebirth or emergence. When this image is turned so the line coming out of the doorway is vertical rather than horizontal, it suggests membranes holding a child safely within a womb. The outside lines form the mother's arms ready to hold the child after birth. Ancient people living in South America as well as in North and Central America would have recognized this symbol.

Kivas are cave-like underground sanctuaries where ritual and ceremony take place with great intention. The kiva represents Mother Earth. One of the Hopi names for the Goddess is Hard Beings Woman. She makes Earth solid. Long ago, she lived in a kiva in the western part of America, the only place on earth that was free of water at that time. Sun lived in the east, but came to her kiva each night, rising again at dawn. The seas began to recede, passing through underground labyrinth channels to the east and to the west. There are many creation stories, but most Hopi communities tell of the first humans emerging up from the underworld; rituals that take place in the kiva harken back to those ancient times. The hole in the floor, the *sipapuni*, is the place of emergence from the preceding world. Hopi men retreat to the kiva to weave their sacred ritual stoles. A ladder propped up on the side and extending through the kiva's roof represents an umbilical cord leading up to the next world. The Hopi still hold that the earth's own *sipapuni* is the Grand Canyon, ninety miles west of Hopi country.

PART ι ~ Red

Initiation

Certain forms, such as the labyrinth, represent explicitly the experience of initiation—entry into the abyss of the mysteries, the pilgrimage of the spirit.

—Joan Halifax

Initiation marks a time when one is ready to begin something new. Many cultures have special rites of passage. Young boys and girls become men and women through various instructional periods such as making vision quests or entering sacred spaces for the first time. Once you're initiated, you can never go back to that earlier uninitiated status. When one is baptized or has a bat mitzvah or bar mitzvah, one is changed—forever.

Egyptian initiates entered a dark pyramid for three days of "temple sleep." A priest remained nearby to protect them while they journeyed until they awakened, reborn. They emerged with new spiritual insights. Every time a Navajo woman is initiated, the world, they say, is saved from chaos. Her initiation keeps the power of creativity alive in her body for the world.

When you walk the path of a labyrinth, you feel as if you're leaving your old world behind and going someplace different. Twisting pathways lead to the center. Cretan labyrinths as well as some Native American maze forms are very womblike, in that their edges are rounded and the paths take on aspects of uterine folds, like the labyrinth in **Mystic** 8.

The image pictured here asks you to remember, or plan for, your own initiations. What are you entering now? Is it the entrance to your very self? Don't be afraid. You didn't fear the womb when you lived in it for nine months. Why should you fear entering the dark sanctuary you now face? You are invited to consider leaving some things behind in order to take up a new way of being. Birthing fills one with joyful potential.

You will not get lost. Labyrinths have only one way in and one sure way out. It is like life. You are born and you will return again, safely, to the underworld. Arms reach

Hunab Ku

out to hold you. While you may feel caught and confused, disoriented, or even lost at times, you are on an exciting lifelong pilgrimage. The kiva ladder is always standing there, ready to help you move between the worlds. Red stands for the strength and courage you possess to help you reach new plateaus.

The crystal-walled underground mounds and caves that the Irish called the *Sidhe* were filled with light. They were literally places of enlightenment. Though it may seem as if you are totally in the dark, you are safe.

Nine is a number of completion, the last number before ten. Three times three, it is a strong number. Edgar Cayce, America's sleeping prophet, said nine signified a termination of the natural order of things—a sign of imminent change. One of the three paths of this image has nine segments; another has eighteen, making twenty-seven, which is three times nine. When you add the digits in twenty-seven (2 plus 7), you get nine again. Watch for nines to appear, sharing their strength and sense of completion with you.

This image invites you into an inner, protected space. You need not fear the journey. Something is about to be finished, now. And something else is poised to begin.

Except a man be born of water and of the Spirit,
he cannot enter the kingdom of God.

—JOHN 3:5

Carved stone, 100 BCE, Sanchi, India

10

Peacock

Peacocks have long been associated with insight and secret wisdom in many countries, across many cultures. In ancient Greece it was forbidden to own peacocks unless you were in the priest or aristocratic class. Mohammed's own mystical journey into heaven, where he was given the vision to establish Islam, was made on the back of a white horse with a woman's head and a peacock's tail. The horse's name was Alborak. It was similar to Pegasus, the horse born of Medusa's female wisdom.

Many ancients believed it took a female spirit to lead one to divine knowledge. It is no surprise, then, that peacock feathers became associated with goddesses and "her eyes" adorned ritual processions in Greece and Rome.

The carved stone peacocks depicted here adorn a ritual burial mound or *stupa*, enshrining relics of the Buddha. This pair of birds appears on the Eastern Gateway of the Sanchi Stupa in India, which is the peacock's native country. Hindu law still prohibits harming the sacred bird, which, incidentally, is also India's national bird. This carving was completed around 100 BCE. Native to southern Asia, peacocks were mentioned in the Rig Veda as early as 1200 BCE. Biblical accounts (I Kings 10) tell of King Solomon's riches. Fleets of ships, the ancient texts tell us, regularly brought him gold, silver, ivory, apes, and peacocks.

PART *i* ~ Red

Insight

Enlightenment is simply sanity—the sanity in which I see my real situation in the living fabric of all that exists.

—Frederick Franck, *The Awakened Eye*

"Proud as a peacock." This is a royal bird with a crown on its head and a hundred eyes on its wings. Peacock calls loudly and raucously to you, as if announcing rain. He defies convention and loves to dance in thunder.

Ovid's *Metamorphoses*, tells the story of how Juno, angry with her husband, Zeus, imprisons his lover, Io, in the body of a milky white cow, and then sets the giant Argos to guard her. Argos is an ever-vigilant guard because his whole body is covered with eyes. Zeus, however, dispatches Mercury to lull Argos to sleep with stories and music, and then Mercury kills Argos, frees Io, and collects Argos's eyes as a peace offering to Juno. Juno casts them over the feathers of her favorite bird, and that's how the peacock got its eyes.

This old story is an alchemical metaphor, where Mercury plays an elemental role. It's a colorful process. Slaying the giant is the black stage of putrefaction, freeing Io from the milky white cow is the white stage of coagulation and distillation, and, if your alchemical experiment goes well, you will eventually reach the peacock stage, where you will see iridescent colors in your beaker. It is at this point, alchemists believe, gold will appear.

Spiritual alchemists are not out to make gold from lead, but to refine and polish the human spirit. As in chemical experiments, the will and the imagination are combined through various disciplines—prayer and fasting, visualization and meditation—until insights rise like iridescent clouds and you achieve enlightenment.

Insights come to adepts when we are willing to enter a kiva or safe place (see **Labyrinth 9**), to go down into the dark night of the soul and come out the other side.

French Jesuit philosopher Teilhard de Chardin taught the process of spiritual alchemy,

Hunab Ku

during which we all change as we evolve toward God. "Someday," he said, "after mastering the winds, the waves, the tides and gravity, we shall harness for God the energies of love and then, for the second time in the history of the world, man will discover Fire." Peacock brings us fire—the fire of love and understanding.

Peacock feathers were once used to rid people of snake's venom; peacocks, after all, were known to kill snakes. Some believed God created angels from peacock perspiration. With such a mythical history, it is no wonder that peacock feathers are still considered good luck.

Peacock tells you that you can see beyond the stone walkway on which you strut. Peacock offers you rainbow eyes with which to see. Peacock tells you of new life. After their feathers fall off when they molt, and they seem to be stripped of color and life itself, peacocks are again clothed in the splendor of brilliant rainbow plumage.

One is the supreme primal number, and ten, completing the cycle of one through nine, is a return to One—a number of perfection. Pythagoras claimed the number ten, the decad, was the archetype of the universe, the great number encompassing everything, good or ill. Judaism uses ten to represent God. Ten men must be present for a Jewish service. Moses received ten commandments, an indication that ten represents moral fulfillment. Even the long neck and rounded body of the peacock suggest the number ten.

The uncontrolled mind does not guess that the Atman is present;

How can it meditate? Without meditation where is peace?

Without peace, where is happiness?

—Bhagavad-Gita

• *Painted stone bas-relief, c. 1800 CE, derived from Aja people (c. 1100 CE), Dahomey, West Africa* •

11

Ouroboros

OUROBOROS IS A GREEK WORD THAT COMBINES "TAIL"(*OURA*) AND "DEVOURING" (*boros*). This image of a tail-eating snake once decorated the walls of a palace of King Ghezo of Dahomey (now Benin), an area of West Africa on the lower Niger River near the Gulf of Guinea. The stripes around its neck were regularly painted red and blue; the rest of the design was white. This sculpture is now in the Musée de l'Homme in Paris. It is called "God of the Rainbow, Servant of Thunder."

Early drawings of this tail-eating snake in Europe were called "All Is One" or "One Thing Is All." The circular snake was often shown half in light, half in darkness, similar to the Chinese yin-yang Tao symbol. Like a Möbius strip, the snake eating its tail presents an endless loop.

Symbol dictionaries usually tie this tail-biter to Africa and consider it to be one of Africa's oldest images, an *imago mundi*—a world image associating opposites, its sinuous lines representing the primordial ocean encircling solid earth. In their *Dictionnaire des Symboles*, Jean Chevalier and Alain Gheerbrant express doubts that any serpent has ever actually bitten or swallowed its own tail. However, they say, this image also relates to the dragon (see **Serpent 7** and **Dragon 33**). They say the ouroboros is "a celestial symbol, the power of life and of manifestation, it spits out the primordial waters of the Egg of the world, which makes it an image of the creating Verb."

Ouroboros seems to create a perpetual motion machine. Like the yin-yang symbol of the Chinese Tao, the ouroboros eternally loops. Early Greek alchemists used this tail-biter to show how all creation is devoured and melted, dissolved and transformed once again in a self-restoring engine of creative energy.

PART i ~ Red

Unconsciousness

*At the still point in the center of the circle one
can see the infinite in all things.*

—Chuang Tzu

The American writer Flannery O'Connor once said, "The truer the symbol, the deeper it leads you, the more meaning it opens up." This snake image is a powerful archetype—a cosmic picture—showing us what eternity looks like, and inviting us to realize the oneness of all things. It's a sacred hoop holding together all we deem necessary for life. In many cultures, world serpents are said to hold the earth safe. From Norse mythology comes the Midgard Worm, which circles Middle Earth with its tail in its mouth, holding all things fast. Russians call the circle snake *Koschchei* or "Deathless." This female serpent fertilized herself by swallowing her own tail. She surrounded the land mass, and the Greeks called her *Okeanos* or *Oceanus*—ocean. And within these primordial waters float all things unconscious: dreams and visions, intuitive flashes, and spontaneous fantasies. C. G. Jung claimed that this unconscious region is both personal and collective. It is from this psychic realm that we experience synchronicities—real occurrences that are not connected by any rational rules of cause and effect (see page xvii).

An ancient Chinese legendary hero, Fu Shi, was begotten by a dragon whose body ended in a snake's tail. It was to him that the numerical system of the *Book of Changes* or I Ching was given. This collection of oracles claims that life is an all-containing continuum. And in spite of the chance quality we may feel, all life is, indeed, ordered. Jung believed the I Ching, with its eight *pa-kua* trigrams that can be combined into sixty-four hexagrams, organizes archetypes into a certain pattern that we may read. Understanding these archetypes hinges on accepting a perception that time is not linear (from A to B, and then to C and D), but rather that it is a flow, a field, which crisscrosses and spirals. We exist, then, in a living system of acausal orderedness. Together we create synchronistic events, Jung says, that are "acts of creation in time."

Hunab Ku

Ten plus one equals eleven, or what the Chinese call the Tao. Eleven is a self-sufficient prime number. It moves beyond the perfection of ten to a place of enduring energy. In Kabbalist tradition, eleven means knowledge.

Like the ancient circling serpent, red is also an old, primal color. It curls at the base of your spine, waiting to move up and bathe your body with robust consciousness. Ouroboros invites us to move from our unconscious state into an awakened, conscious understanding. Each of us manifests ideas from the vast undulating ocean of our dreams and meditations. What is emerging for you? In your dreams, you will remember. The ouroboros tells us that we hold all the answers within ourselves. The Enveloper, the All in One assures us of our well-being and our place in infinity. The circle goes on spinning forever. Our Creator truly is a circle whose circumference is nowhere and whose center is everywhere. What do you sense circling you today? What comes from your personal unconscious and our collective wisdom to enliven you?

Remember what you have seen,
Because everything forgotten
Returns to the circling winds.

—NAVAJO CHANT

• *Solar disk, 800 BCE, Babylon (Iraq)* •

12

Sun

THE SUN HAS BEEN KNOWN BY MANY NAMES: SULIS, SOL, SUL, SHAMASH, Helios. The name *Solomon* (*sol-amun*) means "sun god." Ancient fire rituals marked the year's turnings: solstices and equinoxes. A perfect eight-pointed star is formed on one of the stones in Stonehenge when the winter solstice sun falls on it at dawn.

The solar disk often appears in Babylonian art as a four-pointed star with twelve wave-like rays in groups of three emanating from its center between each point. Sometimes the solar disk appears as an eight-pointed star, the symbol of Ishtar—a radiant, divine being "filled with beauty and resplendent light." The sun image pictured here, part of the Sipper Stone Tablet, was dedicated by a ninth-century Babylonian king. The solar disk rests on an altar, and three smaller stone figures stand in awe of its radiance.

In some cultures the sun was a symbol of a glorious warrior, a fiery, active male embodiment, galloping across the sky. In others, the sun was a feminine symbol of new birth and renewal. Egyptians had three words for the three daily phases of the sun: *Kheperi* for the infant morning sun, *Re* for the powerful noon sun, and *Atum*, the weaker, but very creative evening sun.

SUN
12

PART *ii* ~ Orange

Success

The Sun, the hearth of affection and life, pours burning love on the delighted earth.

—Arthur Rimbaud

Since early times, the sun has been a symbol of a deity, appearing all around our planet in images of wheels and spirals and rays. Ancient Indian Vedas refer to the sun and light as the supreme good and truth. Brahma was the Most Excellent Ray. The Egyptians called their rulers Ra, the name for the golden sun. Balder is the sun god of the Scandinavians, and Cymbeline is Celtic for "Lord of the Sun." Sun, rulers, and power—a common trilogy. People once wore amber and gold to borrow some of this power.

We all recognize the sun as the most important object in our sky. Ancient astrologers, using stones and stars, concluded that the sun and its mate, the moon, were singularly different from all the other sky beings. Astronomers still use a circle with a dot inside—a powerful image—to denote the sun. The dot or point in the center is our true self, anchored within love. Any point can be the center of the universe, if all is really One, as was discussed in **Ouroboros 11**. Each of us has a personal circle, and all our individual circles are contained within the larger circle we call the Source, God, Father, Mother, the Eternal Force, Allah, or whatever name we might choose. When we draw circles around ourselves to keep others out, we fail to embrace the power that is ours.

From the sun's power comes our source of food; it is our main source of energy. Everything starts with sunlight. Thom Hartmann, in *The Last Hours of Ancient Sunlight*, reminds us that from the dawn of our humanity, probably two hundred thousand years ago, we have depended upon the sun to nurture the earth, providing us with plants, trees, and the results of buried trees. Our past successes have been built on stored ancient sunlight in the form of burning wood, coal, and oil. But our fossil fuels will not last much longer. Maybe forty more years, if we're lucky—that is, if our population can

SUN
12

Hunab Ku

somehow level off and we can hold to our current rates of consumption. Alternative energy sources must not be overlooked or put off. But as Hartmann challenges us, we can change our story. We can redefine success. "Culture is not about what is absolute, real or true. It's about what a group of people get together and agree to believe. Culture can be healthy or toxic, nurturing or murderous."

A dodecagram has twelve points. There are twelve astrological sun signs, and the earth makes one orbit through those signs every year. There are also twelve gods in the Brahman zodiac. Many great teachers have had twelve followers: Jesus, Osiris, Quetzalcoatl, Arthur, Buddha. The number twelve seems to be, for us, a common symbol of cosmic order.

Powerful creative energy comes from orange. Your health, your energy, and your sexuality lie in your orange energy chakra, which is centered in your reproductive organs. Orange, the opposite of blue, is a bold color, a color of worldly triumph. Wake up! Sense its positive energy in you as you view the image pictured here and read these words. Let Sun's fiery rays flow through your entire body. Meditate under the sun, perhaps at dawn. Orange stimulates your thyroid gland and tends to expand your lungs. It also stimulates your spleen and pancreas and aids in your circulation. Radiate with Sun's splendor. Feel, now, your sense of strength and purpose. Fruitful and powerful actions can result from your positive thoughts and feelings—your sunny, vital thoughts. Brilliance is yours, in all its forms. Today Sun teams up with your thoughts, your movements, and your success.

When the Sun rises up, purification comes to the earth made by Ahura, purification to the flowing waters, purification to the waters of the wells, purification to the water of the seas, purification to the water that is standing. Purification comes to the righteous creation, which is of the Beneficent Spirit.

—SUN LITANY, ZOROASTRIAN *Khorda Avesta*

SUN

12

PART ii ~ Orange

Limestone relief statue, c. 20,000 BCE, Laussel, France

13

Venus

THE EIGHTEEN-INCH-TALL EARTH MOTHER FIGURE PICTURED HERE IS THE "Venus of Laussel." It is a carved limestone relief located over the entrance to a cave in Dordogne, France. The woman holds her left hand over her belly. With her right arm she raises a bison horn, a lunar crescent that is marked with thirteen incised lines, perhaps suggesting the waxing days of the moon. This figure was carefully carved sometime around 20,000 BCE. Evidence exists to indicate it was once painted with red ocher.

Rock carvings of human couples making love decorate the cave walls, likely creating a fertility ritual environment. The Sanskrit word for menses is *ritu* or "ritual." While the image pictured here is very old, even earlier goddess figures have been discovered that may date back three million years. The Romans venerated Venus; the act of "venerating" carries echoes of her name. Sacred mountains in medieval Germany were called *Venusbergen*. Venison is named after her, as well, recalling her stag companion.

Is this faceless female mother figure pregnant? Or ready to become pregnant? The position of the left hand indicates that possibility. Conception can take place on the fourteenth day after a woman begins menstruating, and she has clearly marked thirteen notches on her raised horn.

In *The Great Cosmic Mother*, Monica Sjöö and Barbara Mor suggest that patriarchy turned the number thirteen into a bad omen to negate the influence of matriarchal religion. Friday the thirteenth is a good example of this. Friday is named after Freya or Frigga, the Scandinavian goddess. Friday the thirteenth was a sacred holiday; the Swedish St. Lucia's day is December 13; the Greek Hecate's day is August 13.

PART ii ~ Orange

Fertility

The union of feminine and masculine energies within the individual is the basis of all creation. Female intuition plus male action equals creativity.

—Shakti Gawain, *Living in the Light*

Venus's astrological sign is the sign we still use to represent "female," a circle over a cross. The circle, or sign of the womb, connected to the cross, both anchors women to the earth and connects them to the heavens. Even in ancient times, the planetary forces of Venus and Mars were considered direct opposites (perhaps when the United States elects a female president, we will consider landing on Venus). For more Mars and warrior insights, see **Scorpion 3** and **Weaver-Warrior 8** from the red palette.

In esoteric traditions, Venus's day was Friday, Freya's Day. Venus became the Empress in tarot traditions, symbolic of births beneath the sun; she was the pregnant Earth Mother, the Horn of Plenty. Though Venus is usually associated with green and copper, which tarnishes to a verdigris green, is her associated metal, we have chosen to place Venus in the orange palette. Here Venus represents the fertility chakra, the creativity arena. The orange chakra center has been called her special abode. Her womb offers growth for all.

The image pictured here points to Venus, the most brilliant body in the heavens. Venus shines twelve times brighter than Sirius. She says, "Come into my cave. See my sacred cave images creating new life. Motherhood is a sacred task. Blood is hallowed here. Come in. Here you are blessed." The word blessing comes from an old word, *bledsian*, meaning "to hallow with blood."

The Mayans, who believed there were thirteen heavens, charted seven heavenly systems, the solar system being but one. They calculated a year on the planet Venus to be 583.92 days long. And without the aid of computers, they determined a year on Earth to be 365.2420 days long—more accurate than the Roman calendar. They used a special glyph for zero, and with only dots and bars they could count backward and

Hunab Ku

forward four hundred million years. They had thirteen clans of warriors and seven tribes, both key numbers in their elaborate matrix. Thirteen, three dots over two bars, represented the movement in all things.

This prehistoric female image lends you compassion to spark fertility and health in your life. Whether you are actually pregnant or nurturing creative acts, take time to bless yourself and those around you. To be truly creative, you need your own place, whether it's a studio, a room, or a corner somewhere. In Sanskrit, the orange chakra is the *Svadhisthana*, which means "one's own place." This is the seat of pleasure and passion. See **Giant 22** for a balancing view of fertility; both images help you with your emotional identity and your feelings. Anodea Judith says in *Chakra Balancing* that the demon of your orange energy center is guilt. Guilt tells us we shouldn't be feeling a particular way, but Venus reminds you to honor *all* your feelings.

Heavenly Aphrodite, much hymned, Lover of laughing, seaborn, birth-giving Goddess ... Maker of marriage, Mother of desire, Source of persuasion, Grantor of favor, Worker in secret, Seen and not seen ...

—ORPHIC HYMN

VENUS

13

PART ii ~ Orange

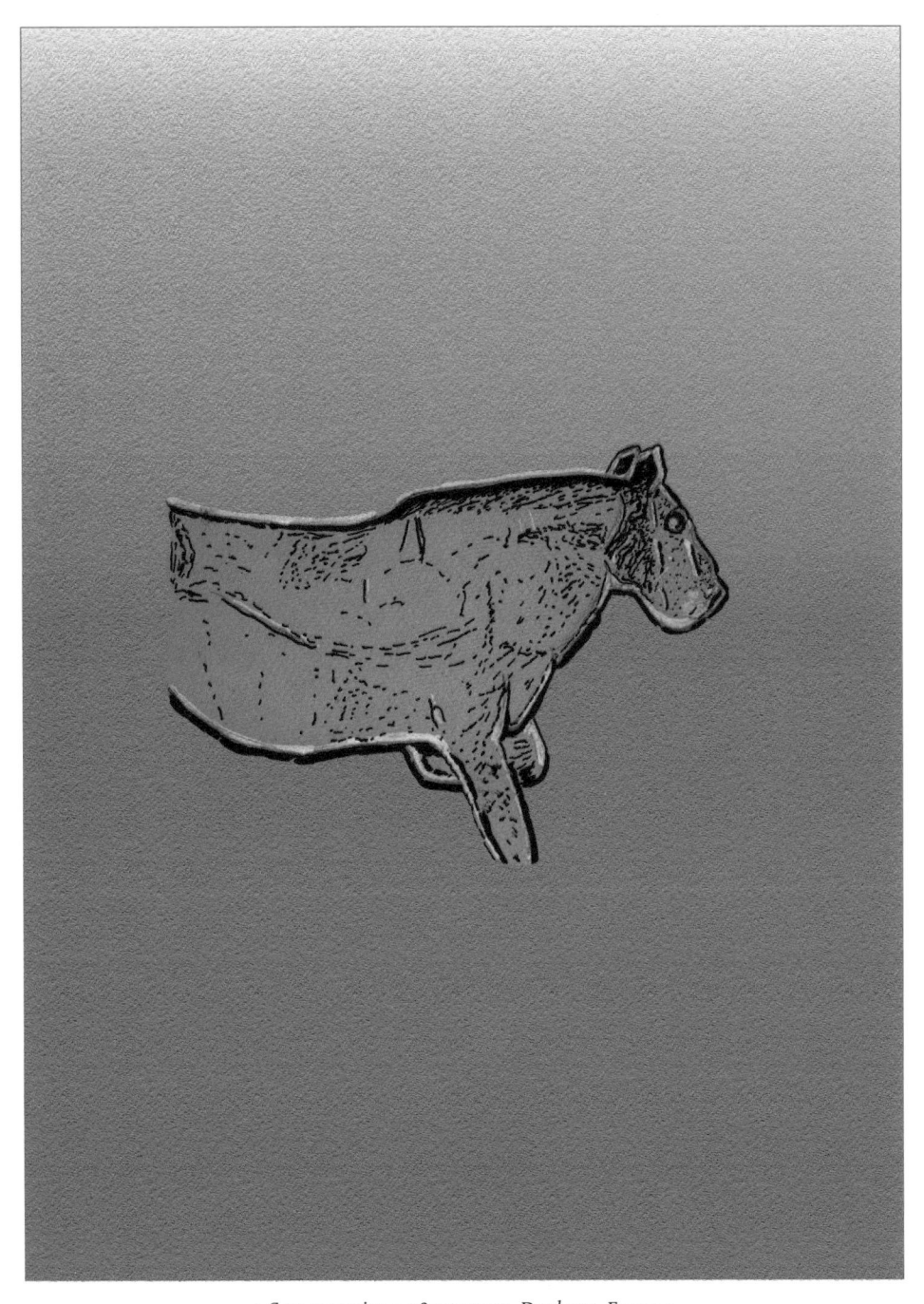

Cave engraving, c. 18,000 BCE, Dordogne, France

14

Lioness

THE ENGRAVING PICTURED HERE OF A LIONESS IS CUT INTO THE WALL OF A cave at Les Combarelles in Dordogne, France. Wall art is difficult to date, but experts believe this one was created sometime between 18,000 and 14,000 BCE. Decorated European caves can be found from as far south as Portugal up to the north of France, and also from Georgia to Siberia. The famous caves at Lascaux, in Dordogne, were rediscovered in the 1940s after the main entrance collapsed 15,000 years ago. Inside, often on white walls, there are about six hundred paintings and fifteen hundred engravings like our lioness. The Grotte des Trois Frères at Ariège (see **Shaman** 15) has over a thousand figures with more found yearly as clay is removed from cave walls. In the Dordogne area alone, over thirty caves contain graphic images. When ice covered much of the world, people deep in these caves sculpted and painted, leaving their works behind.

Five lions appear in a decorated gallery of a cave at Les Combarelles in Dordogne. Hundreds of the other figures first discovered by Abbé Breuil in 1901 were partial images, but in this particular cave gallery 291 figures are recognizable. Besides the lions, there are horses, bison, bears, reindeer, mammoths, ibexes, oxen, stags, hinds, and a fox as well as a rhinoceros.

Cave art, both portable and stationary, can be found all around the world, most of the images going as far back as this lioness and some much further. In Zimbabwe in Africa, pigment has been in use for 125,000 years. No one is sure, of course, just what all this Paleolithic art meant or what it was used for. Some speculate, from prints still existing on the floors of some of the cave galleries, that dancing and ritual must have been performed there.

PART ii ~ Orange

Protector

I found God in myself and I loved her fiercely.

—Ntosake Shange

Once goddesses—Asherah and Ishtar, Cybele, Hathor, and others—were regularly depicted with lions and lionesses. They were called Lady of the Beasts, Mistress of Wild Things, or Lion Lady. When these powerful regal animals weren't carrying a goddess on their backs, they drew goddesses in chariots, flanked their sides, assisted in childbirth, and protected the dead. An Orphic hymn "To the Mother of the Gods" calls her "nurse of all" whose "fast running chariot is drawn by bull-killing lions."

Imperial lions adorned ancient gates and terraced walls, and stood as royal sentries throughout the ancient world. On the Greek island of Delos, a row of marble lions still guards the sacred lake where Phoebus Apollo was born. Sekhmet was Egypt's lion-headed goddess (see also **Sphinx** 12; *sphinx* means "secret place of the lion"). Sekhmet sported many titles: Lady of the Place of the Beginning of Time, the One Who Was Before the Gods, and the Great One of Magic, just to name a few. Her statues usually show her seated on a throne, but the sculptures are done with such intensity that one can almost imagine her roaming the desert at night, hunting and protecting her young. The word for lion, in Egypt, meant the eastern and western horizons and the darkness of night. In Iran, where the ancient Mithraic beliefs once flourished, initiates rode lions bareback.

The astrological sign of Leo, the lion, is ruled by the sun. Proud, loyal, but prone to be quick tempered, a Leo is strong-willed, yet very affectionate.

In a pride of lions, it is the females who hunt. Listen to this image—you'll hear her roaring with conviction, the cave reverberating. Her golden fur ripples in torchlight. Orange generates a sense of pride and self-preservation. It shows a strong sense of identity and healthy assertiveness. The tawny lioness is proud and ambitious. She

Hunab Ku

encourages you to dare to protect those who need protecting. Your physical strength may be tested, but you will remain strong. Believe in yourself. The lioness cuffs and disciplines her young, but loves them fiercely. She revels in her physicality, but saves her strength for the big push. After hunting, she stands back and allows the males to eat. Today, sense your Lioness energy. Roar with confidence.

Fourteen is a number of movement and change. What is moving and changing for you? Numerology often treats numbers greater than ten as integers to be added. In looking at fourteen, then, we might add one plus four and get five—a number of wholeness (see **Earth 5**). Five is also the number of the human, the one meant to be protector of all creation. If the verses in Genesis, telling the story of Adam and Eve, are read substituting "responsibility *for*" for "dominion *over*," we learn we are to care for and be responsible for the "fish of the sea, and the birds of the air, and the cattle and all the earth, every creeping thing that creeps upon the earth." *We* are the protectors.

This day your child I have become, I say.
Watch over me.
Hold your hand before me in protection
Stand guard for me, speak in defense of me.
As I speak for you, speak for me.
As you speak for me, so will I speak for you.

—NAVAJO PRAYER

LIONESS
14

PART ii ~ Orange

Rock carving, c. 3200 BCE, Newgrange, Ireland

15

Mother

Spirals curve around cave walls and ancient artifacts all over our planet. One of the earliest spiral images dates from 24,000 BCE: a mammoth tusk dotted with seven spirals found in Mal'ta, Siberia. In Australia, spirals are symbols of the primary life source and mark the paths of ancestors. Hopi people see the symbol for Mother Earth within each spiral.

The triple spiral pictured here can be found deep within a barrow hidden inside a circular earth mound at Newgrange in Ireland's County Meath, thirty miles north of Dublin. It is one of hundreds of stones engraved with megalithic art in Ireland. Its entrance was discovered in 1699. The barrow maintains a constant temperature of between forty-five and forty-seven degrees Fahrenheit.

One myth about Newgrange tells how the Mother Goddess created the mound by dropping stones from her apron. According to Irish legend, the *Tuatha De Danaan*, magicians from the sky, the Lords of Light, first lived in this "wonder hill." When the winter darkness seems almost unbearable, the solstice comes and on that single December sunrise, a shaft of light enters the barrow, strikes this spiraling trefoil, and illuminates the entire passageway. In this image of the triple spiral, each of the three spirals has five rings moving toward its center.

MOTHER

15

Part *ii* ~ Orange

Intuition

I know the way of all things by what is within me.
—Lao Tzu

Spirals call forth vortices of energy. If we look at **Ouroboros 11** and imagine it spinning, the motion represents a desire to reunite, to get back to our oneness. Black holes in space are giant and mysterious vortices. We see this expression of energy in the microcosm too—in hurricane eyes, in tornadoes, in water going down a drain. In early Hebrew and Babylonian texts, God manifested through a whirlwind. All creative acts enter our dimension through spirals of energy, turning and pulsing, like the Hunab Ku itself.

Why is there a triple spiral on the Newgrange rock wall? Some believe it marks the three moon phases—waxing, waning, and full; others find rich symbolism in the Mother Goddess herself—mother, maiden, and crone, the three phases of a woman's life. Others see the Christian Trinity—the Father, Son, and Holy Spirit. There is completeness in three. Perhaps it relates to the birth experience—mother, child, and other—and the divine plan behind each birth, the divine plan behind all acts of creation. Or perhaps it marks three flowing rivers, each independent, yet intertwined.

Each of us observes and understands our reality in various ways. We take tests to determine who we are and to understand how we react to life. One such typology separates people into sensates or intuitives. Sensates (the S people) rely on outside data; those who rely on inner data are called intuitives (the N types). Intuitives don't seem to need detailed information; they rely on patterns and gut feelings, flashes of insights, and an inner understanding. We are all perceptive, but we don't all honor or act upon our intuition. The poet Robert Browning said, "Truth is within ourselves, it takes no rise from outward things." Even Albert Einstein, whom we might think would have relied on empirical data, said, "The really valuable thing is intuition." Intuition lets us know something, but we are never sure exactly how we know it. Maybe you

Hunab Ku

discovered it in a dream. Maybe Mother or the angels sent it to you. Archimedes met up with his intuitive ideas in a bathtub, watching his body weight displace water. Friedrich August Kekulé, the nineteenth-century German chemist, saw an ouroboros in his dream one night and woke up to draw the benzene molecule closed ring. Poets often "get" lines while walking. Sometimes, as with Coleridge, they receive whole verses. Mozart put his musical gifts this way: "Whence and how they come, I know not . . . nor can I force them." People hear things and act on them, often with astounding results. One night in the fall of 1941, as the war raged over London, Winston Churchill left his offices. His aide opened his usual car door, but Churchill later told his wife, Lady Clementine, that something said to him, "Stop!" He went around to the other side of the car and that saved his life, for a bomb exploded and had he been on his usual side of the car, he no doubt would have been severely injured.

The triple spiral invites you to circle and float and know that Mother spirals on forever. There is no end, only cycles. The mother image invites you to follow its pathways of harmony and to cherish life's ebb and flow. This image incorporates the line and the circle, allowing all possibilities. Claim your intuition. Trust what may seem like chaos. For a time, things may appear to spin out of control. Spirals may be shorthand codes to remind us there really is no end—only many rebirths. Many beginnings.

Gaia, mother of all, splendid as rock
Eldest of all beings; I sing the greatness of Earth.

—GREEK HYMN, SIXTH CENTURY BCE

MOTHER
15

PART ii ~ Orange

• *Reed ideogram, 3000 BCE, Sumer (Iraq)* •

16

Water

PICTURES AND SYMBOLS THAT REPRESENT WORDS ARE CALLED IDEOGRAMS. The ideogram pictured here is a bundle of reeds tied in a knot, standing for Inanna, the Queen of Heaven and the mother of deities. It was carved in stone and dates from around 3000 BCE.

Marija Gimbutas, an archaeologist studying Neolithic Europe, said that of the 210 common core ideograms she isolated, the ones that didn't relate to moon signs (crescents, the circled cross, horns, eggs, and fish) related to water and rain. Water ideograms included V shapes, zigzags, chevrons, M shapes, meanders, and spirals. It appears that most if not all early ideograms were inscribed or painted to ensure and value life.

Situated near the Tigris and Euphrates rivers in what is now Iraq, the early city-states of Sumer featured ziggurats dedicated to the divine feminine. It was there that literature was born. Many of those hymns and prayers remain today.

The Epic of Gilgamesh, an ancient Sumerian text, tells of a worldwide flood. Enki, the water god, flooded the Sumerian lands with his *semen*, the Sumerian word for water. Inanna, whose other names commonly used in the Mesopotamian region included Ishtar, Astarte, and Asherah, was represented by a sacred knotted bundle of reeds. In this desert land, it is understandable that people called her the River of Life.

PART ii ~ Orange

Movement

All things are swirls of energy, vortexes of moving forces, currents in an ever-changing sea.

—Starhawk, *Spiral Dance*

The ancient art of geomancy, practiced first in China, is called *feng shui*. It means "wind and water." Practitioners of this science lay out buildings and cities and arrange households according to the earth's *chi* or *qi*, its energy meridians. Cosmic breath moves energy about the earth, and human architecture can direct and purify the movement of energy within the home, just as acupuncture interacts with energy and healing in the body. By balancing pairs of opposites, luck and health can be assured. Feng shui teaches that there are five elements: wood, fire, water, earth, and metal. Each has productive and destructive cycles, and they interact with one another. Geomancy came to Africa in ancient times. Fa, the God of Truth, representing the movement and freshness of water, came to the Yoruba and Fon peoples of West Africa from the east. He made a palm tree grow. The tree had sixteen branches and produced sixteen palm nuts, symbolizing the sixteen signs of geomancy. Oracular sayings, based on the number sixteen, are still used in some African folkways.

Water, whether still or moving, shows us release and renewal. Wind and water create movement. Water sustains us from the time it cushions us as embryos to the day we die. Without water, we will, indeed die—perhaps within three days. The Sumerian word for womb is the same as that for the sea. Seawater and blood are nearly identical; the only difference is seawater has more magnesium, and blood has more iron. We are born through the powerful movements of uterine water. Our first word is likely to be "Ma," which for the ancients meant the letter M, the symbol for mother as well as for moving water. Many cultures celebrate a ritual similar to Christian baptism. The Maori mark their children with water on the brow as a daily ritual of protection.

Hunab Ku

The ideogram pictured here reminds us that the Goddess restores life, just as water restores health and well-being. Every lake and river has its own unique pattern of movement. However, many of them now are experiencing "fevers," for they are far from healthy. Under a microscope, a healthy droplet of water looks like a complicated flower. If the water is polluted, the image is ill-defined, fuzzy, and far less complex.

Water is yielding, yet conquering. It extinguishes fires, forms steam, and solidifies into ice; it is always changing. Water has no form of its own, molding itself to its container. The word *rhythm* comes from the Greek word meaning "to flow." In stories and legends, water usually represents our unconscious. The water image invites you to be less rigid and more fluid.

Look to your dreams, for Water may be speaking to you there. Look to history and myths to see what you might learn from Water. In the Bible, Joseph got to Egypt by going down into a well, and his people returned by passing through the Red Sea. Inanna's knot symbolizes the re-creative womb. The Ankh, the sacred knot of Isis (see **Ankh** 27), was an ideogram for life itself. Sacred Egyptian mysteries were called *shetat* or "she knots." When people wove or knitted string or yarn into knots, it was believed they could control wind and weather and call up water. Bundles of knotted grains are still powerful symbols of Mother Earth's fertility. Knots encourage the eye to move, as in elaborate Celtic knotwork, and to dance on mystic paths. What moves you today?

The great sea has set me adrift; it moves me. As the weed in a great river Earth and the great weather move me, have carried me away and move my inward parts with joy.

—INUIT SONG OF UVAVNUK, A SHAMAN WOMAN

WATER
16

PART ii ~ Orange

Olmec pottery figurine, 600 BCE, Tlatilco, Mexico

17

Child

From the village of Tlatilco, lying on the outskirts of Mexico City, comes the Olmec pottery figurine of a seated child that is pictured here. It is a white-slipped hollow figure, about 14.5 inches high, dating from about 600 BCE, and it is part of a private collection. Tlatilco may have first been settled around 800 BCE. Teotihuacán, with its great pyramids, was called the Place Where the Gods Touch the Earth. It lies about thirty miles northeast of Tlatilco. Seashells permeate the main pyramid there, perhaps proving contact with the coast and older Olmec sites. It is estimated that about 150 people may have lived there.

Olmec art was created long before the Classic Mayan or Aztec times. Olmec culture flourished on Mexico's tropical Gulf Coast from about 800 to 400 BCE, when the main temple complex on a remote island, now called La Vente, was defaced and abandoned. Olmec sculptures and monuments were often made of small serpentine blocks filled with colored sand. Colossal stone heads were common, usually carved from basalt; numerous smaller figurines of serpentine or jade have also been found.

Like most Olmec Gulf Coast art, the child pictured here is naturalistic, not abstract. It may have even been a portrait of an actual baby. Portrait sculpture in Olmec art is rather common. Many child figures have been discovered, all anatomically correct and all in child-like proportions. They have expressive faces, some crying like this one. Almost all of them have almond-shaped eyes.

CHILD
17

PART ii ~ Orange

Birth

Childhood is the nearest thing to true life.

—André Breton

Birth, according to Monica Sjöö and Barbara Mor in *The Great Cosmic Mother*, is "the supreme paradox of aloneness, when a woman in sweating and groaning solitude brings forth the continuity of human life." Regardless of how many people encourage her breathing, or how many midwives surround her, a woman, alone, is responsible for pushing new life out into the world. It may be the most supreme act of sacrificial giving we humans ever do. Women *give* birth. The baby simply receives this gift, full of assurance that food and warmth will follow. The number of this image, seventeen, is an expression of eight (when you add the digits, seven plus one). In the West, the eight-pointed star is the Star of the Magi, the star that heralded the birth of Jesus.

Why is this little Olmec baby crying? Perhaps she suspects that not all babies are wanted and many die on their way to being born. Babies can suffocate in the birth canal; many more suffer hunger and illness, and perhaps worst of all, abuse, once they arrive.

Or this baby girl may have begun to suspect she is separate from her mother, from the Source, and she is puzzled and frightened. She has survived birth stress; the cord has been cut. Yet she knows she will always continue to need her true mother, her *Mecitli*. Crying is a distress signal sent out to the wider world. "Here I am! Listen to me! Pick me up. I need to be close to someone who smiles at me."

Some of the oldest Neolithic images are of large women, goddess figures, sitting on a throne and giving birth. These images affirm that giving birth is a sacred act. Sitting or squatting is a natural birthing position still practiced by many traditional cultures. Western midwives have tried to bring back more natural birthing practices, but it's been difficult for midwives ever since the Middle Ages when providing herbs and teaching muscle-relaxing techniques to women in labor meant being labeled as witches.

CHILD 17

Hunab Ku

What is begging to be born in your life? What are you willing to *give* birth to? How will you do it? Who will be your midwife?

The Olmec child pictured here reminds you to honor the child within you. Let her play and feel safe. Red-orange, the color of amber, is filled with playfulness and mischief. Within its hues, it holds the energy of children, full of uninhibited feeling. Along with this child, you are beginning a great adventure.

When you were born, you cried and the world rejoiced . . .
Live your life so that when you pass to the Great Spirit,
The world will cry and you will rejoice.

—LAKOTA PRAYER

CHILD
17

PART *ii* ~ Orange

• *Hopi petroglyph, traditional, Springerville, Arizona, United States* •

18

Meander

SNAKES AND WATER TRAVEL IN IRREGULAR LINES. THEY MEANDER. THE JAGGED lines in the Water Clan image pictured here were found written on rocks in Arizona, but similar ideograms appear all over the planet. Although it looks like simple decoration, this ideogram, a meander, was a visible metaphor for water. Meanders usually appear as V shapes and chevrons and were associated very early with waterfowl and female images. These zigzag markings appear not only on rocks, but on early pottery, spindle whorls, loom weights, altars, and all sorts of figurines.

The Water Clan, one of seventeen major clans within the Hopi Nation, used the collection of meanders pictured here to mark onto rock walls the record of their having passed "this way." Every clan made four directional pilgrimages before they made their permanent home in the Southwest. According to Frank Waters in *Book of the Hopi*, "Only when the clans had completed these four rounds of their migrations [meandering to the ends of the earth] could they come together again forming the pattern of the Creator's universal plan" and claim their rightful spiritual power.

Clans left petroglyph signs everywhere they journeyed, showing which clan had been there and on which of the four migrations they were traveling. Some Hopi believed that the Mayans were a lost clan that meandered far south and began a new story, never to return.

The Meander River still flows through eastern Turkey, home to ancient goddess sites at Ephesus. Like a meandering snake, it slithers to the Mediterranean Sea. It's more silted up now than in earlier days, but you can still find it on maps.

PART *ii* ~ Orange

Reversal

My hosanna has come forth from the crucible of doubt.

—Fyodor Dostoyevsky

Everything flows—but not always forward. Meander shows how water bends and twists back on itself, all the while flowing at its own pace. Meanders and chevrons, two Neolithic aquatic signs, often appear on images of birdwomen. Marija Gimbutas points out that the bird goddess had a dual nature. Like the doubling back of the meander image itself, the bird goddess gave life and took life (see **Vulture 13**). Red bird's feet were commonly drawn on cave walls. Drawings of figures wearing bird masks and having pendulous breasts appear regularly. Two such figurines have been found, both from around 23,000 BCE. The bird goddess, as an image of Mother Earth, with decorative meanders, found her way onto vases shaped like water birds. She also appeared in the old stories, as geese, cranes, and swans. The character M is just a portion of the meander sign.

V shapes and M shapes, as part of what Gimbutas calls the "Old European script," were in common use between 5300 and 4300 BCE, and eventually many of the signs migrated into Classical Cypriot and an old Minoan language found on Crete that is still not deciphered. Later these letters made it into our modern written languages.

Things may not be going as smoothly for you right now as you'd like. Be patient. And expectant. Detours and reversals can be birthing times, offering new directions and fresh-flowing possibilities. Trust ancient river beds to carry you along paths you may currently think are totally blocked. But water persists and paths turn. Patience can reverse many courses. Reversals are a natural part of forward movement. Disappointments and detours lie along many paths. You may feel stagnation. Obstructions, like rocks in a river, seem to pop up. But you can row around them. They need not take you down.

MEANDER 18

Hunab Ku

The number eighteen points to the material side of your nature, the part balancing your spiritual side. Eighteen is associated with upheavals, revolutions, and wars. The meander image pictured here is similar in some respects to the tarot card Hanged Man, showing an image of a person hanging upside down and generally looking at ease with the suspense. It is an image filled with faith in an outcome that may be different from the obvious one. A crucifixion can turn into resurrection. To keep from meandering for too long, you may have to take an unorthodox upside-down view of your situation. There may be difficulties, loss, and even sorrow. Remember Dostoyevsky's words: Hosannas come from crucibles of doubt, and from reversals.

O heroic one, Ishtar, the immaculate one of the goddesses,
Torch of Heaven and Earth, radiance of the continents . . .
You alter the fates and an ill event becomes good . . .
Lengthen my days, let me live, let me be well.

—BABYLONIAN PRAYER

MEANDER

18

PART ii ~ Orange

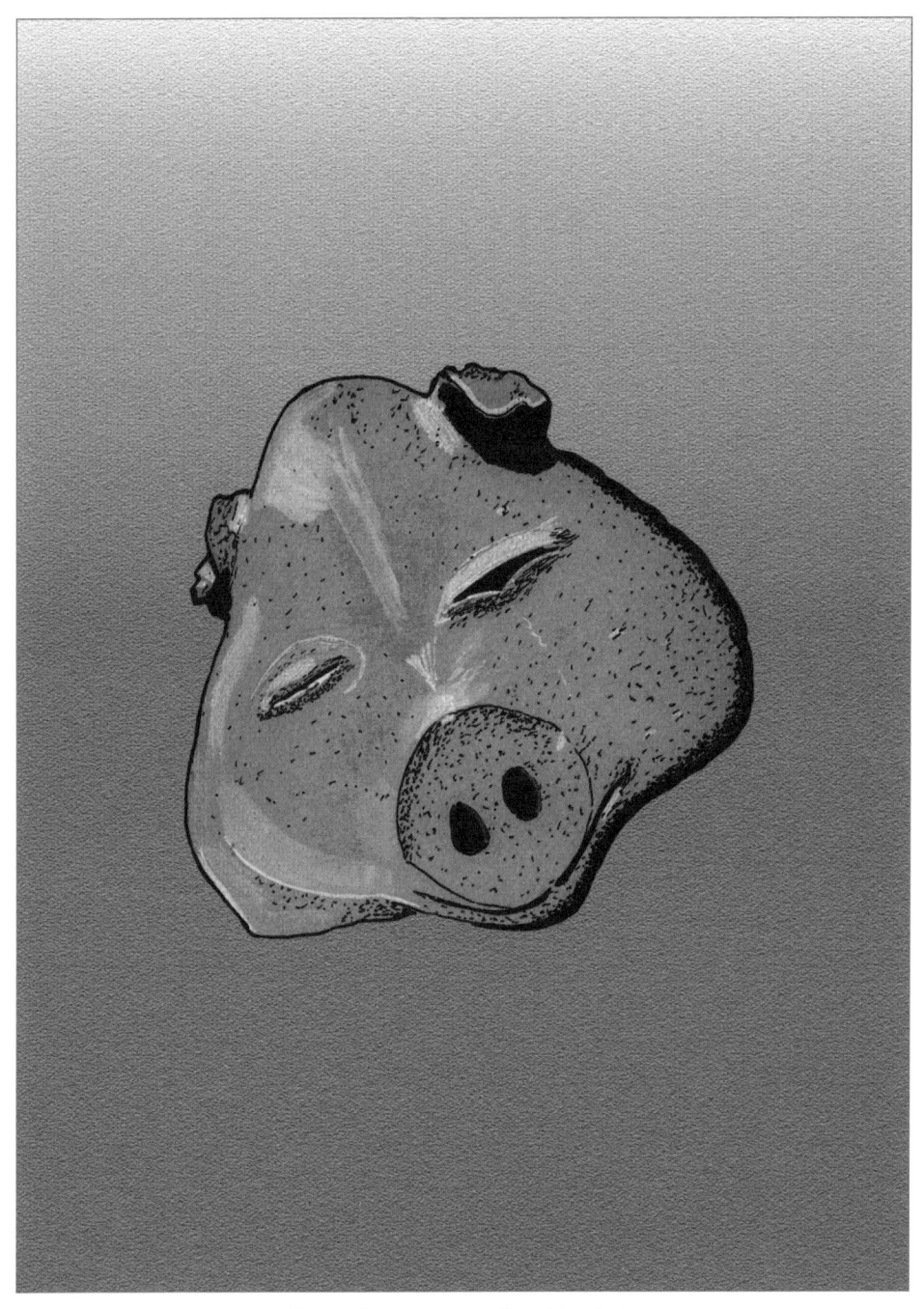

Clay mask, c. 4500 BCE, Vinca, Macedonia

19

Player

THE CLAY MASK PICTURED HERE OF A PIG, 7.5 INCHES HIGH, WAS FOUND at Vinca near Stip in Macedonia. It dates from 4500 to 4000 BCE. The sow was the sacred animal associated with the Pregnant Goddess, perhaps because of its fast-growing rounded body. Many sculptures and vases featuring the sow have been uncovered throughout Greece and central Europe. Some were carved in marble around 3000 BCE and can be seen in an Athens museum. Reliefs and paintings often feature sow-masked dancers.

For over eight thousand years Mother Earth and her pig effigies were connected to seed planting and farm fertility. Suckling pigs were later sacrificed to Demeter and her daughter, Persephone, in Greece. During the October harvest season in Europe, for thousands of years up to the eighteenth century, country women mixed sacrificial suckling pigs that had been buried in the earth with seeds to be planted to ensure an abundant harvest. Some clay pig sculptures have been found embedded with grain, furthering the connection between pigs and crops.

PART ii ~ Orange

Sensuality

We are making hay when we should be making whoopee; we are raising tomatoes when we should be raising Cain or Lazarus.

—Annie Dillard, *Pilgrim at Tinker Creek*

Among many early people, the pig was considered a sacred animal. *Sacred* comes from the Latin word for both "holy" and "unclean": *sacer*. Small wonder, then, that we have been confused by why certain folks refuse to eat pork. Was it because, like the horse, the pig was once associated with the goddess culture and therefore taboo? Or was the pig somehow unclean? The pig had religious significance for early Israelites as well as people in Egypt, Syria, Asia Minor, and India. Early Egyptians encouraged pigs to trot along the fields, pressing seeds into the ground.

Animals were sometimes sacrificed and later eaten, to replace the ritual killing of a ruler. Usually they were goats or rams, lambs or kids, to take the place of the sacrifice of firstborn children, which was also common at one time. Pigs were often eaten at special ceremonies, which set the pig apart rather than declaring it unclean.

Vishnu was called the Boar God, and it was said his sacrificial blood held great creative power. He claimed the whole universe is made of sacrifice. Boars were offered to goddesses: Astarte and Demeter. Freya, the Mother Goddess of Scandinavia, was sometimes called the Great White Syr (sow); her chariot, legend says, was pulled by boars. In Polynesia, Pele, the fire goddess of volcanoes, was thought to have a hog child as a lover or spouse. The tusked boar was sacrificed in her honor. Young boys also sacrificed boars as a masculine rite of passage.

In the Buddhist tradition, Marici was called the Diamond Sow. Seven pigs attended her on her throne. The Magical White Sow and her seven porcine ladies-in-waiting also appear in Celtic myths. Culhwch's name meant "womb or hiding place of the pig." In Scotland her name is Orc, and the Orkney Islands are sacred to her. Even the Isle of Man, it is said, has fairy pigs.

Hunab Ku

PLAYER 19

Nut, the Egyptian sky goddess, "ate" her "piglets" at dawn—she ate the stars—and then rebirthed them again the next night. When people excavated the old site of Troy on the northern coast of Turkey, they found statues of pigs studded with stars.

Cowrie shells, shaped like tiny vaginas, are considered women's symbols in many cultures. In Latin, the shiny white shells were called *porcella*, "little sow," and the word *porcelain* is connected to both the pig and the cowrie shell itself with its appearance of china. The Greek term *choiros* was used for the female genitals; it also means "pig."

The pig mask encourages you to play, to be open to surprises, to accept the absurd, to dare to break free of your chains. "Embrace life," she seems to say, with all its pleasures. "Accept your body and your sexual energies, your feelings and your passions. Celebrate the moment—for it is all you have. This very moment." In Gaelic the divine mother's name is Muc Mhor. Indeed, she is much more!

Masks allow us to step into another time, another persona. The orange pig mask invites you to understand that *all* is play. Orange celebrates sexuality and the life force, and it is the positive color of good cheer. Even the number nineteen is playful; add the numbers together and you have ten, add one and zero and you are back to one, to the beginning.

Your cheeks are like halves of a pomegranate behind your veil...your rounded thighs are like jewels, the work of a master hand...I am my beloved's, and his desire is for me.

—SONG OF SOLOMON

PLAYER

19

PART ii ~ Orange

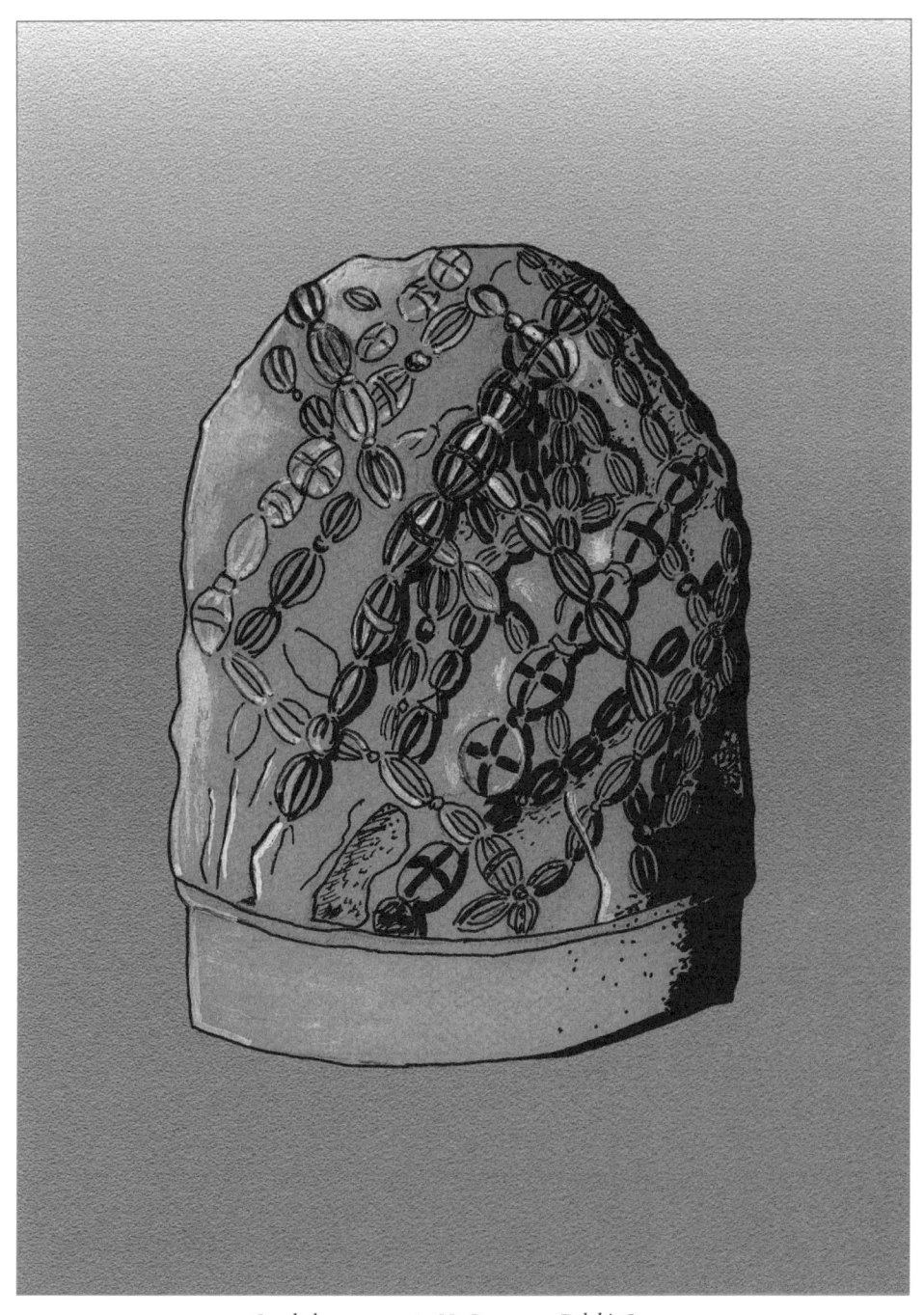

• *Omphalos, 1400 BCE, Mt. Parnassus, Delphi, Greece* •

20

Mountain

THE CARVED STONE PICTURED HERE, CALLED THE OMPHALOS—THE NAVEL OF THE world—once marked the spot where Mt. Parnassus emitted sulfurous vapors. Virgil says Zeus sent out two eagles and where their paths crossed, there was the Om-Phallos, the center of the world. It was there, on the slopes of the three-thousand-foot Mt. Parnassus, north of Athens, that the Pythia priestesses welcomed visitors seeking wisdom. This carved container housed a python underground.

The priestesses' sanctuary was originally called Delphyne, after the Greek word *delphys:* the Womb of Creation. It is from this same word that dolphins are named. The Delphyne or Pythia were young teenage girls who were trained to invite psychic messages; they ate bay leaves and drank water from the goddess's sacred spring. There is speculation that they ingested venom extracted from the fangs of poisonous snakes. Sitting over a crevice in the mountain on a three-legged birthing stool, they entered an altered state, and other women interpreted their words for the seeker. A verse was then written with no spaces between the letters and with no accents, and it was up to the person seeking insights to interpret and understand it.

Legends about the site preserve the change from prehistoric matriarchal culture to our historical patriarchal one: it was here that Apollo "made war" on the Python, or the Mother-Creator. Even after the Delphic shrine was taken over by Apollo, and a Doric temple built to him, a priestess called the Pythoness acted as the oracle; however, male priests interpreted and controlled the oracle's messages. Severe earthquakes have now destroyed much of the site. The Emperor Theodosius finally forbade oracles altogether in 385 CE and closed the temple.

This conical stone with its bead-like pattern was originally carved from a meteorite. A serpent design encircles and protects it. Only a Roman copy in marble now survives.

PART *ii* ~ Orange

Revelation

Here on the mountain I have spoken to you clearly.... Here on the Mountain, the air is clear and your mind is clear; as you drop down into Narnia, the air will thicken. Take great care that it does not confuse your mind.... Remember the signs and believe the signs. Nothing else matters.

—C. S. Lewis, *The Silver Chair*

World navels such as the one at Delphi appear all over the earth. Researchers notice they appear in fairly predictable geometric patterns. A navel or sacred center can be natural, constructed, or even imagined. Silbury Hill in England is called the goddess's navel. Jerusalem's Rock and Temple Mount is the omphalos to Christians, Jews, and Moslems. Many believe it is the planet's sacred center. Even prior to Solomon's temple, the Canaanites worshiped Baal there. The Chinese thought there were sacred mountains on each of the four horizons. The Oglala Sioux believe Harney Peak is the center of the world. The Inca said Cuzco was the world's navel, the omphalos set there by the first Inca. Ancient Ireland was divided into four kingdoms meeting at the fifth kingdom, the Hill of Uisneach, the Celtic omphalos.

Mountains, mounds and temples, pyramids and ziggurats are all considered gates into heaven—dwelling places of the gods and goddesses. The Tibetans call Mt. Everest the Goddess of the World. Fuji. Ayers Rock. Maccu Picchu. Shasta. Olympus. Golgotha. Meru. Mecca. This is mystical geography, for as Black Elk of the Oglala Sioux once told Neihardt: "Anywhere is the center of the world."

The Delphi navel stone represents all mountains and encourages you to listen to your own center. Revelations come in many forms, including your own dreams and meditation times. You may be about to receive a new discovery. Ask yourself where your summit is and why you continue to climb. What will it mean to reach the peak? The mountain symbolizes your search for meaning.

MOUN-
TAIN

20

Hunab Ku

Revelations exist in most traditions. Mayan calendars revealed the birth and death of great cultures. Biblical prophets foretold the coming of the Prince of Peace. Nostradamus claimed to see future dictators like Napoleon and Hitler. The Hopi people watch the heavens for signs. Edgar Cayce, the great American prophet, predicted coming earth shifts and alterations in geography. Greg Braden, in his book *The Isaiah Effect*, says, "Prophesy... allows us to witness the future consequences of choices that we make in the present." Each of us makes choices about the future. Revelations can ring archetypal warning bells to correct our present course.

Just as Delphi is a central earth chakra, the orange genital chakra, *Svadhisthana*, is sometimes called the *hara* (one of the lesser chakras) or center belly chakra. Orange is red's raw energy tempered with yellow's insight.

The mountains... I become a part of it...

—NAVAJO CHANT

MOUN-
TAIN

20

PART ii ~ Orange

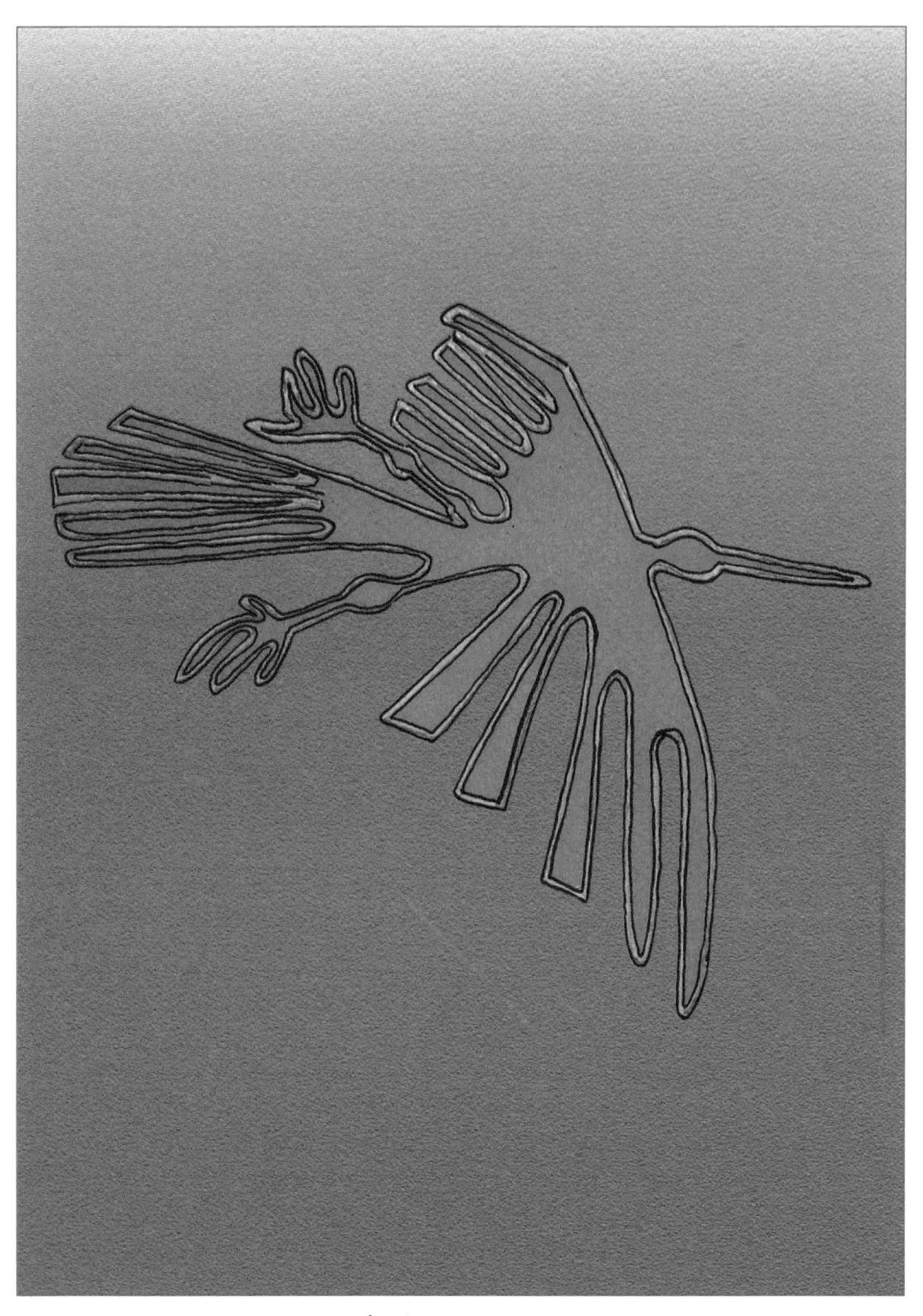

• *Desert drawing, 100 BCE, Nazca, Peru* •

21

Hummingbird

There are 320 species of hummingbird, all of them in North, Central, and South America. The largest hummingbord is found in the Peruvian Andes; the giant hummer can grow up to 8.5 inches long. Perhaps it is no coincidence, then, that the hummingbird appears in giant form among the mysterious Nazca Lines.

The image pictured here is one group of Nazca Lines found in southern Peru, where these stony murals stretch for miles across the Palpa Valley. They were created in the extremely arid desert called Pampa de Ingenio in the foothills of the Andes. We know the hardworking Nazca people brought water from the mountains in aqueducts, but it is unclear how or why they laid stones in the desert to create these enormous animal figures. Made of stones, pebbles, and red sand, they seem like aimless lines until seen from the air. The lines were created on the desert floor around 100 BCE. Eighteen of these large-scale birds appear along the Ingenio River. They range from 30 to 300 yards long. The one in this particular drawing has a 140-yard wingspan.

A hundred giant figures in all are preserved in this two-hundred-square-mile area. What were they for? Why did the artists go to such lengths? The people who created these enigmatic outlines in the Nazca region may have been making a giant astronomical calendar marking movements of constellations and planets. Or the figures might be large labyrinths on which to ritually walk. Or perhaps communication markers of some as-yet-unknown technology are buried beneath the figures, humming, like the bird shown here. According to ancient Mayan teachings, the hummingbird is an otherworldly creature. Blue and green hummingbirds are associated with the first two days of their thirteen-day cycle and of their first two heavens: the god of fire and time and the god of earth.

HUMMINGBIRD

21

Part ii ~ Orange

Vitality

Joy is the holy fire that keeps our purpose warm and our intelligence aglow.
—Helen Keller

By beating their wings twenty to twenty-five times a second, hummingbirds are able to hover, fly backward, and even fly upside down. Vitality in motion, they also can achieve speeds of up to twenty-five miles an hour. By adding the integers in twenty-one (two plus one), we get three: two wings and one tail working together to produce dynamic flight. The Tao Te Ching says, "Out of the One comes the two; out of the two comes the three; and out of the three come the ten thousand things."

Vitality is one's life spirit, the source of all our creativity. You have it within you, but you must be awake to react to it and rejoice in it. Native Americans believe hummingbirds bring love. They open hearts. NASA has measured a "hum" of electromagnetic frequencies generated both by Earth itself and by the subtle life force in human bodies. We are "humming" birds! All living beings—all stellar beings—give off frequencies of varying degrees. Dowsers can pick up earth energies. Sensitive people can pick up energies flowing through humans as well as animals. We live in a rhythm of energy. Helen Keller called it *holy fire*.

If she were with us today, Keller would encourage us to dispense with sluggishness. She might ask, "Why are you bored? Open your heart. You are vital to the world." *You* are the only person who can do what you do, smile the way you smile, affect the world the way you affect the world. The hummingbird celebrates flight for flight's sake. What could be more joyful than doing something just for the sheer fun of doing it!

Since the nineteenth century we have come to understand that although energy can be transformed, it cannot be created or destroyed. Energy exists. The energy exhibited by the hummingbird is kinetic energy. The energy running through us has been described in many ways: *prana, chi, qi,* juice, charge, kundalini, *josh*. Certain yogic practices focus one's bodily energy by controlling circulation and producing

HUMMING-BIRD
21

Hunab Ku

heat. Tibetan monks can wrap themselves with wet sheets and go sit in mountain snows. By meditating they are able to dry the sheets with the fiery heat their bodies generate. They call this *tumo*. The !Kung people of the Kalahari call it the boiling *n/um*, a trance state generated by dancing. The Hindus use *jajval* for burning and *jvalit* for possessing fire. Christian mystics called it a burning love of God. Michael Murphy in *The Future of the Body* describes how athletes, too, feel this mystical vitality. Murphy believes we all can experience "the unitive awareness, selfless love and redeeming joy that crown human life."

When our brains absorb high frequency sounds, we are stimulated and our energy actually increases. However, lower frequencies, like your TV and airplanes, decrease our energy. When we hum, making that nasal sound with our lips closed, we stimulate our inner ears and our vestibular system, which is linked to balance. It's been proven that people who practice regular humming give themselves an inner massage that improves clarity, balances their hormones and increases their antibodies, strengthening their immune system. Humming, even ten minutes a day, will also benefit our blood pressure and improve our sleep.

All of us have felt our energy drained by certain environments, certain people, certain illnesses. As humans, we are capable of receiving and sending energy via our attitudes, our expectations, and our degree of openness. Our health and vitality depend upon feeling that holy fire.

Wearing my long wing feathers as I fly,
I circle around, I circle around
The boundaries of the Earth.

—Arapaho Ghost Dance Song

HUMMING-BIRD

21

Part *ii* ~ Orange

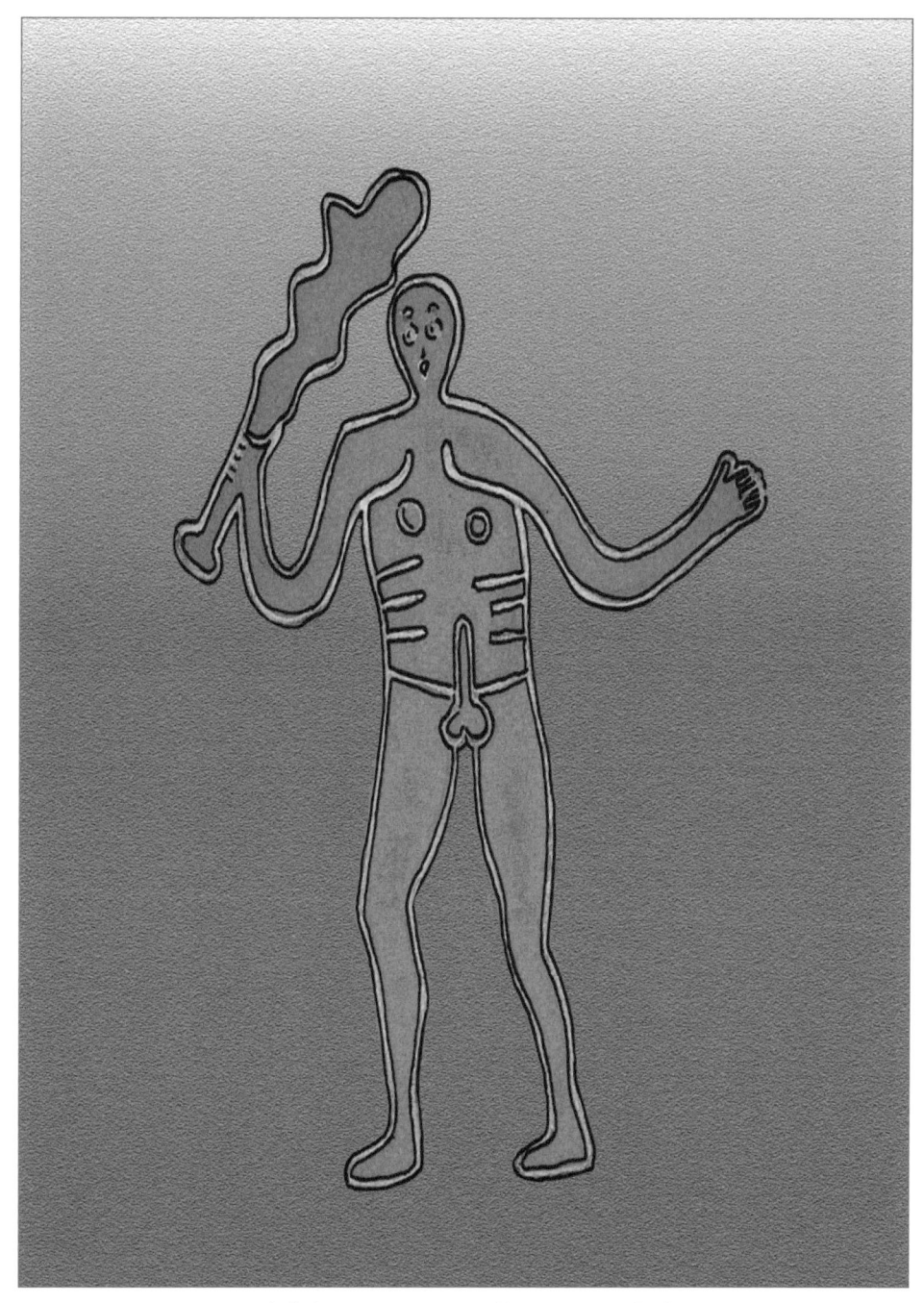

• *Chalk figure, 100 CE, Cerne Abbas, Dorset, England* •

22

Giant

THE CERNE GIANT STANDS 180 FEET TALL AND WIELDS A CLUB 120 FEET LONG. He can, therefore, be seen in all his phallic glory throughout the Cerne Valley. The chalk outline was carved by cutting through turf to the chalk below. He stands on a hill between Dorchester and Sherbourne in southwestern England, Thomas Hardy's country. Like the great White Horse at Uffington (see **Magician** 26), the Cerne Giant's outlines were scoured and cleaned every seven years, traditionally on May Eve. Couples probably still enjoy celebrating the coming of spring by sleeping with the Giant. He was said to cure barrenness, for he is without a doubt a fertility figure, given his thirty-foot erection. The National Trust now scours the outline with the help of local villagers.

The village of Cerne Abbas with its medieval streets and thatched yellow stone houses lies at the foot of the Giant's hill. No one knows precisely when this figure was carved, but some experts believe it was around 100 CE; however, like many ancient sites, the hill figures may have been created over earlier existing sites. Ancient earthworks and barrows surround the Giant. There are other carved human effigies, sometimes called "long man" figures, like the one in Sussex near Windover Long Mound. There is some speculation that the one in Sussex was intended to picture the constellation of Orion. In 603 CE, St. Augustine came to take over the sacred well at Cerne and founded an abbey hoping to convert the pagans there. In 1764 William Stukeley, secretary of the Society of Antiquaries, first called the Cerne Giant and his club Hercules, or Helith. Hercules was often portrayed with a club and a lion's skin in Celtic statuary of the Roman period. Recent archaeological research revealed a buried outline beneath the Giant's outstretched arm that could be the image of a draped animal skin.

PART ii ~ Orange

Control

The opposite of control is celebration ... celebration is about energies dancing.

—Matthew Fox, *The Coming of the Cosmic Christ*

Like phallic symbols in India, such as the lingam, and other obelisks around the world, the maypole figure pictured here represents the masculine energies planted into the earth's womb. We see phallic images replicated in skyscrapers, rods, scepters, spears, and guns. This archetype says, "I am a virile king. I am one who can produce seed. Growth is assured by my virility."

An early Saxon god was Heil, which literally meant virility. "Hail! Be alive! Be of good cheer." Helis and Heil are very close to Helios, and may, in fact, derive from the Saxon word for the sun. The Cerne Abbas Giant appears to be a masculine solar deity.

Hercules was, as the Greek myths tell it, the strongest man on earth. He was not an earth giant. But he was a son of Zeus and, although not considered one of the gods, the Olympians needed his arrows and club to kill the lion of Nemea; kill the Hydra with nine heads; bring a golden-antlered stag back alive; capture a rampaging boar; clean out, in only one day, some stables housing thousands of cattle that hadn't been cleaned for years; drive away a plague of birds; go to Crete and capture the Minotaur; capture some man-eating mares; bring back the Amazon queen's girdle; capture a monster's oxen; bring back some golden apples from a location that no one knew; and finally, as his twelfth task, go to the underworld and bring back Cerberus, the three-headed dog. Manly feats, all. But as the mythologist Edith Hamilton says, "Intelligence did not figure largely in anything he did and was often conspicuously absent."

Brute strength can make one a hero or a felon. Wielding clubs of any kind often causes pain, rape, and death. Ask any male soldier, and you're apt to hear that he has been trained to think of his gun and his penis interchangeably, for both are raping tools.

GIANT 22

Hunab Ku

Some people choose to dominate. Interestingly enough, there are cultures with no word for rape, for the concept of controlling someone else's body is unthinkable to them. Using sex slaves has gone on in Judeo-Christian and Classical Greek times and continues throughout the world today. Abuse and the need for control come, Riane Eisler says, from living within a dominator trance perpetuated by rigid hierarchies and painful punishments. As long as the female body, as well as young boys' and girls' bodies, are considered male property to be bought, sold, traded, used, violated, destroyed, or discarded, all of us will be held in bondage. The author of *The Chalice and the Blade* and *Sacred Pleasure,* Eisler has much to say about how we can move from the dominator model to a partnership model of interaction.

Perhaps Giant comes to encourage you to curb your controlling instincts; allow the power "with" and not "over" people and events to be your guide. Giant tells you that you have great ideas and giant-sized possibilities; don't limit yourself to pettiness. Orange is self-assertive and ambitious. This powerful sexual energy center creates desire and visualization. Tibetan monks often wear orange robes to balance the energy they are not using in this second orange chakra. Orange is a push-pull color; it represents both desire and frustration. Add the digits from twenty-two and the result is four, the number Pythagoreans called the root of all things. An intellectual number. A number defining the powers of the soul: mind, science, opinion, and sense. Twenty-two also doubles the risk of the Ram, two. With the use of control comes great risk, just as the doubled spirit of *Dreams* (**Moon** 22) increases your *Wisdom* (**Owl** 2).

Anger of fire; fire of speech; breath of knowledge; wisdom of wealth; sword of song; song of bitter edge.

—Druidic Chant

GIANT
22

Part ii ~ Orange

87

• *Cartouche, 3000 BCE, Egypt* •

23

Star

SIRIUS IS THE BRIGHTEST STAR IN THE HEAVENS. ALTHOUGH IT IS 8.6 LIGHT-years away from Earth, it shines twenty-three times more brightly than our sun. Sometimes called the Dog Star, Sirius appears in the constellation Canis Major. In Tibet, Sirius is celebrated in an annual festival called *Rishi Agastya*. *Rishi* is Sanskrit for "sage" and also the "giants of the elder race." Throughout all of Northern Europe, giants were called *risi*.

The hieroglyphic for Isis/Sirius is written by combining the obelisk, the half-moon or eye, and the star within an oval or cartouche.

The Dogon people, the Mali of the Sudan, also believe in an elder race, and they think this elder race came from Sirius. The Dogons measure time by the orbit of the white dwarf star Weight, which circles Sirius every fifty years. The Dogons have a long mysterious history of knowledge about this star and its seed star or eye star (see **Womb 6**). The *Nommos*, the ones who came from Sirius, the Dogons say, will come again on the path of the rainbow. All of creation, they believe, came from the heavy star that circles Sirius. They call it the Germ of All Things.

Babylonians and Dogons believed amphibious beings with fishtails—*Oannes*—came from the Sirius system and founded their civilizations. Called Ancient by the Egyptians, brilliant Sirius was thought to embody Isis and Osiris. During the Middle Ages it was a coppery red color, and it is now seen as a greenish, steel blue. In Egypt, after the summer solstice, Sirius reappears on the horizon after being hidden for seventy days, marking the beginning of the Nile's annual summer flooding. This appearance was the harbinger of fertility. However, they also called Sirius the Death Star or Scorching One when it appeared to withhold needed rain. Egyptians measured their year of 365.25 days by Sirius's rising.

PART *iii* ~ Yellow

Inspiration

> I have a terrible need... shall I say the word?... of religion. Then I go out at night and paint the stars.
>
> —Vincent van Gogh

Isis's name means infinite space and infinite stars. When she appeared in the night sky, in the form of the sparkling star Sirius, Egyptians knew the Nile would flood, causing rich silt to bless their fields. Isis came, shedding tears over her dead husband, Osiris; with this, she brought the Egyptians life once again.

On any clear night, we can see about two thousand stars with the naked eye. Of these, about one-third are, like Sirius, binary star systems—two stars that revolve around each other. Sirius, the Dog Star, can be found by locating the three parallel stars in Orion's belt and then following the line they draw, rather down and to the left, to the brightest star in Canis Major. Astronomers figure the Sirius supercluster of stars is about 490 million years old. Sirius has companion stars—masses of dozens of white dwarfs, each weighing about two-thirds of our sun's mass. That's extremely dense! Because of the varying temperatures of stars, some, such as Sirius, Rigel, and Regulus, appear blue; others appear more orange, such as Vega and Aldebaran; still others, like the famous Garnet Star, Cephei, are deep red. Some stars look greenish gold. Double stars appear very brightly colored. Astronomers measure a star's brightness by a magnitude; zero is the brightest (Sirius is −1.5), and fourth magnitudes are fainter, with nebulae or clouds of gas and newly formed stars being the faintest of all. Nuclear explosions from hydrogen gas cause all the twinkling we see in the night sky. Some stars are a hundred times larger than our sun, and some are only one-tenth the sun's mass. When a star no longer has much fuel at its center, it expands and its surface cools. Some become exploding giants—supernovas. Some pulse and are called pulsars. Some become black holes. Nothing in the sky remains static.

Hunab Ku

It is easy to be inspired by the night sky. One breathes in, in-spires, sighs, and exhales in total awe at the canopy of brilliance overhead. Stars connect us to our immortality as nothing on Earth can do. When a star, or most likely an asteroid or comet, "falls," we sense that something greater than ourselves has touched the earth.

Young stars and suns are always yellow. Yellow brings out our wisdom and understanding, our passion and our creativity. Yellow is the color of the solar plexus chakra (the *Manipura* chakra), our self-identity. Our ego. We are fired up with starlight. It is here that we have a strong sense of our own will and action, our own mastery. The stars inspire us with their life-giving warmth.

The number twenty-three, the date in July when Sirius rose before the sun in Egypt, is two plus three. A five-pointed star or pentagram, sometimes called Solomon's Seal, evokes the number of man in many traditions. The famous image of Vitruvian Man by da Vinci mirrors the hermetic knowledge that the body can create a pentagram. Two times three creates a six-pointed star, the Star of David. All are royal stars.

When you see the cartouche of a star, an obelisk, and a half-moon or eye pictured here, you see your own creativity and inspiration. Be at peace, knowing you are linked to a higher plane. Star lights your way, so you can, in turn, light the way for others. Yellow fills you with its intellect and generosity, calm and peace. Just as the Star of Bethlehem guided the young child's visitors so long ago, stars can guide you as well. They can warm you and guide you to a higher place.

What do the stars do? What do the numbers say? What do the spheres revolve?
O souls that are lost and saved, they relate, they sing, they revolve—your destinies!
—HERMES

STAR
23

PART *iii* ~ Yellow

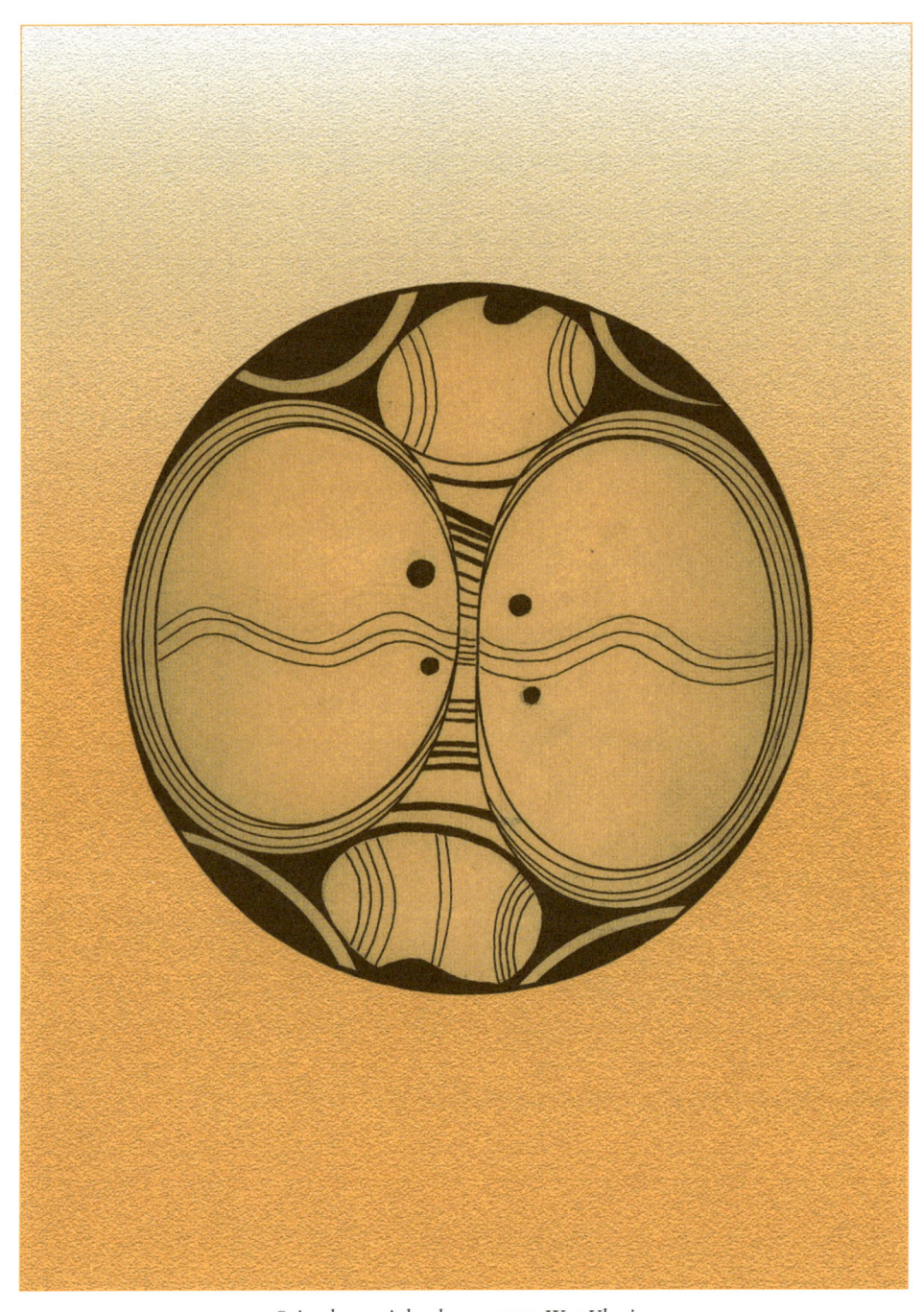

• *Painted ceramic bowl, 3500 BCE, West Ukraine* •

24

Twins

THE CERAMIC IMAGE PICTURED HERE, PAINTED IN BLACK ON RED, WAS discovered in the western Ukraine. It was created around 3500 BCE. It seems to portray abundant fertility: twin eggs in a womb joined by three sperm-like snake lines.

A fetus starts out as female, but may become male. In some traditional cultures, a hermaphrodite was considered superior to either of the two sexes because that person was seen as more total, closer to perfection. In some Native American communities in North and South America, the *berdache* (the Europeans' term for two-spirit person) or "he-she" is valued as a person who can bridge the sexes. A two-gender-divided universe is just one alternative. The Siberian shaman symbolically assumes both sexes. Hermaphroditism is a source of sacred power and a sign of spirituality. The androgyne—*andros* (man) and *gyne* (woman)—points to wholeness, to perfection.

Farm folklore claims that when two things grow together into one unit, it is a symbol of good luck and cause for rejoicing. If twin oxen plow the first spring fields, the farmer is brought much luck; if the farmers are twins, the field, some country folk say, will be protected from all natural disasters.

Two-headed figurines are found in excavations of communities that existed in 25,000 BCE. The folk custom of burying a placenta after birth for fertility and good luck may stem from the ancient Egyptian custom of treating the placenta as if it were the unformed twin of the birth child. The pharaohs' placentae were always saved and buried with them when they died so their twins would not wander the earth forever in search of them. Several sources suggest that this custom holds the origin of the *doppelgänger*, the idea that when we see our "ghost twin" we are about to die.

PART iii ~ Yellow

Androgyny

> My face is a caricature of her, and her soul is a caricature of mine ... we are that perilous pair.
>
> —Rose O'Neil, *Garda*

Twins are connected, yet separate, two yet one. Safely cradled, they stretch and grow, surrounded by a soft womb of possibility. These two eggs are infused with a Gemini nature. They already feel their cleverness. They are anima and animus, Adam and Eve, mirror images of one another.

Castor and Pollux resulted when their mother, Leda, mated with Zeus when he was in the form of a swan. Romulus and Remus founded Rome. People born under the sign of Gemini experience dualism in their interests as if inhabited by "another."

Twins are born to about one in eighty-six mothers. Siamese (conjoined) twins are named after Chang and Eng from Siam, who were joined at their sides. Identical twins are mirror inverted; that is, their features, even down to their fingerprints, are the mirror image of one another.

Twins represent the dual nature each of us embodies: physical and spiritual, human and divine, life and death, light and darkness, masculine and feminine. It was the alchemists' challenge to unite these dualities into one. A *hierosgamos*, or sacred marriage, unites opposites. We live in such split-apartness that each of us longs for "another."

In Middle English, to *twin* something meant to split it, to halve it. But *twin* and *twine* also mean "to join." Yin and yang. Or as the Egyptians saw it, Atun and Nun, the sperm and the egg. Geb and Nut, earth and sky. Isis and Osiris. The **Hunab Ku 39/39** is a twinned image.

Some cultures value twins as very good luck. In others, they are taboo. In Nigeria, for instance, a spiteful curse was, "May you be the mother of twins." The Bantu of the Lower Congo once starved one twin and buried it at a crossroads. Some Amazon and

TWINS
24

Hunab Ku

Australian people believed twins were actually subhuman. The Togo and Masai people, however, feel twins bring good luck to their communities. In Bali, twins are called "the betrothed." In legends and myths, one of the twins is usually stronger and wilier than the other. Consider Jacob and Esau who struggled as fetuses and continued to struggle after birth. Cain, you will remember, killed his twin, Abel. Twins can more easily work with the dark side of their personality since they live with their mirror image.

The poet Shelley wrote of love thirsting after its own likeness. It's true, we find ourselves in our relationships with another. Shelley argued that we strive for our "antitype," our twin and counterimage. The person who makes us whole. That *perfect fit*.

Two eggs come to you in the image pictured. What is each saying to you? You are quick thinking, versatile, and capable of accessing your whole nature. You may begin to notice "an opposite" within yourself that needs integrating. Mercury rules Gemini, so you may feel mercurial or edgy with mood swings. If Gemini speaks to you, no doubt you are intellectual and quick witted, at ease with your mind. But it may be your body that needs your attention now.

Yellow raises one's consciousness. It mixes red and green rays so it both stimulates and relaxes, like twins growing up together. At times, they pull apart, but at other times they are completely in line with one another. The number twenty-four is twelve plus twelve; twelve is six plus six; six is three plus three. Twins, all.

Perhaps you are about to birth an idea or integrate several concepts for an outstanding result. The number twenty-four is thought to be very auspicious.

TWINS

24

Namaste: I honor the place in you where the entire universe resides.
I honor the place in you where, if you are at that place in you
and I am at that place in me, there is only one of us.

—INDIAN GREETING AND FAREWELL

PART iii ~ Yellow

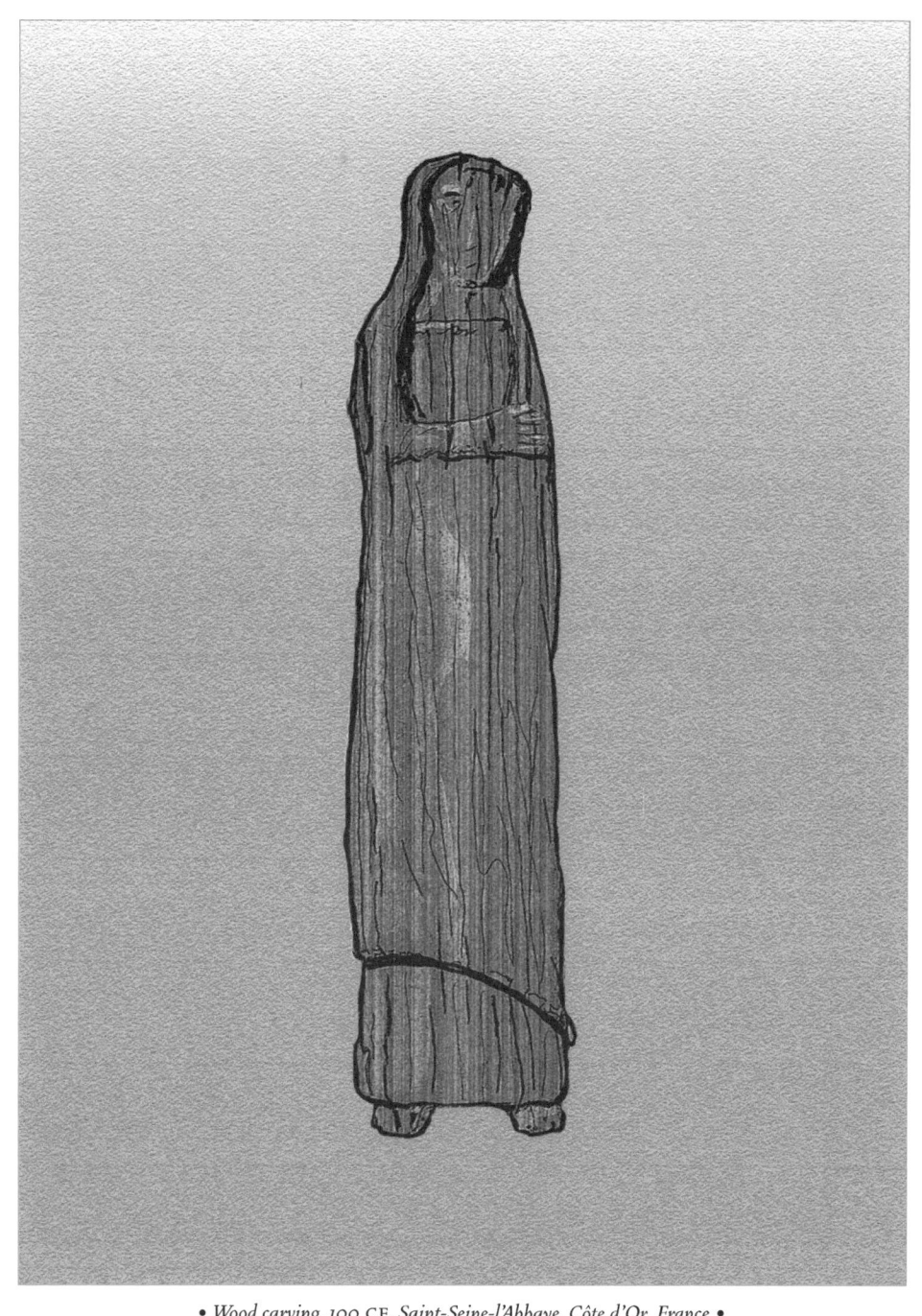

• *Wood carving, 100 CE, Saint-Seine-l'Abbaye, Côte d'Or, France* •

25

Virgin

Near the source of France's River Seine, near Saint-Seine-l'Abbaye in the Côte d'Or lies a sacred pool in the sanctuary of Sequene. In 1964 hundreds of wooden votive figures, including the female figure pictured here, were recovered from the bottom of this pool. The figures are dated as having been deposited there in 100 CE, but they may have originated from a much earlier site.

Sacred wells and pools are common throughout the ancient world. *Cenotes* in the Yucatán Peninsula were watery tombs for real virgins as well as for gold offertory figures. Holy wells appear throughout Ireland and the Cornwall Peninsula, often associated with Brigid, the goddess of healing, blacksmithing, and poetry.

Whether the figures dredged from Sequene's pool were meant to represent divine or human forms is unclear. What is clear, however, is that the figures were crafted by retaining much of the wood's perfect natural form. Echoing this efficient use of line in wooden sculpture, most Virgos have a reputation for practical organization, perfectionism, and critical discernment.

VIRGIN
25

Part iii ~ Yellow

Perfectionism

Perfectionism is daring to embrace the universe itself as our true dimension, daring to steal the fire of the gods, to walk on water or fire unafraid, to heal, to claim plenty in time of dearth, to behold boldly what is desired and become what we have need to be.

—Joseph Chilton Pearce, *The Crack in the Cosmic Egg*

One in myself. That is the meaning of *virgin*. A woman who does not depend on another—especially on a male—for her identity is called a virgin. It traditionally meant "unmarried." Priestesses in early temples were called holy virgins. Their task was to heal, prophesy, honor the dead, and offer their bodies in sacred dance to the Mother. Any children born were called virgin-born children. The angel Gabriel, the divine husband (which is what his name means), came to Mary, and she gave birth to a virgin-born child. Mary was called *almah,* "young woman." In less than five hundred years, the Christian Church turned her into the Blessed Virgin, the Queen of Heaven, and she took on the compassionate and accessible face of the divine feminine. The university we graduate (birth) from is called our *alma mater,* which once meant sacred virgin mother.

The constellation Virgo, or Maiden, with its bright star Spica, is the only female figure among all the constellations in the zodiac. She has, therefore, been long associated with all the familiar female goddesses: Ishtar, Isis, Demeter, Persephone, Astraea or Starry One, Medusa, Artemis, Diana, Athena, Minerva, and, of course, Urania, the Greek muse of astronomy. Virgins dedicated themselves to celibacy in their service to Isis. Spica is one of Virgo's oldest stars and represents her spiked shaft of wheat. Some people believe Virgo was the inspiration for the mythological sphinx (See **Sphinx** 12) as she is near Leo, the constellation many early Egyptians thought to dominate the night sky and lend its leonine nature to the sphinx statues. Virgo is the second largest constellation in the sky, Hydra assuming the largest star path. Every culture has named star clusters, but since 1930 we have been able to commonly identify

Hunab Ku

them. It was then, worldwide astronomers decided to use Latin names to delineate the boundaries of eighty-eight constellations. The Virgo cluster has over a million, million stars, most of them very old and red.

This virgin image pictured here stands with her right arm crossed over her heart, as if embracing all she stands for. She wants things to be done right. To be perfect means to satisfy all requirements, to respond to an ideal. She refuses to be dominated or hurt; she values her body too much. The word *perfect* also means "contented" and "satisfied." She is that. She is also self-sufficient and efficient. Like the statue found in the quiet pool, Virgin often leads a hidden life, preferring academia, health care, child care, or government work. The Virgin is more like Martha in the biblical story of Mary and Martha, preferring to do her work in the kitchen rather than sit and listen to Jesus.

The Virgin might mean you need to stand alone. Perhaps you will work with your tendencies toward perfectionism and put them in balance. Virgo's search for meaning is to serve. Use your tact and skills today; allow your intuition to free you from your rational side. Twenty-five is a number of discrimination, analysis, and perfection, being a perfect fourth of one hundred.

Yellow-gold is the color of spiritual perfection, the color of peace and rest. The image pictured here stands with her arms across her solar plexus, the chakra that rests on the strength of will. This chakra, sitting near the pancreas, handles your energetic fires and regulates your blood sugar levels. Your ego is housed here. Who are you? How will you act? When you have fire in your belly, you are ready to go! To hold this power in balance is your challenge. Team up with **Ram 2** to assess your risks. Yellow is a self-empowering color, optimistic and filled with health and well-being. Yellow foods and yellow colors aid your digestion. For the Chinese, yellow is the color of earth. Yellow is also a moon color, watery and reflective.

VIRGIN
25

All the immaculate perfections, at all times encircle Thee
As the stars surround the crescent, O Thou blameless holy one!
—Mahayana Buddhist hymn

Part iii ~ Yellow

Incised shell, 1000 CE, Mississippian, United States

26

Artist

AN ARTIST LIVING IN THE MISSISSIPPI RIVER VALLEY AROUND 1000 CE INCISED a seashell with the spider image pictured here. Given its two holes, it may have been created to wear as a necklace.

Most Native American people have legends surrounding the spider. Often, as for the Keres Indians of New Mexico, the spider is the creator—Thought Woman. For the Hopi, the Pueblo, and the Navajo people, she spins possibilities. She created the earth by stretching a thread of web from east to west and then one from north to south. By mixing her saliva with earth, she created the first beings, which she covered with her white cape of wisdom, knowledge, and love. As she named things, they appeared. After creating the earth, she sent her two sons to the north and south poles to keep the earth balanced and safe. The Navajo sometimes refer to Spider Woman as Changing Woman. She taught people how to weave, and she is honored in every woven creation. She keeps the universe working and sacred dreams alive.

In Africa, the spider is the hero-trickster, Anansi; he is cunning, resourceful, and creative. In Greece, Athena was called Spider—Fate Weaver. The Fates, three aspects of Aphrodite, were the Spinner, the Measurer, and the Cutter, weavers of destinies. The word *spider* comes from the Old English word *spinan*, meaning "to spin." In Latin *neo* and *necto* mean "spider"—literally, "the wool spinner."

PART III ~ Yellow

Creativity

Whether we are weaving tissue in the womb or pictures in the imagination, we create out of our bodies.

—Meinrad Craighead

ARTIST 26

She hangs there, from her three-strand web, watching you. She senses you are ambivalent about her. Small wonder, since many call her the Devouring One, for she eats her enemies. Sometimes she is poisonous. But, do not fear her; watch her and emulate her movements. She is the part of you that also spins and weaves and creates something from nothing. She risks every time she hangs by a spinneret and then lets go. Just as spider creates that thin filament from the center of her body, so also do you create from within your body. You create from your core, your center.

Web-working and net-working make all people stronger because of the interconnectedness involved. We create when we make decisions and when we neglect to make decisions. We create even when it seems we are idle. "We owe most of our great inventions and most of the achievements of genius to idleness—either enforced or voluntary," said Agatha Christie, the prolific spinner of mysteries. Spiders call us to weave our own webs of responsibility.

The French have a wonderful word for playing with whatever is at hand, and it seems to encompass the essence of creativity: *bricolage*. To be a *bricoleur*, you need only reach out in front of you for whatever is there and play with it. Put it into a new order or disorder. To trust Artist's power, you have to do something worthwhile. Eleanor Roosevelt encouraged us to "do the thing you think you cannot do." Try new things, but don't get caught in tangled webs; remember *you* spin them.

Spider uses large arenas in which to do her work; no task is too overwhelming for her to undertake. And for those of us who grew up with E. B. White, we know what Charlotte was able to accomplish. "Some Pig!" Charlotte most likely had never heard of the opera singer Beverly Sills, yet she lived Sills's words: "You may be disappointed if

Hunab Ku

you fail, but you are doomed if you don't try." Even webs in a barn remind us that all art is sacred.

Volumes have been written about what supports and what destroys creativity. You need to walk your own web's thread to discover what will help your work flourish. Like the fragile seashell pictured here, which lasted centuries, you are much stronger than you think. The yellow chakra is the navel chakra, the point from which you were spun in your mother's womb. The solar plexus is the seat of your emotions. Artists bring what is inside, out. They manifest and continue the creative actions put in place by the original divine Creator. Therefore, we are all cocreators and we are all artists. The Nahuatl people of southern Mexico and Central America say this of artists: "The good painter is wise; god is in his heart. He converses with his own heart. He puts divinity into things."

Spider comes to remind you to bring energetic clarity and divinity to each undertaking. You will be amazed. Opportunities will present themselves; they will fly right into your web, but you must be awake and ready to catch them. Fling those filaments into the void. And use yellow energy to fuel your undertakings. Let yellow keep you optimistic and hopeful as you create.

The number two represents both sides of your brain, which you must draw from in order to create. As an artist, you are intuitive as well as rational. A dreamer and a doer. Six is a balanced number, a symmetrical force. In the Hebrew mystery writings of Kabbalism, six represents beauty and creation. Together, two plus six makes eight, the number of a spider's legs and of infinite possibilities.

ARTIST
26

O God, creator of our land,
Our earth, the trees, the animals and humans;
All is for your honor.

—WEST AFRICAN ASHANTI PRAYER

PART iii ~ Yellow

• *Stamped pottery, 200 CE, southern Appalachia, United States* •

27

Fire

CIRCLES, FLAMES, AND TRIANGLES REPRESENT FIRE. THE UPWARD-POINTING triangle is a spirit-rising, energy-releasing ideogram. The word *pyramid* is Greek for the idea of fire. In India, the triangle represented the deity Agni, the fire god, who consumed sacrifices and was burned on the altar. Ashes were called Agni's seed.

Combining circles and lines in an interlocking design, the Native American fire sign pictured here was stamped into pottery created in the southern Appalachian region of the United States around 200 CE.

This interlaced design is directly related to the sacred fire symbol of the Hopewell mound-building people. For seven hundred years they lived near navigable North American rivers where they created an extensive trading network unrivaled until the modern era. Objects were traded from the northernmost Mississippi valley to the ancient Mayan lands of Central America. Like ancient Egyptians on the Nile, they traveled up and down the Mississippi River by barge. They lived harmoniously in "mound" cities, terraced structures reminiscent of early Central American cities. They used copper from Lake Superior, mica from the Appalachians, shells from the Atlantic coast, and obsidian from the far west. There seems to have been a continent-wide symbolic and aesthetic language shared in the crafts and artwork found throughout the Americas at the beginning of the first millennium.

We know very little about the mound-building culture. It was already just a memory to the Native Americans who encountered the first Europeans thirteen hundred years later. Only their earthworks and selected objects remain to remind us that America was civilized much earlier than most people think. (See **Great Bear 1** and **Serpent 7**.)

PART *iii* ~ Yellow

Energy

Energy is eternal delight.... Energy is the only life.
—William Blake

Long before Socrates was asking his insightful questions in Athens, people understood the world to be composed of four elements—fire, water, air, and earth—and they usually listed fire first. They were the four pillars of the ancient world. Carl Jung believed this fourfold structure of the universe also appears in our psyches. Fire represents intuition and inspiration, air being our thinking function, water our feelings, and earth our senses.

Prometheus rescued mankind, in Greek myth, by giving us fire, much to the sky father's chagrin. Zeus punished him by chaining him to a rock in the Caucasus Mountains. Every day an eagle ate poor Prometheus's liver, and every night he was restored once more to health. This fire from heaven was a metaphor for enlightenment or secret knowledge. Moses, the Bible tells us, saw a bush that was burning but was never consumed. This purifying fire is common when people come face to face with the "I Am."

Quantum physicist David Bohm said, "Matter is frozen light." Physicists tell us atoms are 99.9 percent empty space. This means there's a lot of room for electrons, protons, and neutrons to vibrate and set up energy patterns within these vast fields. Author and theologian Matthew Fox says, "The divine is washing through everything." We all share the same source of light and life. This powerful energy lights up our bodies in fields surrounding us as auras of color. There is a continuous electromagnetic field encircling all living things like threads of fire, weaving in and out. These energy movements often generate heat.

Internal fires kindle our bodies and spirits to perform in new ways. Mystics speak of "burning up for God." Our bodies, which do not stop at the boundaries of our skin, are filled with such divine energy, and some people actually feel as if they are on fire.

Hunab Ku

FIRE
27

Energy—*prana, chi, qi, mana, num, Orenda*—can be seen and felt as a palette of seven colors moving through our bodies. We are nested, like Russian dolls, with many energy bodies. Although our physical body is the only one we can feel with our senses, we also have mental, emotional, spiritual, etheric, and astral bodies, and so forth. Hold your hands close to another person's hands, without touching, and you'll feel palpable pulsations as you move your hands closer and father apart. Hands are particularly sensitive instruments. Our bodies are like the fire image pictured here, with permeable edges and thin boundaries capable of evolving and transforming. French philosopher and anthropologist Teilhard de Chardin wrote about our eventual "omega point," when all consciousness would converge into a unity of love. A contemporary Prometheus, he told us we would then discover fire for the second time. An interviewer once asked French poet Jean Cocteau, before he died in 1963, "If your house were on fire, which object would you take with you?" Cocteau responded: "The fire!"

The Cherokee Indians teach that yellow is the sacred fire of wisdom and the East, source of all illumination and understanding. The yellow chakra in the belly is the seat of the literal chemical fire that converts our food into energy. Think of the number twenty-seven as a fiery upward-pointing triangle, nine on each side.

This yellow pottery symbol, with its carefully woven central lines, reminds us of our Promethean gift: we are filled with fiery energy. Not to dissipate. Not to waste. Not to burn out. Rather, this image says: hold tight to this valuable gift. It fuels your deepest intentions and warms your very core.

FIRE

27

O Agni, Holy Fire! Purifying Fire! You who sleep in the wood and ascend in shining flames on the altar, you are the heart of sacrifice, the fearless wings of prayer, the divine spark hidden in everything, and the glorious soul of the sun.

—VEDIC HYMN

PART iii ~ Yellow

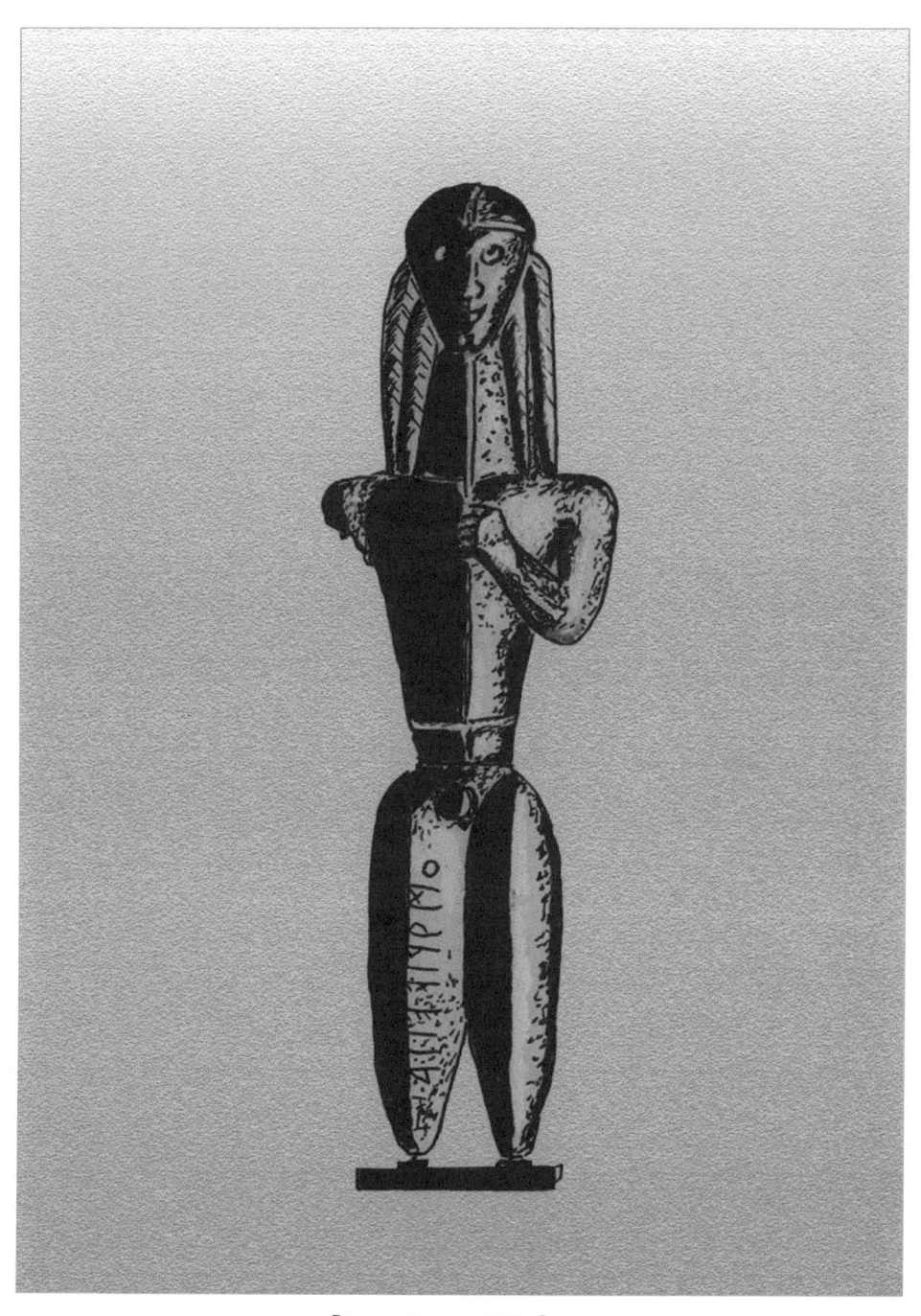

• *Bronze statue, 700 BCE, Greece* •

28

Youth

BETWEEN THE GEOMETRIC AND ARCHAIC PERIODS OF GREEK STATUARY, around 700 BCE, the bronze statue of Youth pictured here was created. It is eight inches high and can be seen in the Museum of Fine Arts in Boston, Massachusetts. Its thighs are inscribed with the following message: "Mantiklos dedicated me to the Far Darter of the silver bow, as part of his tithe. Do thou, Phoibos, grant him gracious recompense."

Some call the figure the Statuette of Apollo. There are numerous examples of youthful Apollonian statues from the same period. In Greek myth, Apollo, the sun god, assumed his twin sister's moon powers. Apollo and his twin sister, Artemis, were born on the sacred island of Delos. Just as Artemis took on the form of the Great She Bear, Apollo assumed the aspects of several youthful animals: mouse, lion, and wolf.

Apollo and Artemis were twins (see **Twins 24**). Apollo represented the sun, and Artemis the moon. Apollo usurped his twin sister's powers of prophecy, magic, and healing, and even her poetry and music. He laid claim to her Muses and even to the Delphic oracle's insights. Go to Delphi today and you will find only his remains, not hers (see **Mountain 20**). He laid claim to her cherry laurel, the plant of poetic frenzy, and its bay leaves, and ever after that, laurel crowns were awarded in the great Greek games.

PART iii ~ Yellow

Growth

The quickest way for a tadpole to become a frog is to live loyally each moment as a tadpole.

—*The Urantia Book*

People who live as perpetual youths usually are afraid to commit and are unwilling to accept responsibility. They always seek adventure, the next new thing. Bodies, usually considered friends, at the time of our youth seem to cause us such embarrassment. We're never sure how we're going to react. Most of us, now long past this stage, think back on it and claim we'd never choose to go through that painful time again. Time seems to drag on and on when we are youths; we long to get to run our own lives, to move out from under our parents' gaze and make our own decisions.

Jungians would call a youth a *puer aeternus,* one caught between the world of the child and the world of the adult. Adolescents are the neither-nors. They are neither children, nor adults. Their peers form their world. Hormones run rampant. Youths need coming-of-age traditions to keep what they perceive as chaos in their bodies from destroying them. Without sacred structures, experimentations of all kinds can cast our youth adrift or reduce rites of passage into purely social events. Under a loving elder's care, a youth can emerge from this time able to contribute to his or her community. We can learn much from ancient people in this regard.

"The vision quest, for example, speaks eloquently of the need to find a guiding light, a higher meaning in life, that gives it authenticity and meaning. When a Lakota Sioux 'cries' for a vision, he is brother to an ancient Greek consulting the oracle at Delphi, a Hindu donning the golden thread in the *upanayana* ceremony, or a Christian receiving the chrism of confirmation. In each case, the participant opens himself to divine guidance and help," say Philip Zaleski and Paul Kaufman in *Gifts of the Spirit.*

With Youth's energy and enthusiasm comes growth. Relationships, projects, and friendships all experience growing pains. What is begging to grow in your life right

Hunab Ku

now? Do you feel you're in constant motion without much forward thrust? What longs to focus and awaken?

Yellow is a hopeful yet volatile color. Children cry more often, color researchers tell us, in yellow rooms, and some allergies flare up when we are surrounded by yellow. Yellow's gotten a bad rap in Western culture, often being associated with cowardice and prejudice. Yet yellow is a sturdy reliable color. Child psychologists have noticed that young children who turn to yellow crayons a lot may long for adult supervision. Dr. Max Lüscher, the well-known color theorist, claimed that yellow "presses forward" and when people choose that color first, in his color test, they have a desire, a hope for greater happiness in the future. If they place yellow in a lesser position, in other words reject it, they have been disappointed and feel isolated. We often gravitate toward colors we feel are somehow lacking within us. Wearing those colors tends to balance out our needs.

The integers of number twenty-eight add up to ten, the number of perfection. The Greek culture of youth, represented by the sun god, Apollo, has profoundly affected our Western view of strength, sports, and performance of all kinds. Youth feels in full control of the physical world and playfully explores every aspect of it. Youth also is poised to explore all aspects of the mental and spiritual worlds and has the boundless energy and drive to do just that.

YOUTH

28

May all humankind likewise offer blessing: Old woman, young woman, wise men and foolish. Blessing of youthfulness, blessing of children—big boys, little boys, big girls and little ones. Bless the wisdom of the holy one above us; Bless the truth of the holy one beneath us; Bless the love of the holy one within us.

—CHINOOK PSALTER

PART iii ~ Yellow

• *Celtic knotwork, 700 CE, Lindisfarne, England* •

29

Triangle

Celtic art had its beginnings thousands of years before monks used it for decorating their intricate manuscripts, such as the triangle figure pictured here from an early Christian document. Celtic knotwork can be found across the British Isles and Ireland. Its mathematical perfection and beauty ornamented standing stones, metalwork, and jewelry as well as the calligraphed page.

This triangular knotwork design adorns borders of the Gospels of Lindisfarne as well as the famous *Book of Kells*. Lindisfarne is an island off the northeast coast of Northumberland and is connected to the mainland at low tide. All of these old manuscripts were painstakingly penned, some designs so tiny and delicate people thought angels had traced them.

Knotwork interlacings are peculiar to the Pictish school of Celtic art, no doubt arising from Scandinavia, but similar patterns have been discovered in the Ukraine and Slavic areas dating as far back as 20,000 BCE. Braiding, plaiting, and basketry use similar knot patterns. They all point to an original notion of the great cosmic loom. Knotwork seems endless, like eternity. Knots were thought to bind the soul to the earth and must be cut or broken, as in Alexander the Great's task of untying the Gordian knot, for the spiritual journey to go on. For some, knots represent the never-ending return of lives. Cords and knots signify various binding forces and protection. A circular chain of knots can become a prayer formula. The Chinese created an earth square of knots called the Knot of Eternity, which, like the triangle pictured here, was also used as a mandala for meditation (see **Ankh 27** and **Water 16**).

TRIANGLE

29

PART iii ~ Yellow

Harmony

All things are penetrated with connectedness.
—Hildegard of Bingen

Triangles are strong, fixed figures. You cannot alter one side without altering the others. A hundred thousand years ago triangular stones were placed above burials. A downward triangle often depicted the female pubic triangle or delta of Venus; an upward-pointing triangle stands for the phallus. A triangle shows, with its sacred geometry, a concept of three in one. Plato, drawing from Orphic and Pythagorean sources, called these threefold aspects of ourselves "same," "other," and "essence."

Triangles with a dot were signs commonly used by people of the Upper Paleolithic, Magdalenian, and Neolithic cultures to represent female fertility and honor the divine feminine. In India, dots within a triangle still symbolize the seeds of life. *Bindu*, a dot, is a basic building block of life. In Tantric traditions, the downward-pointing triangle is known as the Kali Yantra, a symbol for the female vulva. In Egypt and Arabia, the triangle pointed to the mother lunar goddess in her three forms. The Egyptian triangle hieroglyph means "woman," just as it still does for the Gypsies. The triangle, or delta, stood for All Mother. Through her triangle are born all powers of unity. The triangle, as the symbol of the trinity, shows how, as in the Christian tradition, the Father, Son, and Holy Spirit are united into one.

The Greek letter "D," or *delta*, is formed by a triangle. It is used to represent Demeter, the divine mother. For Pythagoras, the triangle represented wisdom. Baking triangle-shaped cakes for the goddess of wisdom was long a tradition. In Australia, the Aborigines danced in a large triangle, calling it the Mother's genital center.

Like the triangle, our third chakra offers balance, stability, and harmony. The philosopher Plotinus discovered a note struck on one musical instrument sets up sympathetic vibrations on another; all sounds are either in sympathy or in antipathy with other sounds. Either they are harmonious or inharmonious. Harmony creates

Hunab Ku

a pleasing, systematic weaving, a congruent arrangement of parts into something pleasing to the ear or eye.

The universe seems to be in numerical harmony with all of life. For instance, a lunar eclipse occurs on the same date every eighteen years. In an average lifetime of seventy-two years, we see four of them. On average we have seventy-two pulse beats and take about eighteen breaths a minute. The Egyptians noticed that if one lives for seventy-two years, one has lived 1/360th of a cosmic year of 25,920 years. Women's menstrual cycles correspond to movements of the moon, which travels one cycle in 27.5 days. Planets and stars also create harmonies, which our ears are not tuned to hear. Whales can sing on one side of the ocean and be heard on the other.

"The triangle is the universal shape associated with the attainment of desired goals, and with the ability to envision new possibilities," says Angeles Arrien in her book *Signs of Life*. Meditate on this image and visualize your goals as being accomplished. The triangle is a symbol of wholeness. By embracing all parts of ourselves and all parts of the world we live in, we sense an interconnectedness in all things. The Chinese have a saying: "If you pull one grass root you always get the whole meadow." If one knot comes untied, the whole begins to unravel. What seems unharmonious in your life right now? What seems to be fraying? Triangle represents fire, the energy of life. Is your energy being depleted or replenished? Do you feel held taut as the lacings in this triangle?

TRIANGLE

29

Sleep, dream, and ecstasy are the three doors opening upon the Beyond,
whence come to us the science of the soul and the art of divination.
Evolution is the law of Life; Number is the law of the Universe;
Unity is the law of God.

—PYTHAGORAS

PART iii ~ Yellow

Petroglyph, c. 1000 CE, Chaco Canyon, New Mexico, United States

30

Trickster

THE COYOTE PETROGLYPH PICTURED HERE WAS INSCRIBED ON A CHACO Canyon wall in New Mexico. Chaco Canyon formed the center of ancestral Pueblo culture between 850 and 1250 CE and was a hub of ceremony, trade, and administration for the prehistoric Four Corners area of the southwestern United States. The coyote, like the raven, is a Native American trickster. Tricksters, which are usually male, are frequently promiscuous and are always outrageous, inventive, untamed, deceitful, and impulsive, offering humor and self-mockery. They exist to overturn laws and to call people back into harmony. They challenge our sacred cows and show us things inside out. Coyote, and all tricksters, test our beliefs. The old grandfather coyote of ancient Mexico showed people the gaiety of sex. His name was Ueuecoyotl, which means "worthy ancestor."

Like the Water Clan totem (**Meander 18**), this image represented one of the original Hopi clans and can be found in caves and on canyon walls all along their ancient migration routes. The coyote is seen in different forms, sometimes running, usually laughing. These drawings create an ancient travelogue, recording the Hopi people's treks around Arizona and New Mexico. One coyote, shown with two circles near it, states that the clan had completed only its second round of its four-round journey. The coyote drawing pictured here, with its tongue out, indicates one particular group visited this spot and then hurried on ahead. The Hopi believe that they settled in a place where they needed rainwater to survive so they would always depend on the gods and their own ability to call up storms. The Hopi also believed that the lost tribe of the ancient Maya became soft and unconnected to their spiritual world when they were tricked into living in a tropical paradise instead of completing their migration rounds.

TRICK-
STER

30

PART *iii* ~ Yellow

Confusion

A truly sacred world allows for a sense of mockery and play that turns the weight of reality around.

—Kenneth Lincoln, *Native American Renaissance*

Tricksters appear, as do the Tibetan *dakinis*, to deliberately upset the status quo. They appear in our lives to throw a curve ball, to make us rethink our goals. Just when we think we're in charge, Coyote or some other manifestation of Trickster—such as the American Br'er Rabbit, the Egyptian Anubis, the Greek Hermes, the Scandinavian Loki, the Indian Krishna, the Egyptian Hermes, the Polynesian Maui of a thousand tricks who could snare the sun and slow it down, or the African Spider Anansi—leaps into our consciousness. Why? To wake us up and to humble us. Tricksters pull the rug out from under us and say, "Hey! Maybe your ego isn't so almighty after all. Maybe you don't have all the answers. Maybe, just maybe you have a few limitations."

Artists are tricksters and they break rules. So are martial arts masters. Gentleness can thwart an attack. Fugues can turn a theme upside down. According to John Briggs and F. David Peat in *Seven Life Lessons of Chaos:* "A work of art's simultaneous concords and discords subtly peel back our abstractions and reflex for making algorithms, showing us something that shines beyond them or lies glimmering within them."

Huge crop circles appear overnight thanks to Tricksters of this planet or some other, and they confuse us. In their intricate complexity, they seem to say, "Hey! You think you know all of earth's mysteries? Guess again!"

Trickster comes into our lives in the guise of chaos. But he's a wily survivor and he lends us his techniques. He subverts systems and, like a whistle blower, breaks down power structures. He enables us to see things in fresh, new ways. Trickster engenders creativity and innovation. He stands things on their heads to help us see them in new ways.

Hunab Ku

Poets often speak of their doubts and uncertainties, their ambivalence, and their struggles as paving the way for and actually helping to birth their poems. Trickster offers us unexpected insights by allowing us to see differing points of view. Briggs and Peat paint creative chaos in a context of "inadequacy, uncertainty, awkwardness, awe, joy, horror, being out of control…"

Albert Einstein offered three ways of working: out of clutter find simplicity; from discord, find harmony; in the middle of difficulty find opportunity. We could add a fourth: out of confusion find clarity.

Why is the coyote pictured here, with his tongue hanging out, leaping into your life right now? Are you being tricked into thinking in a new way? Were you taking yourself way too seriously and now Trickster is saying, "Why not laugh about this?" Briggs and Peat say, "Chaos theory teaches that when our psychological perspective shifts—through moments of amplification and bifurcation—our degrees of freedom expand and we experience being and truth…. Our true self lies there." Trickster is your strange chaotic attractor. He sneaks up on you before you know it and tests your beliefs. Ralph Abraham, author of many mathematical books, says, "Repression of chaos results in an inhibition of creativity and thus a resistance to imagination." Trickster tugs at your ankle and dares you to imagine.

Somebody's playing a trick on you; maybe it's yourself. The number thirty is three tens, completion and wholeness tripled. Trickster has come to make you whole!

TRICK-
STER

30

Eshu, do not undo me, do not falsify the words of my mouth.

Do not misguide the movements of my feet.

You who translate yesterday's words into novel utterances, do not undo me.

—YORUBA PRAYER TO THE TRICKSTER GOD

PART iii ~ Yellow

Men-an-Tol stone, 3000 BCE, Cornwall, England

31

Wheel

THERE ARE MORE THAN NINE HUNDRED STONE CIRCLES IN THE BRITISH ISLES. Standing stones may be early astronomical observatories mapping various alignments and serving as calendars. Stones often marked solar and lunar prayer sites. Some believe these particular stones near Land's End in Cornwall were linked to star positions that can be sighted along the two tall standing stones. The Men-an-Tol or Crick stones at Sennen Cove, on the Penwith Peninsula, were raised sometime around 3000 BCE. While this holed stone looks like a wheel, it is actually polygonal, about four feet high. The triangular *menhirs* on either side are about eight feet high. In Welsh, *men* means stone, and *hir* means long. Like many stone clusters in Britain, this one is thought to be a complex of stones marking a Neolithic burial chamber. These stones were once part of a large stone circle.

Large stones with holes were thought to possess healing power. Skeletal bones were passed through a hole in the stone, symbolizing passage to the otherworld. The hole symbolized a rebirthing from death to life.

If a child had rickets or scrofula, the patient was passed through the opening, as if birthed into a new, whole life. Adults suffering from ague or fever and chills could be restored to health by the stone's curative powers, if they crawled through the hole "nine times against the sun."

The phallic stones with the vaginal holes are considered to be fertility stones. Women, seeking pregnancy, visited the stones, sometimes passing their clothing through it, and later visited the stones again, in search of a safe childbirth.

PART *iii* ~ Yellow

Change

You cannot make the Revolution. You can only be the Revolution.
—Ursula Le Guin, *The Dispossessed*

When things change and transform it means we're alive. Every one of our cells dies and is reborn within a seven-year period. We embody constant change. The Taoist Chuang Tzu, who lived several thousand years ago, said, "The essential feature of the universe is the constant flow of transformation and change." Like a wheel, we are in constant motion. Wheels are symbols of journeys. But when movement seems to be too chaotic, we long for order.

Chaos theory comes to us from mathematical minds inspired by physics. It is a science that says we live in a huge system of process, not stability. Everything, including human beings, is in a process of becoming something else. Chaos theory reaffirms the notion that everything is in flux. Within a larger whole, however, chaos and order are not mutually exclusive. We may not see the order because it is part of a larger hidden pattern.

When Gandhi considered change, having, in his own passive way, helped effect great change in India and around the world, he asked, "What will the effects of this change be upon the weakest individual in our society?" Gandhi taught us that it is people who put plans and policies and governments in place, and it is people who can change them.

We are told that earth changes resulting from global warming, which can profoundly affect the melting ice caps, can happen very quickly. We once thought it took thousands of years, but now we know that great change could happen within a handful of years. Passage may be painful. Ask the caterpillar.

Caterpillars don't just add wings to their existing bodies. A butterfly is not just a "better" caterpillar. It's not just a variation on a theme. A butterfly is through and through something that never existed before. Once caterpillars convince themselves

Hunab Ku

it's time to spin those cocoons, they are committed to complete transformation. They literally turn to mush. Then, around several tiny remaining cells called imaginal buds, a new life takes form.

What are we creating from our imaginal buds? What do we imagine might change? What if transforming ourselves and our world is truly the only task we have? Krishnamurti said that in order to transform the world, we must begin with ourselves, and what is most important is our intention.

What do you *intend* to change? What things in your life act as your change agents?

Mythic archetypes, such as the wheel pictured here, often announce times of change and deepening. Wheel suggests you are ready for a rebirth; getting through the birth passage may be frightening and even painful, but it will lead you to something completely new. This image may be your wheel of fortune, telling you that very good luck is around the corner.

Yellow seeks movement and change. Yellow draws us out into the world, encouraging new experiences and challenges. Like fire, it rises up to destroy and transmute one form into something new.

The Tao Te Ching says, "We join spokes together in a wheel, but it is the center hole that makes the wagon move." Go to a still inner place and find your center; roll with the change that is happening in your life.

WHEEL 31

God grant us the serenity to accept the things we cannot change, the courage to change the things we can, and the wisdom to know the difference.

—SERENITY PRAYER, ATTRIBUTED TO ST. FRANCIS AND A CULDEE CELTIC PRAYER

PART iii ~ Yellow

Wall drawing, 100 CE, Catacombs, Rome, Italy

32

Dove

THE SKETCHED DOVE WITH AN OLIVE BRANCH IN ITS BEAK PICTURED HERE can be seen on the walls of a Roman catacomb. Catacombs had rooms with niches in the walls for burial called *columbaria,* from the Latin for "dovecotes." The catacombs were once sacred to Venus. The olive branch and the dove once meant the peace of the goddess. Olive branches have been associated with peace and fertility from the time of Greek legends. Since people hid in these underground passageways, a few miles from the city, fearing for their lives, this image must have offered them comfort. Perhaps they, too, would be able to fly away from the Colosseum's killing field.

The holy island of Iona, off the coast of Scotland, may be named for the Semitic word *ione,* or "dove," which is related to *yoni,* or "vulva." St. Columba, who sailed there from Ireland (which also means "dove"), founded his monastery on Iona and brought Christianity to Britain.

PART *iii* ~ Yellow

Peace

Peace I leave with you; my peace I give to you; not as the world gives do I give to you. Let not your hearts be troubled, neither let them be afraid.

—Jesus, John 14:27

Doves appear to be charged with divinity. Noah sent a dove out from the ark and knew the waters had receded enough for life on earth again when it returned with an olive branch in its mouth. The Psalmist in Psalm 55 says, "O that I had wings like a dove! I would fly away and be at rest." Solomon called his lover, his dove. His perfect one. At the time of Jesus's baptism, a dove came and rested on his head. The feminine dove symbolizes the Holy Spirit.

These peaceful birds swoop in and out of most sacred texts. White birds are associated with many early goddess figures, such as Astarte-Aphrodite. Romans called her Venus, the Dove. Sometimes called Irene, she was the Dove of Peace. Legend tells us people sacrificed doves to various goddesses, including Tiamat, during ritual recitation of Babylonian creation stories. Ever since, doves have been sacrificial symbols of healing, peace, and grace.

Sophia, the dove, is one of the names for feminine divine wisdom. Dove, along with **Serpent 7**, are two images repeated in sacred legends all around the world. Jesus tells his disciples, according to the book of Matthew, that they are to go among the people and "be wise as serpents and innocent as doves." Barbara Walker points out that this was no random metaphor, but a traditional invocation of the Syrian god and goddess. A portion of the Uxmal ruins in the Yucatán, with its serpent images, was a building called the house of doves. Early creation myths speak of a dove brooding on the waters and finally laying an egg, the earth, and a serpent coiled around the egg seven times to give birth to everything in the world.

The star cluster we call the Pleiades receives its name from the Greek for "a flock of doves." Well over two hundred stars make up this identifiable constellation, but seven

Hunab Ku

sister stars are the most visible. Alcyone is the central star. God asks Job, "Canst thou bind the sweet influences of Pleiades?" The Mayans felt that sweet influence as well and created a calendar based on the cycles of the Pleiades.

Our dove is firmly perched in our yellow palette, the place of feelings. What does peace feel like? In our bellies we know certain places feel different from others. A hospital feels different from a country club. A small town feels different from a teeming city. A loving action feels much different from one of disrespect. Peaceful feels different from anxious, nervous, jittery, or fearful.

Dove comes to you as solace and a promise of some inner release. Doves, as they once did in the Yucatán, still carry messages. What message comes to you from the emotions in your yellow chakra? Listen to your gut feelings and act purposefully on them. Dove offers an olive branch and an invitation to fly with her across open waters. Give up judgment, conflict, and worrying. Fly free and come home.

Make us into tribes and nations that we may know each other, not that we may despise each other.

—MOSLEM PRAYER FOR PEACE

DOVE
32

PART iii ~ Yellow

Wooden ship, 850 CE, Oseberg, Norway

33

Dragon

DRAGONS IN ALL CULTURES ARE MYTHICAL SCALY FLYING SERPENTS THAT flare their nostrils and scorch whatever gets in their way. Some dragons live with fire under mountains and in caves; some live in water, down wells and in lochs. In Hawaii, the dragon is a direct descendent of the Mother goddess, Mo-o-inanea, or Self-Reliant Dragon. Most dragons have glaring eyes. That is fitting, as the word *dragon* comes from a Greek word meaning "to see."

The dragon depicted here is a watchful beast. About 850 CE a seventy-foot-long wooden ship was buried on the west coast of Norway, near Oseberg. This carved oak dragon head decorated its prow. A skeleton of a middle-aged woman was found in a grave robber's trench near this ship. All the jewels and metal artifacts had been removed, but the items left indicate this was a state burial. Archaeologists speculate that the woman buried on this ship may have been Queen Asa, daughter of a king and mother of the royal line of Norway. All the artifacts on board were related to women, including a painted four-wheeled cart and four intricately carved sledges together with the skeletons of ten horses: one pair for the cart and one pair for each sledge. Kitchen utensils, including a hand mill for grinding flour, grains and fruits, tapestries, and three looms were excavated from the ship. Another female skeleton was on board, but there were no weapons, no implements of war. Only the dragon protected them as they "sailed" to Midgard, the otherworld.

PART iii ~ Yellow

Fear

*We are as ignorant of the meaning of the dragon as
we are of the meaning of the universe.*

—Jorge Luis Borges

Dragons flick their tails and breathe fire across our entire planet. They've left their images on many cultural artifacts: Chinese tapestries, Roman pennants, ancient pottery seals, Anglo-Saxon shields, Eastern rugs, and even Algonquin Indian rock paintings. They dwell on mountaintops or in lakes and deep wells. They emanate fire and lightning and often guard treasure, as in *Beowulf*. Fire-breathing "worms" floated through many European legends. They raided rural towns until heroes, like St. George, struck them down. Many dragons in the old stories are female: Grendel's mother; Tiamat, the Babylonian female sea creature; Mo-o-inanea, Hawaiian mother of dragons. These self-reliant figures of chaos, isolated and destructive, must, it seems, be struck down.

The Chinese consider the dragon to be a beneficent force, a light-giving deity, and the symbol of imperial authority. The gentle dragon's breath brings rain. Its body is formed from the parts of nine different animals: a camel's head, a deer's horns, a cow's ears, a snake's neck, a fish's body, a carp's scales, an eagle's claws, a spirit's eyes, and a tiger's paws. The emperor was called a "true dragon." His throne was a dragon's seat. His pen was a dragon's brush, his clothing was a dragon's clothing; even his beard was called the dragon's beard. Dragons are the symbolic lynchpins of *feng shui*, or geomancy. As the spirits of wind and water, they can be found where clouds gather and streams slither. *Lung mei* are dragon veins that network the earth's surface. Megalithic people knew of these lines and tapped them with standing stones like acupuncture needles.

Ken Carey in *Return of the Bird Tribes* points out that love vibrates rapidly. Fear has a slower rate of vibration. "Those who channel fearful energies find that as time passes, the fear vibration grows heavy, depressing. Eventually it brings sleep, gloominess,

Hunab Ku

discouragement, despair. The love vibration brings enthusiasm, energy, interest, perception."

Dragon fears are those parts of us we dare not name, dare not confront, dare not love. We are afraid of what we don't know (see **Saturn** 33). A powerful, mystical wise part of yourself is now emerging. Dragon is guarding the door to your heart. To rise into your heart chakra and move on to the green palette, you must overcome the fear and survival issues in your lower realms. Bo Gyllenpalm, a Swedish management consultant, describes fear as an acronym: Forgetting Every Available Resource. You have deep and wonderful resources; don't forget them.

It is fitting that Dragon, with its green, scaly skin, leads us into the green chakra. One of the most valuable and symbolic green stones is the jade. The Chinese once believed jade is formed from the earth dragon's semen; it embodies the vitality of life itself.

Don't minimize your yellow power to create, whether physical actualities or ethereal ideas, whether positive or negative images. If you are confronted by a mischievous or even malevolent thought, laugh it off. Fear is often just a matter of perspective. Turn it upside down, and you'll see it for the illusion it is. Laughing melts most fear into mist. Raise the slow vibrations of fear into quickened love. The Tao Te Ching tells us: "There is no greater illusion than fear… whoever can see through all fear will always be safe."

He who knows the joy of Brahman, which words cannot express and the mind cannot reach, is free from fear.

—*Taittiriya Upanishad*

DRAGON

33

PART *iii* ~ Yellow

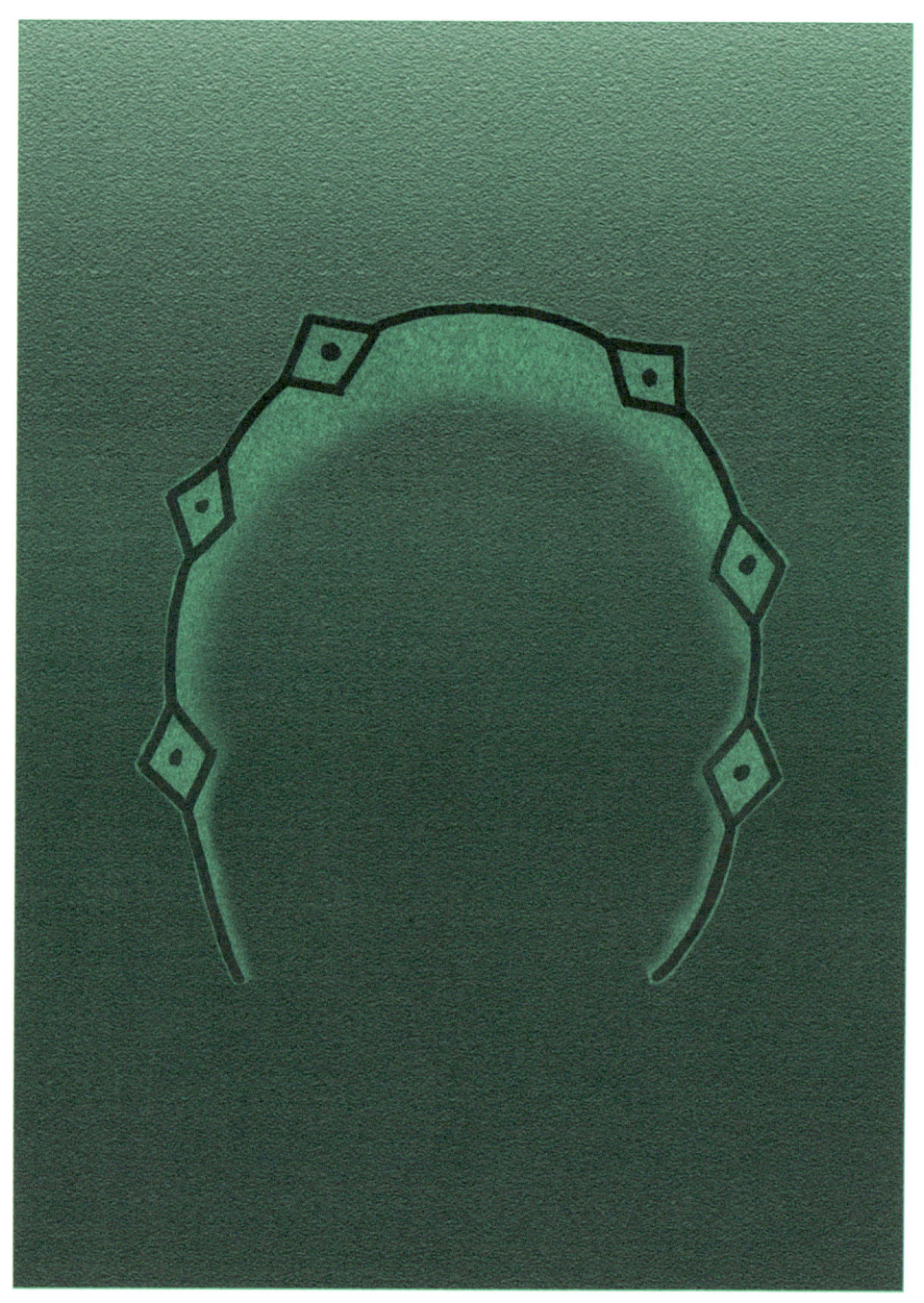

• *Pictograph, traditional, Plains, United States* •

34

Constellation

THE NATIVE AMERICAN SYMBOL FOR CONSTELLATION PICTURED HERE COMES from the Plains and Lakes people from the central part of the United States. It is one of an extensive and beautiful vocabulary of pictograms.

The Pawnee people often arranged their villages to mirror constellations. The shape is a sacred hoop, and the circle is always left open for others to come into the community. Pleiades, part of the Taurus constellation, for instance, is an open cluster of several hundred stars, though seven are the brightest. These seven stars are associated with seven sisters or seven maidens. It is from these stars, many Native American cultures claim, humans came to live on the earth.

From 2000 BCE or earlier, the Egyptians divided the night sky into thirty-six constellations. The morning sun rose in front of a different constellation every ten days. Ancient Greeks reduced this number to twelve. Every month, the rising sun was seen in front of a different animal in the zodiac, or *zodiakos*, Greek for "a circle of animals." The stargazing magi of Persia redefined these divisions around 300 BCE when they created the Chaldean Tables, the first recorded star map. Constellations generally carry Latin names, and the brightest stars in the constellations often have Arabic or Greek names. In 1930 the International Astronomical Union officially divided the night sky into eighty-eight constellation names we can all agree upon. Constellation boundaries, like most communities, are irregular in shape, and they are named because of their positions relative to one another.

PART *iv* ~ Green

Community

We have come to the place where we must decide either to live as one people, or perish as fragments.

—Wendell Berry, *The Hidden Wound*

CONSTEL-LATION 34

The Milky Way galaxy is "powdered with stars," as the poet John Milton wrote—a billion stars and ten billion planets. Since the Babylonians began stargazing, constellations have been named and watched as regular star patterns.

The word *community* can mean a village, a neighborhood, a city or town, or a place with no boundaries such as an Internet community. True communities cherish, as do Native American communities, the young and the old, the rich and the poor. People, like stars, die as fragments, but we live as whole beings. Communities create wholeness in their semicircle of friendship.

The image of community pictured here has six "eyes." We must look into each other's eyes and recognize each other when we are in community. We are relatives.

When geese migrate in their V formations, they show us how communities are formed. As each bird flies, it creates an uplift of air for the one flying immediately behind it. The leading goose assists the one following. When a bird falls out of formation, you can see it beating a path to get back in line because, according to bird researchers, the whole flock can fly 70 percent farther than each bird can fly by itself. When the goose at the front of the V gets tired, it rotates back and another takes its place. And if a bird should be injured, two others fall out of formation and follow it to earth to protect it.

Strength comes from alignment. Seek others who share your hopes and your joys. Open your eyes to see what is around you. You may be surprised at the communities and gatherings waiting for your arrival. Communities are strong because of the individuals in them, compensating for each other's weaknesses and supporting each other.

Hunab Ku

In a book called *The Vermont Papers* by Frank Bryan and John McClaughry—a call for rediscovering homeland and having faith in small things—the authors define community this way: "A bond between the past and present which extends into the future, where people interact on a personal level, have shared identity, values and traditions, sense an organic bond to each other, possess the power to make many of the decisions about their common lives and feel a responsibility for extending mutual aid to their fellows in need. Community becomes a place of repair and solace and a scrapbook for shared memories."

The integers of thirty-four (three plus four) added together make seven, as in the constellation of the seven sisters of the Pleiades. Green is a community color, a heart color. It is associated with nature and growth, but it also has the ability to nurture growth, as good communities do. Christian Huygens realized, back in 1665, that when he put his pendulum clocks in the same room, they began ticking in tandem. The theory of entrainment suggests things *want* to harmonize. And hearts, when aligned, beat together in a community of welcoming beings.

The green chakra, *Anahata*, lying in the center of our bodies near our heart and our lungs, balances the three palette colors above and the three below and connects our body and spirit. The fourth energy center relates to our respiratory system and, along with the thymus gland, helps our immune system stay strong and healthy. This first green image invites you into a peaceful, centered place.

CONSTEL-
LATION

34

Remember, remember the sacredness of things

Running streams and dwellings

The young within the nest

A hearth for sacred fire

The holy flame of the fire

—Pawnee, Osage, Omaha song

PART *iv* ~ Green

• *Bronze statue, 500 BCE, Greece* •

35

Centaur

The classical definition of a monster calls for combining two species in one body. In the case of the centaur, a human's head, arms, and torso are joined with a horse's body. Perhaps the name, which means "those who round up bulls," suggests that the real origin of the centaur comes from the rough cattle breeders of northern Greece who rode horses more than they walked. Homer is credited with having first named this human-equine creature.

The Greek bronze statue pictured here was crafted around 500 BCE. The idea of a man-horse originated in the Near East between 1750 and 1150 BCE and was most likely brought to Mycenaean Greece by the Hittites.

CENTAUR
35

PART iv ~ Green

Action

Life is either a daring adventure or nothing.

—Helen Keller

CENTAUR

35

There are several interesting myths about how centaurs came to be. The poet Pindar provided one of the earliest ones. Hera was in love with a disreputable mortal named Ixion. Zeus was typically jealous and created a cloud image of Hera, fooling Ixion, and Ixion's union with this illusion produced Centaurus, a centaur.

In another form of the centaur story, the Titan Chiron made the mistake of fighting the young Olympian gods, and Apollo punished Chiron by making him half horse. But Chiron prevailed and became a beloved and wise teacher of apprentices like Achilles, Jason, and Hercules. Chiron taught them hunting skills, medicine, music, and divination.

Hercules accidentally shot Chiron with a poisoned arrow. Because the pain of the wound never lessened, the centaur gave up his place in immortality to Prometheus, and at his death Zeus gave Chiron a place of eternal remembrance in the heavens as the constellation Sagittarius.

The Greeks, well acquainted with horses, transferred stallion qualities to the fabulous centaur figure. Centaurs, Chiron aside, were generally cast as wild, sexually charged, and violent males usually wearing shaggy beards. Shakespeare called them the "Dreadful Sagittary." Hindu texts describe horse-men wizards in Central Asia as *asvins*.

According to Pindar's story, Centaurus was the child of the Greek goddess Hera and a mortal man. The divine and the mortal came together in this wonderfully balanced creature—having female and male, god and human, horse and human aspects. Author Sheila Farrant, in *Feminist Guide to the Zodiac*, points out that the centaur represented female wisdom and inspiration guiding male energy and vigor. Centaur, taking on the connotations of the Sagittarian archetype, expands awareness, motivates, and inspires. His symbol is the arrow; he is a straight shooter, direct and articulate.

Hunab Ku

Centaur, therefore, encourages you to take action regarding justice issues. Be outraged when people are being treated unfairly. Pythagoras taught that courage in action tempered by prudent thought is part of the ideal of justice. The Vermont-based theologian William Sloane Coffin, in *Credo*, says, "Truth is above harmony. Those who fear disorder more than injustice invariably produce more of both."

What is your catalyst for action? Sagittarius, as a fire sign, is quick to move, to reach resolutions. Where do you sense some hesitancy? Centaur offers you his cool logic and muscular body to spur you forward. You are clever and quick; set your goals and hit your targets. Others will see your actions and learn from you. Like Centaur, you have your feet on the ground, and you know what needs to be done. You are grounded, yet a visionary, restless and optimistic.

By eating green foods and surrounding yourself with natural green, you build strong muscles, bones, and tissue cells. Green elevates your blood histamine and stabilizes your emotions.

The integers of the number thirty-five (three plus five) add up to eight, a number of action. This is also the **Weaver-Warrior 8** number. You combine spirit and courage to bring action in will and deed. The **Eagle** 35 offers you courage, as well. Action is energy with a purpose. Off you go!

| CENTAUR |
| 35 |

As you wish that others would do to you, do so to them.

—JESUS

PART iv ~ Green

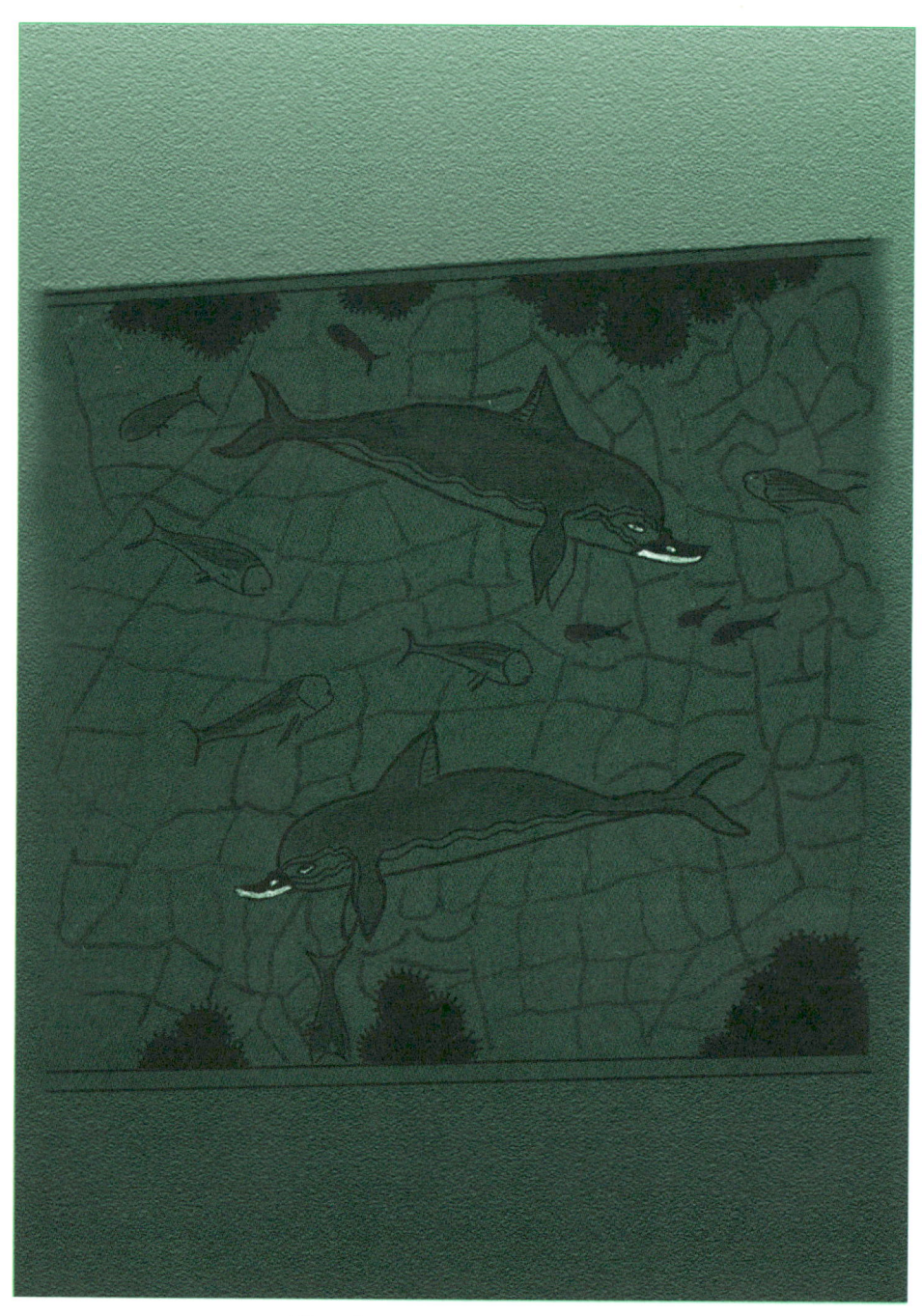

• *Minoan fresco, c. 1400 BCE, Knossos, Crete* •

36

Dolphin

MOST COASTAL COUNTRIES HAVE NUMEROUS ACCOUNTS OF DOLPHINS swimming with people, saving drowning people's lives, and generally nurturing humans. One modern theory is that dolphins' sonar actually aids in childbirth. Dolphins are mammals and breastfeed and nurture their young. Their name, *Delphinus*, comes from the Greek word meaning "womb" (see **Mountain 20**).

The blue and gold dolphins pictured here can still be seen swimming across a wall fresco in the queen's room, located in the east wing of the Palace of Knossos on Crete. In ancient Greek culture when dolphins appear in cemetery art, they signify the soul swimming into the otherworld.

DOLPHIN

36

PART iv ~ Green

Addiction

Dolphins are the angels of the animal kingdom.
—Barbara Hand Clow, *Eye of the Centaur*

Playful dolphins beg you to come in the water to swim with them. The dolphins' breathing regimen, forced on them because they are land mammals adapted to permanent sea life, produces a constant fine-tuned altered state of consciousness. They are addicted to deep breathing. It's hard to tell where the sea stops and they start, for they are one with their environment. They click and use sonar to see; nothing is hidden from them. Their senses are so keen, they can virtually see through you. Everything is interconnected on our planet; therefore, when dolphins get caught in tuna nets, so, on some level, do we. When dolphins wander off course and beach themselves and die, so does a part of us. All lives are intertwined.

At times, one's Pisces nature lives in the substrata of denial and addiction. When we try to lose our pain, refusing to face our shadows (see **Saturn 33**), our spirits sink into the depths.

The Buddhists have a wonderful concept of the universe called the Diamond Net of Indra. They say there is a vast net containing everything, everywhere, and a multifaceted diamond is caught at each nexus point in the net. Like a sparkling hologram, each diamond reflects every other diamond. Looking at one, you see the entire net throughout space and across all time. If you shake one piece of the net, all other parts tremble; each is codependent on the others. The author and theologian Matthew Fox says one reason we have such tremendous addiction problems in our culture is that we have no sacred place to get intoxicated with the mysteries of the universe. We need reentry points into that Net. Thomas Aquinas said you change people by delight and by pleasure. Dolphins, with their smiles and movements, seem to know that.

Fox has also pointed out that our arrogance is toxic and needs to be washed out, for it is tearing us apart. Spirit cannot be found in a bottle, a pill, food, sex, wealth, our

Hunab Ku

body shape, or a shopping mall; rather it is in our hearts, minds, and imaginations. Fear closes down our hearts, clamping shut our heart chakras, the outward manifestation of which all too often is addictive behaviors. On the other hand, joy expands our hearts, and we no longer need to be dulled with chemicals or material things. Addiction is, as John O'Donohue points out in *Eternal Echoes*, "obsessed longing." Dolphins encourage you to examine your longings.

Green's heart chakra carries a burning desire to help—to help others and to help yourself. Green is a creative and procreative principle in our lives. In Sanskrit the heart chakra is *Anahata*, which means "unstruck" or "unhurt." It lies at the very center of our being, bringing balance and peace. Listen deeply. Breathe, as dolphins breathe. Your heart chakra governs your lungs. How might you release and avoid taking in more of the toxins that harm your lungs?

Pisces is a water sign, and people under this sign have a natural creative ability to heal; however, they may overlook their intuition and immerse themselves in ways to forget problems. It's easy to talk about doing things differently, but Dolphin reminds you to follow through. Thinking about swimming and leaping is not the same as actually swimming and leaping. Neptune rules this sign, which means you may find it comfortable to float through life. Dolphin reminds you to live your life fully. The entire ocean is yours.

The digits that form thirty-six, three and six, add up to nine. Like humans, dolphins are mammals and carry their young in the womb for nine months.

DOLPHIN
36

We call upon the creatures of the fields and forests and the seas, our brothers and sisters the wolves and deer, the eagle and dove, the great whales and dolphins, the beautiful Orca and salmon who share our Northwest home, and we ask them: Teach us, and show us the Way.

—CHINOOK BLESSING LITANY

PART *iv* ~ Green

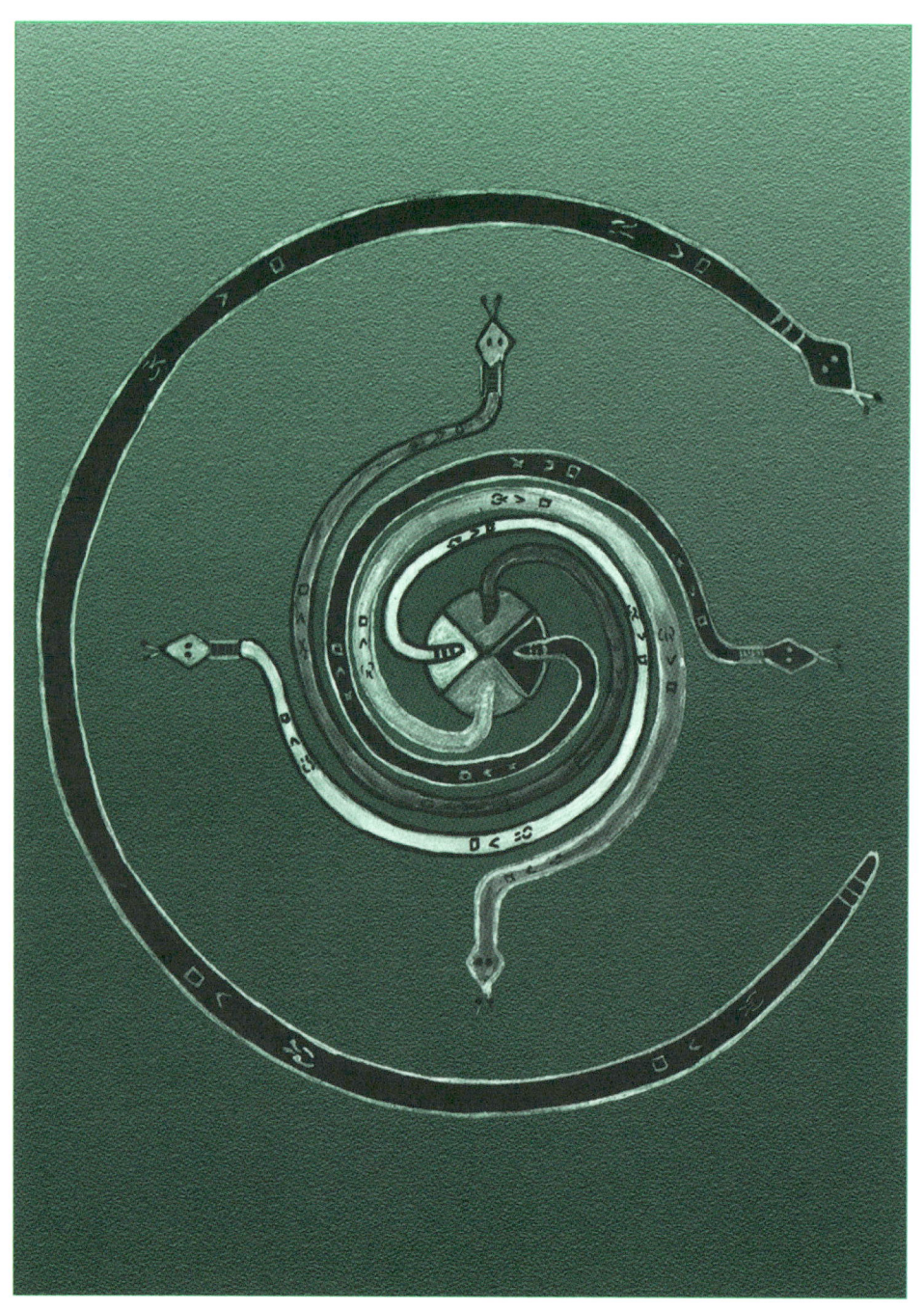

• *Navajo sandpainting, traditional, United States* •

37

Healer

NAVAJO SANDPAINTINGS ARE RITUAL MANDALAS FOR HEALING (see *Dreams, Moon* 22). They tell stories about myths, helping to restore harmony and health. The sandpainting pictured here is a circle of four serpents with a fifth serpent forming an outer boundary. Each serpent's tail is connected to the center. The four directions are faced; the universe is in balance.

Sandpaintings are used in conjunction with ceremonies, some lasting two, five, or even nine days. The person being healed often sits in the middle of the sandpainting as the healers chant. When people are fragmented, they need to regain harmony. The healer's work is to restore balance to the one who is ill and also to the entire universe. Sandpaintings are destroyed once the healing ceremony is finished. The *hataalii*, or singer, who creates the sandpainting is restricted to exact templates and geometric renderings as storytelling devices, protectively handed down from medicine people to apprentices. The circling snake, similar to **Ouroboros 11**, is a common Native American motif, a guardian of health and safety.

Sandpaintings are not intended to be art; rather, they are powerful ritual tools designed for specific healing. Recently a group of Navajo elders went to create a sandpainting for a New York museum. They said they would have to include a flaw in it somewhere, and when the museum director asked them if they couldn't do it perfectly as they would for a ritual, one elder replied, "Are you crazy? Do you want every woman in Manhattan to become pregnant?"

PART *iv* ~ Green

Wholeness

*Wholeness is like a flower with four petals. When it opens,
one discovers strength, sharing, honesty and kindness.
Together these four petals create balance, harmony and beauty.*

—Marie Battiste, *Reclaiming Indigenous Voice and Vision*

Health and healing can be restored in numerous ways. Serpents come to teach you about one of the oldest ways of restoring balance. Look at the serpents pictured here, and feel their completeness. Everything is encompassed within their boundaries. Light and dark. Day and night. Heat and cold. Female and male. Youth and age. Wellness comes when you acknowledge all your opposite aspects. Feel their polarities sweep through your body. They teach you about centering and holding.

Surely no phrase is more bandied about in our present culture than "health care." We seem trapped in a paradox of having to have drugs and not wanting pharmaceutical companies to profit; we depend on nature's pharmacy, yet we destroy her wealth of healing plants and trees at a suicidal rate. We live with food scares, yet depend on food for our well-being. Even Hippocrates, who lived over two thousand years ago, said, "Let your food be your medicine and medicine your food." Nature is the source of all healing. Yew trees are used for chemotherapy; natural antioxidants from pine trees protect against heart disease and stroke. Even snake venom has been used with stroke patients to dissolve blood clots.

The serpents pictured here (see **Serpent 7**) wrap their healing coils around you. Their rattles call you back to health. Their rattles remind you of a death rattle, but you need not be afraid. Healing helps you overcome your fear of death, for you know that death is but a part of life—another opposite to be integrated into your consciousness (see **Released Soul** 6). Without the knowledge of death, life would hold little wonder. Knowing that physical life will end one day makes each day more vibrant, more alive, more whole.

Hunab Ku

This sandpainting image comes to you as a healing community, a family, bringing a tradition of wellness. Sandpaintings hold soul sickness, and when the wind blows the colored grains away, your wholeness remains undisturbed.

How might you take better care of your body? Let Healer swirl through you and help you get rid of any negative elements in your body and in your living style. Green is a serene color, and it invites you to rest and relax. Feel Healer bringing you patience, growth, rejuvenation, harmony, forgiveness, and above all, healing. Opening the heart chakra, like painting with sand, requires a combination of deep understanding and a tested technique. Reconcile the opposites within you and sense equilibrium and wholeness. Investigate what *holistic* means to you. Each of us is called to be a healer—to ourselves, to others, and to our planet. Illness need no longer be viewed as a victimizer, but rather as a teacher.

Thirty-seven is the largest whole prime number in the *Hunab Ku* collection. Its integers, three and seven, are also prime numbers. Together they add up to ten, a number of perfection and completion. Health is a manifestation of our inner harmony and comes as a gift from ourselves to ourselves.

HEALER

37

May you be at peace, May your heart remain open. May you awaken to the light of your own true nature. May you be healed, May you be a source of healing for all beings.

—Metta Meditation of Loving-Kindness, a Tibetan Buddhist prayer

Part iv ~ Green

• *Minoan wall mural, 2000 BCE, Knossos, Crete* •

38

Air

Excavations on the Mediterranean island of Crete have so far revealed four large palaces: Knossos, Phaestos, Malia, and Zakros. The main deity here was always the Mother Goddess, who was portrayed with snakes, lions, birds, and stars. Walls were intricately painted in multicolored frescoes contrasting with the dazzling white-veined blocks of gypsum used to cover the floors and walls.

The lilies or irises pictured here are a part of a wall painting, now restored after severe earthquake damage. To the left of these three flowers stands a wasp-waisted princely figure assuming a postured, dance position. His long flowing black hair is partially covered by a plumed hat, and his short tunic shows off his muscular legs.

Romans later believed irises purified the air and called them the flowers of Venus.

According to an early rabbinical tradition from around 2000 BCE, the same time the wall mural pictured here was being painted, Adam's first wife, Lilith, was named after the lily.

PART *iv* ~ Green

Breath

Breathing is an act of prayer.
—Frank Waters

When we breathe our lungs expand, our bodies obtain life-giving oxygen, and we expel toxins. The Indian yogic breathing practices traveled to China and elsewhere, along with the Buddhist religion. The Dalai Lama has said, "When you inhale, you breathe in all the sufferings of beings and dissolve them into yourself, and when you exhale, you breathe out your own happiness, and cause happiness to others. This is just a visualization, but it builds great inner strength." Breathing is an act of prayer. Breathing connects our consciousness and our unconsciousness, in a way we may never fully understand. And through our breath, we connect our individual bodies to a larger field we might call the universe.

Sufis teach us four ways to breathe. These four ways are outlined in *Awakening* by Pir Vilayat Inayat Khan. Breathe all four ways and imagine the effects.

1. *Earth* breathing: Breathe in through your nose and out through your nose. This sends your wastes and toxins to Mother Earth, and she kindly accepts them (see **Earth 5**).

2. *Water* breathing: Breathe in through your nose and out through your mouth. This bathes you in water and washes away all your impurities (see **Water 16**).

3. *Fire* breathing: Breathe in through your mouth and out through your nose. This lights up all your chakras, and your body will feel as if an incandescent flame radiates throughout you. You become a shower of light (see **Fire 27**).

4. *Air* breathing: Breathe in through your mouth and out through your mouth. Imagine yourself as light as a bird. If you suffer from an addiction of any kind, Pir Vilayat says, you can release it and connect with those ideals you once cherished. Soar on a cushion of air.

Hunab Ku

An intake of breath and audible outpouring, as in a sigh or a cry, is the first sound we make on earth. In the beginning was the word; in the beginning was the breath. Deep breathing will help to purify your body, as the Venus flowers pictured here remind you. You are unfolding in new ways, just as the lily or iris opens from bud to flower. You are opening up to love. Simply note your own breath. Besides opening your windows, you can create breathing space by moving furniture and objects so they do not stagnate your breathing. Sometimes just getting rid of dusty papers and books, dirty carpeting, or old dried flower arrangements can do the trick. Surround yourself with roundness, like the petals of the lily and colors of the sky. Air comes to you to remind you to breathe. Sense your breathing; fall into its rhythm, thankful for every one of the 23,040 breaths you take daily. Breathing enables meditation and grounds you once you leave the meditative state. The Hebrew word *ruah* means both "spirit" and "air." Breathe in the divine.

The integers of thirty-eight (three plus eight) add up to eleven, which is made up of two ones. Meditate on two other images to connect your unconsciousness, **Ouroboros 11**, to your consciousness, **Universe** 11. Combine as many pairs of opposite numbers in *Hunab Ku* as you can. "The greater the tension between pairs of opposites, the greater the energy that comes from them—the stronger its constellating power," C. G. Jung said.

The red, orange, and yellow palettes represent your physical realm; the blue, indigo, and violet palettes are your spiritual realm. And lying in the center, balancing all these colors and ideas, uniting the tensions, are the green images. Thinking of how all these colors swirl and harmonize our very selves might help us better understand how all of life is balanced. In the green images, you access the part of you that is caring, is compassionate, has empathy, accepts without judging, and finds peace and contentment.

AIR

38

I add my breath to your breath, that our days may be long on the Earth.

—Pueblo prayer

PART *iv* ~ Green

Mayan glyph, 500 CE, Central America

Hunab Ku

THE MAYA WHO LIVED IN THE YUCATÁN PENINSULA OF TROPICAL MEXICO abandoned their pyramids and cities around 830 CE, after a half-millennium of enjoying a very advanced civilization. Experts still struggle to decipher their pictogrammatic writing and their intricate calendars. The glyph pictured here, the Hunab Ku—a core sign of their sacred calendars, or wheels of time—is an essential clue to understanding the Mayan sciences and myths (see page xii). Literally translated as "One Giver of Movement and Measure" or "One Source of Limits and Energy," the Hunab Ku depicts movement and energy—the principle of life itself—in a balanced design reminiscent of the Eastern yin-yang symbol. It is the galactic core, found at the center of the Mayan wheeled calendars, and it was thought to be the essence that coordinates the star systems. The Hunab Ku is like the Hopi *sipapu*, a tunnel or passage linking different worlds, a star gate.

José Argüelles described the Hunab Ku, the principle of life beyond the sun, this way: "Hunab Ku may be described as possessing a simultaneous spin and counter-spin motion radiating outward from a center-point of indescribable energy that pulses at a particular rate…[it is] the principle of life and all-pervading consciousness imminent in all phenomena."

PART iv ~ Green

Lover/Relationships

Everything that exists is an expression of relationships, alliances and balances of energies, powers and spirits.

—L. David Peat, *Lighting the Seventh Fire*

In Tantric yoga, Shakti sleeps near the base of your spine and when awakened, she travels up to be united with Shiva at the top of your skull. The two are made one. Yin and yang combine in a sacred marriage of male and female, body and spirit, conscious and unconscious. When you enter the symmetry of the Hunab Ku, you feel this same awareness of wholeness. The ancient Egyptian teacher Hermes explained this symmetry: "As above, so below."

We long for real relationships, for unity, but, as Vaclav Havel, president of the Czech Republic, said in a speech in 1994, "We find ourselves in a paradoxical situation... there appear to be no integrating forces, no unified meaning, no true inner understanding of the phenomena in our experience of the world.... The abyss between the rational and the spiritual, the external and the internal, the objective and the subjective, the technical and the moral, the universal and the unique constantly grows deeper." The archetype of the Hunab Ku speaks to this abyss.

Each side of the Hunab Ku contains the seed and essence of the other side. There are no rigid lines; rather, each side curves, like a lover, into the other. That is the way of all loving relationships. Without one, the other is incomplete. Love is the doorway to passion and compassion. When you are in love, you know how all animate and even inanimate beings are connected. Plato called Eros "the desire and pursuit of the whole." John, one of the four authors of the Gospels, says, "Let us love one another, for love is of God and he who loves is born of God and knows God...for God is love." Only through love can opposites be transcended. The Maya use an expression for this love: *Lak'ech*. Literally translated, it means "I am another you."

Hunab Ku

Hunab Ku represents the joining of opposites. Your masculine, left, exploring, experimenting, discovering, radiating, thrusting, analytical side effortlessly combines with your feminine, right, containing, intuitive, consolidating, processing, feeling, playing, cooperative side. And all this happens at your center. The Mayan word for center is *yaxkin*. *Yax*, or "green," means the center of the cosmos where the tree of life grows, green and balanced.

Found at the center and heart of this book, number thirty-nine is the product of three thirteens. Carl Johan Calleman points out that all people in Mesoamerica shared the view that there were thirteen heavens. Their numbers one through thirteen create a "thirtnight" or thirteen days. In Spanish they call it a *trecena*. Physical time and spiritual time meld into one at the center.

Hunab means "one state of being," and *Ku* means "God." When you look at the Hunab Ku image, you know you are one with God, one with the ultimate essence, the source of all. You know this within your heart chakra, the place within your chest where *prana*, the life force, resides, where our breath, our mind, our spirits, and our bodies are joined.

HUNAB KU

39

May it be loving before us;

May it be loving behind us;

May it be loving above us;

May it be loving below us;

May it be loving all around us; In loving it is begun.

—NAVAJO PRAYER

PART iv ~ Green

Gold plaque, 1100 CE, Huaura, Peru

Cross

THE CROSS IS ONE OF THE EARTH'S MOST COMMONLY RECOGNIZED SYMBOLS. It reaches out to the four directions, intersecting the horizontal with the vertical, showing where forces, whether spirit and body or male and female, meet in a central place. Crossroads are sacred spots, hallowed ground. An X marks holy places, as in making the sign of the cross over one's heart. The cross stretches forth its arms and embodies all that exists. The X is used in early runes as a mark of protection. The cross symbolizes the tree of life, mirroring the Hunab Ku itself. The swastika, dating back to 10,000 BCE or even earlier, was named after the Sanskrit word *amen*, or "so be it." The Nazis later defiled it, using it in reverse, so it spun anticlockwise, a direction some languages refer to as against the sun.

The bird cross pictured here is a gold plaque nearly 9 inches tall and 7.5 inches wide. It dates from around 1100 CE and was discovered in the Chancay Valley, near Huaura, on the central coast of Peru.

PART iv ~ Green

Connection

I believe in Christianity as I believe that the sun has risen, not only because I see it, but because I see everything in it.

—C. S. Lewis

CROSS

38

In prehistoric Egypt the Tau or T, shaped like a gibbet, is often surmounted by a circle. This is called the *crux ansata*, the magical key of life (see **Ankh** 27). The sign of the cross is used in Christian rites such as baptism. By drawing a line of clear demarcation between ourselves before and after baptism, the two lines represent one's old self and one's new self. These signs of blessing in the Christian church are intended to renew our sense of connection with all who participate.

Long before Christ came to earth in the form of the man called Jesus, an East Indian sage was meditating and later described what he saw. Deep down under the mountains, near the earth's central point, he saw a cross. Upon it hung a male-female human being, having at its right side a symbol of the sun and at its left side a symbol of the moon. Over the rest of the body were various sea and land formations.

On the cross, everything hangs in balance. Christians believe Jesus's body hung between life and death, between earth and the cosmos. The cross is the cosmic tree, reaching into all layers of our being, above, below, and across. The cross's vertical axis is creative and penetrating; its horizontal axis is receptive and all-inclusive. Cross reminds you that you are rooted in matter, in your body, in solid structure, and your head is open to the creative forces from above; therefore, you can reach out to all, with compassion. Even sacrifice.

The custom of setting up a scarecrow, the effigy of a human hanging on a cross, has been used to ensure the fertility of fields and gardens since ancient times. Sacrifice and protection have long been linked to an image of the cross.

This image may have come to let you know you're at a crossroads. We often meet important new ideas and new people at a crossroads. Something in your life is now far-

Hunab Ku

reaching. Cross, however, can also mean you are irritated at something, and that irritation is preventing you from connecting to something or someone that could prove beneficial to you both. Perhaps someone needs a hand stretched out to them. Cross could also mean that you are called to sacrifice something in your life. Give something up. Exchange it for something better. Cross also reminds you that you are connected to the planet and everyone and everything on it, as well as to the larger universe.

We are all connected. The Internet and World Wide Web have proven to be outward symbols of our connectedness, but we also share a common inner net that we can access. The cross is an intersection of two lines. They intersect at the point in the center, just as our upper and lower chakras meet at the heart chakra. Our heart is our point of connection to All That Is.

The integers of thirty-eight (three plus eight) add up to eleven. Each line of the number eleven could form a linear dimension of the cross. The ancients thought eleven meant sin and transgression, further embodying Christ's sacrificial mission on earth. In China, eleven, two ones perfectly balanced, is the number of the Tao.

CROSS

38

We give thanks to you gentle Four Winds, for bringing clean air for us to breathe from the four directions. Thank you, Grandfather Thunder Beings, for bringing rains to help all living things grow. Elder Brother Sun, we send thanks for shining your light and warming Mother Earth.

—MOHAWK PRAYER OF THANKSGIVING

PART *iv* ~ Green

Petroglyph, c. 800 CE, New Mexico, United States

Bard

Kokopelli, the Native American storyteller and music maker pictured here, similar to many petroglyphs found on rocky walls in the Four Corners area of the southwestern United States and in Mexico, was created near Hope, New Mexico. Kokopelli, or Kokopilau, the flute player, is related to a Hopi ancestral spirit, the kachina Kookopölö, as well as to the singing cicada. The first petroglyphs were carved in this area about three thousand years ago; some think Kokopelli's images began appearing around 800 CE. Kokopelli was, since early Anasazi times, a mythical Hopi symbol of fertility, replenishment, music, dance, and mischief. The Hopi are believed to be the most direct descendents of these ancient folk whose name means "the ones who came before." Besides images of Kokopelli, the Anasazi left behind the ruins at Mesa Verde.

Kokopelli marked the migrations of various Hopi clans. Upon entrance into this, the fourth world, they were met by Eagle, who shot an arrow into two insects that carried the power of the sun. The insects' melodies healed their own pierced bodies, and they scattered seeds over the barren earth from the sacks on their backs and warmed them with their playing. *Koko* means wood and *pilau* means hump.

Kokopelli's hunchback was thought to be a bag in which he carried gifts and seeds, like an early Johnny Appleseed, from village to village. He warmed the earth with his breath and melted winter snows into spring flowers. Sometimes, like the chalk giant in England (see **Giant 22**), he displayed his long penis, symbolizing human fertility as well as nature's fertility. Like the coyote, he can be a trickster (see **Trickster 30**). The flute he carries is associated with the reed through which migrating people emerged from the third world into the fourth world.

Part iv ~ Green

Song

The Song still remains which names the land over which it sings.
—Martin Heidegger

The bard, or *bardagh*, kept history alive in Celtic oral traditions. Irish bards went to school for twelve years; they could read at least 150 different oghams or lines etched on stone or carved onto sticks, and they memorized hundreds of stories and songs. The word for "to teach" in Old Irish literally means "to sing over." The bards' task was to reform morals and customs, to secure the peace, and to praise all that is excellent. Like all ancient singers and storytellers, their job was to spread truthful knowledge.

The spiral behind the Hopi bard pictured here spins energy from the sun into song. Song calls people to gather, to breathe together and become still together, like the center of the spiral, and then dance out its whirling energy together. Song and the spiral represent one's life force. The belief that divine energy concentrated itself in mounds, hills, rocks, and trees made those places sacred to early people. Spirals often appear in such places, perhaps to show people the Milky Way and help them remember they were connected to the stars. Or to remind them that they were one with earth's spiraling energy vibrations.

Aboriginal Australians believe stories and songs are embedded in the earth and people are charged, like the bard, with carrying these precious reminders of their past to people in the future. People walk long distances, following song lines, and as they walk, they sing their portion of the story until someone else picks it up and carries it on.

Some bards play harps, their strings vibrating with stories of long ago and of what might yet be. Kokopelli's flute reminds you to sing your own song lines. You carry your family's memories. Like the old French troubadours, you can compose your own sacred stories and songs. Come alive with sound (see **Sound** 29).

BARD
37

Hunab Ku

In the Baroque period, musicians believed that music could directly affect and help to balance our bodies. In 1701, Prague musicologist Thomas Balthazar Janowka wrote that music affects our hearts in eight ways. They are: love, grief and lamentation, joy and exultation, rage and indignation, pity and tears, fear and desire, boldness and vigor, and finally, wonder.

Listen to your inner music now. Pipe your dreams. You cannot play wrong notes, for the green palette is nonjudgmental. Green, as a combination of yellow and blue, is the balancing color between the hot and cool colors. Share your music and your stories with others as the ancient flute player did, to heal and to entertain.

Old Irish kings brought their bards along into battle to record the scenes in song and to honor the victors. Bards are removed enough from the action to be objective, yet involved enough to empathize. Musicians feel empathy in their hearts, in their heart chakra, the place where we all *know* things.

The integers of thirty-seven (three and seven) add up to ten. These integers, one and zero, resemble a flute and a mouth open in song. Like music and stories, the number ten returns us to wholeness. Swahili storytellers end their stories this way: "If the story is beautiful, its beauty belongs to us all. If the story is not, the fault is mine alone who told it."

Music is a perfect union of sense, emotions, and intellect. Music allows us to explore emotional situations that are not easily verbalized in other ways. Bard suggests you should let music come into your life if it is not already present. And if it is part of your living and breathing, invite even more of it. Like a bard, spread your truthful musical knowledge.

BARD
37

Since I was cut from the reed bed, I have made this crying sound; Anyone apart from someone he loves understands what I say.

—Rumi, "The Reed Flute's Song"

PART *iv* ~ Green

• *Futami Rocks, Shinto, Honshu, Japan* •

Bridge

THE TWO ROCKS PICTURED HERE, ONE LARGER THAN THE OTHER, LIE OFF THE coast of Japan's Ise Sima National Park. The Futami Rocks, or *Meoto Iwa*, are called the Married Rocks. The husband rock, or embodiment of Izanagi, one twin in a brother-sister pair of deities, has a *torii* gate on the top. *Tori* means "bird," and *i* means "to roost": a bird roost. *Izanagi-no-kami* is "He who invites." The female twin and wife is *Izanami-no-kami* or "She who is invited." The rocks are said to have sheltered Izanagi and Izanami after their union produced all the islands that now form Japan.

The two deities stood on the rainbow, the Heavenly Floating Bridge, and thrust a spear down into the water, churning it and forming islands, the Great Eight Islands as Japan was once called, along with lesser islands in the archipelago.

After birthing the land, ancient Shinto belief teaches that the couple went on to have forty children, including the god of fire. An intricately braided rice straw rope links the two rocks, and each year on January 5, a new rope bridge is ritually placed on the shrine.

PART *iv* ~ Green

Passage

*This world is only a bridge; you may pass over it,
but you should not think to build a dwelling place upon it.*

—*The Urantia Book*

BRIDGE

36

In Japanese, the image pictured here is described by the word *shikake*. It means a clever plan or artful trick. Once the beautiful rice rope is tied onto the rocks, the whole scene takes on a deeper meaning. Simple rocks now become the symbol of marriage or union. The artful image creates a bridge for spirits who are separate, but wish to be united. This is holy ground. Many people come here at sunrise to sense a very special blessing, and no doubt, to be married. The shrine gate or *torii* is not a real gate, for it holds nothing up. Rather it shows visitors they are entering a holy place. Spirits, or *kami*, keep watch over all who visit.

We take bridges for granted today, but the evolution of the bridge was an important step forward in cultural growth. Bridges widen our interactions and open up possibilities hitherto denied. Perhaps Bridge indicates that it's time you passed over something, moved through something, went beyond something. Don't underestimate your connections. Like the Futami Rocks, you may be about to engage in a new partnership. Like the straw braids, you will find what connects you or what needs to be renewed.

The heart chakra seeks bonding to another. This chakra is the place of unity, of coming together. It encourages you to affirm others, to thank them, to appreciate them, to honor them, and to welcome and nurture them. When we feel and express gratitude, our heart opens.

Forgiveness can offer a passage from a locked and rigid stance to a free and open attitude. The heart takes in and gives out. One must love and be loved in order to become whole.

Adding the integers of thirty-six (three and six) together, we get nine. Take a look at the other nines, and see how those images relate to Bridge: **Labyrinth 9** and **Scarab** 9.

Hunab Ku

See what Labyrinth (*Initiation*) has to say about your rites of passage now. Also look at the other number thirty-six to see how **Dolphin 36** might be related to the passage you are contemplating.

What will bridge the gap? What might you have to give up before crossing this bridge? Who will be crossing it with you?

Green has been called the gate of wonder. The effects of color have been well documented. Green, for instance, elevates blood histamine and stabilizes our emotions. It is the sacred color of the Moslems because it represents paradise with its eternal gardens. Children love hues of longer wavelengths: reds, oranges, and yellows. Adults, on the other hand, prefer hues of shorter wavelengths: blues and greens. These latter colors tend to have relaxing effects both physiologically and psychologically. The Zoroastrians in ancient Persia practiced a form of color therapy based on light, and various papyrus accounts tell us Egyptians, certainly back to 1500 BCE, used color for healing purposes. Let green take you now, across a bridge, to wherever you are called to be.

BRIDGE

36

Please, divine spirits, legions of heaven and earth, answer our plea. And just as the dappled horses of heaven perk their ears at the slightest rustle, hear our meek prayer.

—*Amatsu Norito,* SHINTO PRAYER OF HEAVEN

PART *iv* ~ Green

Stone sculpture, 500 BCE, Guatemala, Central America

35

Eagle

The Mayan stone head or *hacha* pictured here is from El Baul, near the Pacific Ocean in Guatemala. It is one foot high. It was a ball court marker from the Early Classic period around 500 BCE. I-shaped ball courts have been discovered throughout the Classic and Post Classic Mayan eras. Stone rings were set up high on the courts' slanted walls. A solid latex ball, about the size of a grapefruit, had to pass through the ring in order for a player to score. Only a player's hips, feet, or elbows could come in contact with the ball. Players wore elaborate protective pads on their knees and arms, along with padded wooden belts around their waists. In post-game ceremonies they hung *hachas* from these belts. The figure pictured here may have been a decoration for such a yoke. Skulls on display indicate the game may have been played "for keeps," and the losers' lives may have been forfeited.

Bloodletting rituals, perhaps imitating menstruation, were thought to bring Mayans closer to their gods. Blood was given freely, as a ritual gift. It was sacred when drawn from any part of the body, but most sacred of all was blood drawn from the tongue or penis. The blood "birthed" the gods and opened the otherworld for visions.

Mayan twin heroes played on a ball court, according to the seventeenth-century Quiche Maya *Popol Vuh*, "Book of the People." They outwitted the underworld's lords of death via their game, a clue to the ritualistic importance of ball games.

Eagle masks and figures connected to the mythical thunderbird were thought to bring rain, for lightning flashed from its eyes and its broad wings created the beating thunder. The Sioux honor births by gifting each baby with an eagle direction: east is yellow eagle for far sight; south is green eagle for innocence; west is black eagle for introspection; north is white eagle for knowledge. When one is nine years old, the eagle's powers begin to manifest themselves.

PART iv ~ Green

Courage

Courage is a willingness to act from the heart, to let your heart lead the way, not knowing what will be required of you next, and if you can do it.

—Jean Shinoda Bolen, *Gods in Everyman*

Our word *courage* comes from *coeur*, the French for "heart." When we "take courage," we enlarge our hearts, allowing them to grow vast enough to encompass our enemies and our friends, the opposing team and our own. In Mayan ball games, players displayed feats of heroic strength. They often gave their very life for the game.

Eagles have long been associated with storms and war, patriotism and battle. They are farseeing and unblinking. It was thought that eagles could look into the sun without being blinded. When eagles fly into our space, they carry otherworldly connotations. For the Lakota Sioux, it was courageous to pluck an eagle's feather while it still lived. They call feathers "prayer helpers." Native Americans value the eagle feather, not only for representing bravery and courage, but as a prayer link to the spirit world. The eagle embodies spiritual courage. Jung has written about the alchemical process of changing the dragon into the eagle, fear into love. Romans believed their emperor's soul was housed in an eagle after his death. Eagles often circled over funeral pyres, lending even more credence to this belief.

Eagle swoops and dives onto its prey from impossible heights. It can do so because its vision is extremely keen. Courage implies flying bravely into a situation after you have seen it as clearly as possible. Folly, on the other hand, is flying blindly into a situation, hoping a sharp beak and strong wings will be enough.

The digits of this number, thirty-five (three plus five), equal eight. Take a look at both eights within *Hunab Ku*. You will find that courage embodies the **Weaver-Warrior 8** and the **Mystic 8**. It takes great courage to be brave enough to travel mystical paths. That, indeed, is what the Mayan warriors were doing.

Hunab Ku

When we wish to embolden someone, we often say, "Take heart!" The green heart chakra links our confidence with our sheer force of will. Some legends say the emerald was brought to earth from another planet. Others claim God gave the emerald to Solomon. The Kabbalist meaning for green is victory.

Mayans and other early Central American people valued green stones, such as jade, as did the Chinese, as far back as seven thousand years ago because of the stones' spiritual properties and wore them, along with shells and obsidian, as hard currency. Both cultures lavished their full artistry upon jade and traded jade pieces far and wide. Mayans buried certain people with a jade stone in their mouths. The Spanish brought jade back from their New World adventures, believing that the rounded edges of this tough stone resembled the kidneys, and they encouraged Europeans to wear these "kidney stones" to ward off kidney disorders.

Eagle flies into your sight today to encourage you to look, unblinkingly, at what is before you. The time may be right to forge ahead, now. Courage impels you to take action. Courage calls you to enforce justice as passionately as you make love.

EAGLE

35

Eagle soaring, see the morning, see the new mysterious morning; something marvelous and sacred, though it happens every day. Dawn, the child of God and Darkness.

—PAWNEE PRAYER

PART iv ~ Green

Mica sculpture, c. 300 BCE, Ohio, United States

Phoenix

THE PHOENIX IS A LEGENDARY BIRD THAT BURNS ITSELF UP AND RISES AGAIN from its own ashes. Arabian and Egyptian legends claim the phoenix may live three hundred, five hundred, or one thousand years. Some claim the phoenix is a metaphor for calendar cycles. Turkish texts claim the phoenix bears these words on its wings: "Neither the earth produces me, nor the heavens, but only the wings of fire."

The Hopewell people, who lived between 300 BCE and 300 CE in middle North America along the Mississippi River and its tributaries, crafted intricate works of art. The bird's claw pictured here, like many other Hopewell silhouettes, was cut from a sheet of thin mica. It is about ten inches high and can be found at the Mound City Group National Monument in south-central Ohio near the Serpent Mound (see **Serpent 7**).

PART *iv* ~ Green

Hope

Hope is a memory of the future.

—Gabriel Marcel

PHOENIX 34

Life arising out of ashes. That is the phoenix's promise. The phoenix is the firebird that flies on iridescent wings to anyone in need of hope. As the legend goes, it builds a sweet-smelling nest from frankincense, cinnamon, and myrrh. A Middle Eastern desert bird, it comes to Egypt from Arabia every five hundred years, and its body is buried, wrapped in a ball of myrrh, at the temple of the sun in Heliopolis. The Chinese phoenix, the *feng-huang*, which originated in the sun, calls up the sun every day with its song, a perfect five-note melody, and carries five colors on its wings.

The phoenix claw pictured here looks like an angel caught in stop-action photography while raising its right wing above its head. Both the angel and the phoenix come bearing hope on their wings. Phoenix renews your youth and offers you promises of lives beyond this one. Hope, as Emily Dickinson said, is that thing "with feathers / That perches in the soul / And sings the tune without the words / And never stops—at all." The phoenix never stops, for it cannot be killed. The dead bird would leave behind a tiny worm or egg, which formed the new phoenix chick.

The phoenix appears throughout literature from the Greek poet Hesiod, who first mentioned it in writing, to the English Harry Potter stories by J. K. Rowling. A Harvard doctor named Jerome Groopman, in *The Anatomy of Hope: How People Prevail in the Face of Illness*, describes hope as that elevating feeling we experience when we see clearly in our mind's eye, or visualize, a path to a better future. "Patients who are hopeful, largely because of their religious faith and their trust in their physician, have a more rapid return to health and a higher rate of survival." Clear-eyed hope is not optimism, he claims. Rather, it is rooted in "the courage to confront our circumstances and the capacity to surmount them.... True hope has no room for delusion."

Hunab Ku

The phoenix has also been called the *benu* or "heron," the bird that greets the Egyptian barge bearing the dead. This magical bird's egg hatches into Osiris, the sun god who brings hope and resurrection to all. When we cling to our visions of the future we don't give up hope.

In Christian iconography, the color green is attributed to the Holy Spirit, a flaming bird. The heart chakra, related to both fire and air, uses air to burn off the dross and impurities that everyone harbors.

Phoenix represents the trauma of new birth that comes when one age is passing and a new one is being hatched. From the Scandinavian *Ragnarok* to the Book of Revelation, every myth system has its end-of-time stories. Phoenix suggests you have the power to balance what others want you to believe you should do next. Just as a mother's birth pains disappear when the newborn lies in her arms next to her heart, so too are your birthing pains but a phase in the coming of something new.

Phoenix is the final image in the green palette. With its message of hope, it frees you to fly on to the blue palette, and its first image, which is **Saturn** 33 (*Blockage*).

The integers of thirty-four are three and four. Three is a feminine sign, and four is masculine. Together, they unite in hopeful balance. Open your heart chakra, allow green to flame within you, and move beyond the illusion that you are separate and alone, as Phoenix appears to be. With clear eyes, claim your light and claim your shadows, all of your self. Therein lie hope and rebirth.

PHOENIX

34

I still feel joy each time the day-break whitens the dark sky, each time the sun climbs over the roof of the sky.

—INUIT SONG

PART *iv* ~ Green

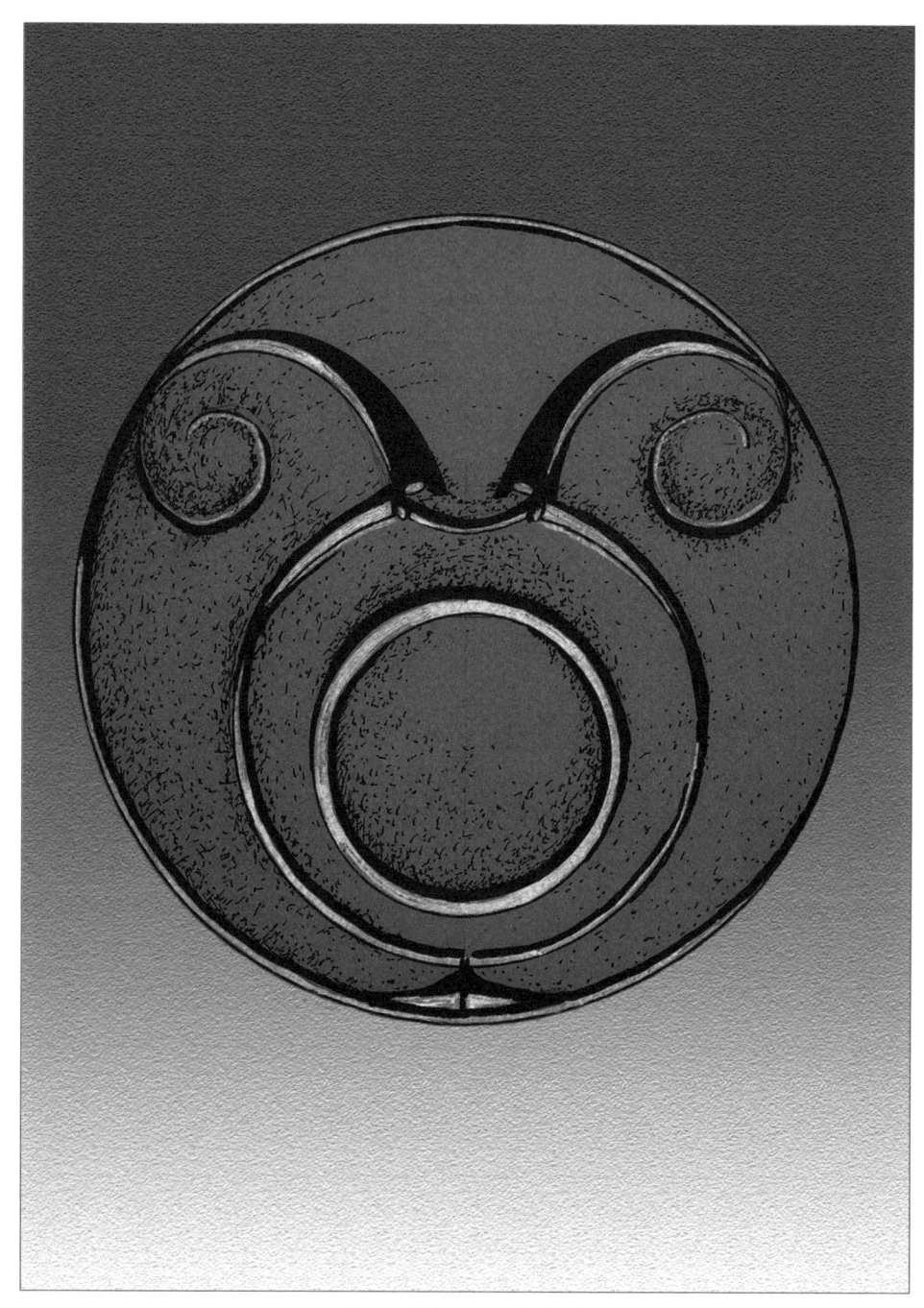

• *Bronze disk, 100 CE, Ireland* •

33

Saturn

Dating back to the first century CE, the Celtic bronze disk pictured here may be abstract swirls, or it may be intended to represent a head and face. Celts believed the soul was centered in the emotions, and the head was venerated as the symbol of life itself.

The Celts migrated eastward across France and into Britain from the Danube and Rhine River valleys between 1000 and 500 BCE. Engraved bronze swords and jewelry such as this disk date back to the first century BCE in Ireland. Bronze brooches often displayed a variety of stylized human and bird heads. If the swirls are seen as eyes, and the circle in the center represents an open mouth, then it is fitting that this image appears in the blue palette. The blue throat chakra (*Visuddha*) opens up communication.

SATURN

33

PART V ~ Blue

Blockage

There are no dark times. There are only people with sawdust in their eyes.

—Nancy Wood, *Many Woods*

SATURN
33

Saturn is the second largest planet in our solar system, and it is the brightest object in the late July sky. It is 736 times larger than Earth and is the sixth orbiting planet from the sun. This may be why Saturday—Saturn's Day—is celebrated on the sixth day of the week. Saturn circles Earth every twenty-eight to twenty-nine years, appearing back in your astrological natal chart as a significant passage in your life. When it returns for the second time, you are about fifty-six and are approaching the time in your life when you are mature enough to enter your "elder" status. Saturn has been called the Lonely Wanderer, although we know now that it has ten moons and three very thick rings.

Like this bronze disk, Saturn is thought to be leaden and heavy. Because of Saturn's traditional alchemical association with lead, someone who is gloomy can be accused of being saturnine. *Saturnism* is still a word in use for chronic lead poisoning. The fifteenth-century philosopher Marsilio Ficino found Saturn at the center of his astrological chart and said, "Well, this is my life. I am going to be sad a lot; I am going to feel heavy. This is my universe."

The ancient Chaldeans called Saturn the Black Sun, Lord of Death. In Babylon, Saturn was called the Star of Law and Justice, and in Egypt, it was the Star of Nemesis and Ruler of Necessity. In China Saturn was the god who presides over the center. Down through the ages, Saturn has been associated with teaching; its lessons can sometimes be very hard.

Carl Jung said that when archetypes are repressed, all kinds of alienation occurs. Shadows can be blocked if our ego gets in the way. When we refuse to look closely at what a particular archetype is showing us, we might be cut off, not just from ourselves, but from nature and all beings, including the spiritual ones, with whom we might have had a relationship. What is dense and heavy in your life right now? Take a good look at

Hunab Ku

your shadow side. But be prepared to get dizzy. Symbols, like Saturn, are never still. A symbol's power is charged by whatever archetype lies behind it.

Marie-Louise von Franz, one of Jung's pupils, has written that the unconscious is made up of many layers and each layer blends with deeper and earlier stages of humankind. Fairy tales and their images delve down deep to layers forgotten or repressed. Tales of ogres, trolls, and nature spirits connect us, and therefore free us, from the shadows lurking in our lower depths.

Countries as well as individuals need to integrate their shadow side to be whole and free. Germany is still struggling with the holocaust. America needs to acknowledge past slavery and exploitation of Native Americans as well as present militarisim, drug use, and sexual exploitation, to name just a few of our cultural shadows.

Let blue help you feel less restricted. It is the color most associated with deliberation and introspection. A dislike of blue might be something to take a closer look at, as well. It could mean resenting the success of others or having a sense of failure. If regret stalks you, let blue enter your life. Express yourself.

The integers of thirty-three (three and three) add up to six, the sixth planet, Saturn. Saturn does not constrict your forward movement or make you unhappy; rather it helps you with what might be blocking you. What is weighing you down? Lean into your pain and your fears and face those shadows. See them, name them, and let them go. Light will come as surely as the summer sun follows the dark night. Matthew Fox exhorts us to "dare the dark."

SATURN

33

Grandfather Great Spirit ... fill us with the Light. Give us the strength to understand, and the eyes to see. Teach us to walk the soft Earth as relatives to all that live.

—SIOUX PRAYER

PART **V** ~ Blue

• *Pitcher, 2500 BCE, Alaca Hüyük, Asia Minor (Turkey)* •

32

Water Bearer

Accomplished metalworkers in Asia Minor fashioned the pitcher pictured here, and it was buried with many other treasured objects in a tomb in Alaca Hüyük. Dating from about 2500 BCE, this bronze pitcher is typical of the exquisite craft of this time throughout the Caucasus, Asia Minor, Armenia, and western Persia. The chevron motif replicates a bird's beak, symbol of a divine bird, associated with water and life-giving moisture.

The city of Alaca Hüyük was rediscovered at the beginning of the twentieth century in north-central Turkey, underneath the remains of a later Hittite city excavated on the Halys River. The site contained thirteen tombs of a local royal family dating from before the Hittites, with artifacts that showed they had skill in bronze and copper work and knew how to hammer, solder, and cast. Alaca Hüyük is only one of many cultures worldwide that mysteriously disappeared at the end of the Early Bronze Age.

WATER BEARER
32

PART V ~ Blue

Service

I am the vessel. The draft is God's and God is the thirsty one.

—Dag Hammarskjöld, *Markings*

WATER BEARER

32

We are entering the age of Aquarius. The Water Bearer takes to heart the words in the Gospel of John: "Greater love has no man than this, that a man lay down his life for his friends." Jesus, born in the age of Pisces and later identified with the fish symbol, ushered in the age of Aquarius—a time epitomized by the word *service*. He "poured out his cup"—his life blood—for his friends. Among his teachings, "Love your neighbor as yourself" stands as a concise Aquarian message.

This image appeals to our higher ideals. But, as in all aspects of giving of one's self, we might feel a bit washed out by it all.

To serve others rather than oneself means to give freely, with no thought to personal reward. Think of service as fluid energy, like water; it flows from one person to another, and on its way, it generates light. As we move out of Saturn into Water Bearer in the blue palette, we are moving away from shadows into a lighter place. When people carry too much fear or hurt, they are so weighed down that it is very difficult for them to serve anyone, even themselves. Unfortunately, damaged areas in our energy fields seem to attract more shadows and darkness, like iron filings to a magnet. Consciousness falls in love with what it knows and tends to repeat its own history. We must empty ourselves of those dark places before we can fill ourselves with light, just as the pitcher must be emptied before it can again be filled.

Sufis tell us that it is only by working through our shadows (**Saturn** 33) that we will be ready for service. Sufis are known as the sweepers, the ones who clean out others' dark areas. When we accept and love what rises up from the blackness of our unconscious, we find light. Working on our own shadows prepares us for a life of service to others.

Hunab Ku

The thirsty wait. Your friends, your family, and your community long for you to pour out acts of kindness on their behalf. Water Bearer suggests it's time for you to become involved. How might you volunteer? People all around you are waiting to benefit from your talents, your intelligence, your sincerity. The homeless, children, abused women, the hungry, the lonely—they're right within reach of your "water pitcher."

The blue palette encourages you to speak out. Your words are of great value. When we speak our authentic truths, our very core resonates with the vibrations of our words. Too often shyness, or fear of being wrong, ill-informed, or ridiculed keeps us from speaking up and speaking out. Water Bearer represents service, and your efforts for others can never be inappropriate. What fills you is beyond your own doing. Trust it.

How are you quenching your own thirst? What are you reading? What are you listening to? What are you watching? Who is informing you? If you feel thirsty, know there is abundant water all around you, just waiting for you to hold out your own glass.

The number thirty-two is associated with communication and working well under pressure. Water Bearer and the color blue remind you of the many ways you can help others relieve their thirst.

WATER BEARER

32

A person consists of purpose. According to the purpose a person has in this world, so does he become on departing hence. So let him frame for himself a purpose.

—Chandogya Upanishad

PART V ~ Blue

Funerary vase, 900 BCE, Knossos, Crete

31

Goat

THROUGHOUT HISTORY, GOATS HAVE APPEARED AS SACRIFICIAL ANIMALS. As the Horned God, the goat was a divine redeemer—the one for whom the Greeks named their tragedies, their goat songs. A scapegoat, then, was the goat given sacrificially. Straw effigies of the Goat Lord, trimmed with red ribbons, are still constructed in Scandinavia in the winter.

In ancient art, goats are often paired with sacred trees; both are symbols of life and regeneration. A goat's horns were thought to be sacred symbols of the moon and God's power manifest on earth. Horns are symbols of sexuality and the fertile seed. The goat was sacred to Demeter, and her rites included goats milk.

Two goats face a series of circles, possibly moon phases, on the vase pictured here, which was used for burying ashes. The vase is nearly seven inches tall, and it's painted light and dark brown on a creamy background. It was discovered at Knossos, Crete, and dates from 900 BCE.

PART V ~ Blue

Practicality

Jars, apples, hillsides and rocks are quite as much a part of God's creation as angels; and since physical objects are right in front of us, God must have wanted us to take notice.

—Jane Roberts, *The World View of Paul Cézanne*

GOAT
31

Capricorn, the sign ruled by Saturn (see **Saturn** 33), can cause a melancholy seriousness to flood over you at times. But look around you, and you will see many wonderful things that can capture your imagination. You can be capricious—as playful as the goats on the vase pictured here, even though the vase's purpose is anything but playful. You are sure-footed, careful, measured, and practical. Like the goat, you can sidestep obstacles in your path, knowing precisely where your next step will land.

The goat has been linked to our lower passions. Early Romans dressed in goatskins and were flogged as a symbol of sacrifice. Goats seem to be linked to atonement in many cultures. Of course real goats have had their fair share of sacrificial moments as well. Thanks to one caught in a thicket, Isaac was spared death in the biblical story (see **Ram** 2).

Goats are practical animals. Wild goats on Mediterranean islands were probably the first animals to be domesticated. They appear to have been an integral part of most Neolithic cultures. There is a Spanish legend about the Milky Way being formed from milk dripping from a goat's full udders. We have named dances after goats: the caper or goat dance, for one. Some Scandinavians still act like *Yule boks*, or "Christmas goats." At winter solstice, they wear masks, make noise, and generally act foolish, like Pan, to celebrate the year's end. This tradition comes from pagan goat games.

Goat reminds you that you are dependable. Or calls you to be dependable. Goat may encourage you to make lists and pay closer attention to details. Goat suggests you are goal driven. Yet, like Pan, you are also free-spirited and filled with joy—open, honest, and uninhibited. Goat can be romantic or outrageously silly while remaining self-disciplined and above all, practical. This may be a time to work hard.

Hunab Ku

The integers of thirty-one (three and one) add up to four. Look at **Father** 4 and **Angel Guide** 4. They have something to tell about how you embody the practical sure-footedness of logic, yet also hold within you the "sacrificial goat" ideal.

A practical use of blue light was discovered in the late 1950s in England. Babies suffering from jaundice, or bilirubinemia, when placed under a blue light, are cured. Imagine the possibilities of using colored lights for healing more conditions. Using full spectrum lighting during the darker winter months can make a profound difference to people dealing with ADD, depression, and even joint pain. Schools that install full spectrum lighting see notable differences in children's emotional states. What if ancient wisdom regarding the practical uses of color and light were rediscovered and widely accepted? Use the images and colors found in this book in practical ways. Listen to what your body needs.

GOAT

31

Let me see if this be real. Let me see if this be real, this life I am living.

Ye, who possesses the skies, let me see if this be real.

This life I am living.

—Tewa Prayer

PART ᚡ ~ Blue

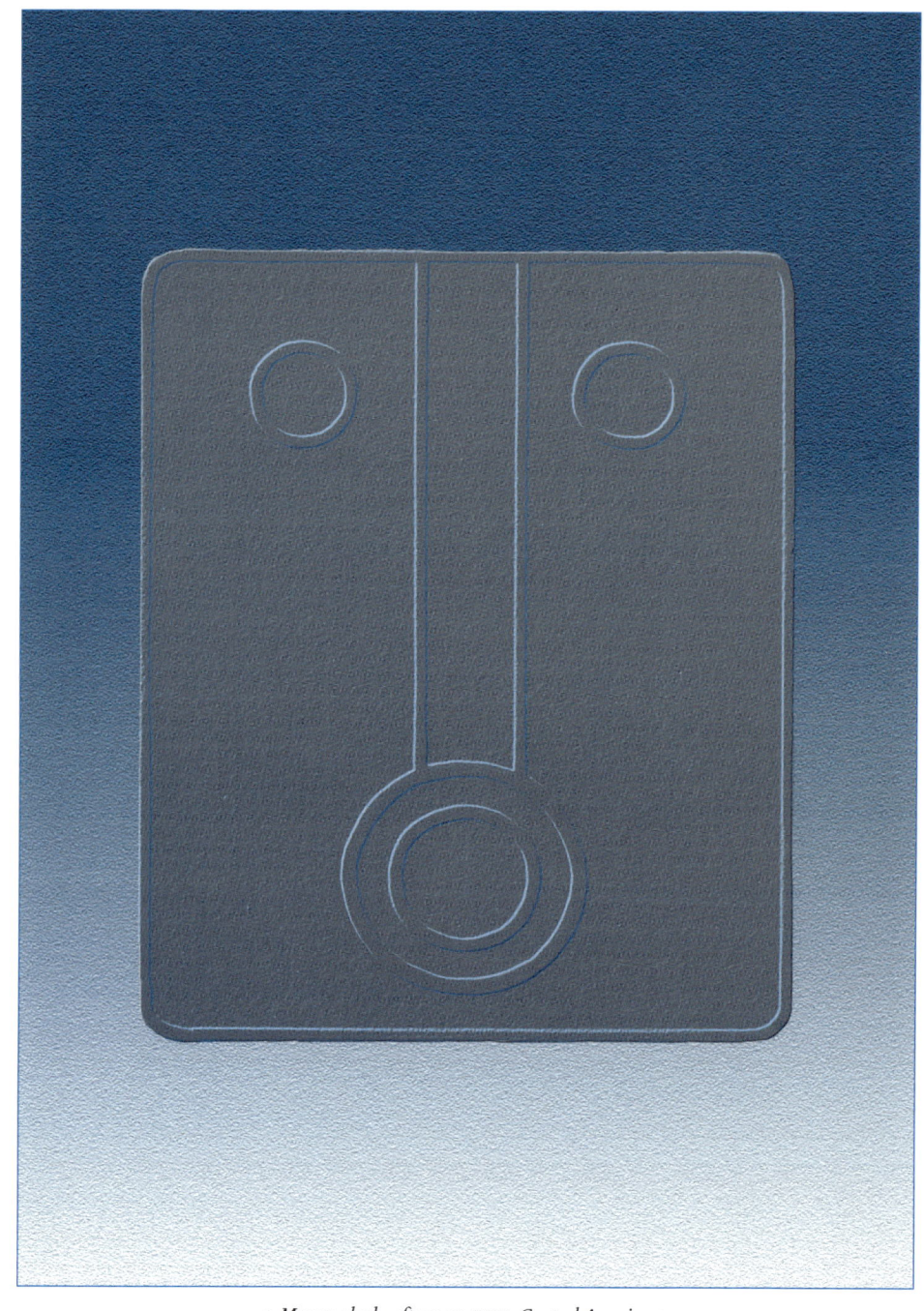

• *Mayan glyph, after 300 BCE, Central America* •

30

Teacher

THE MAYANS FLOURISHED IN CENTRAL AMERICA FOR OVER A THOUSAND years from 200 BCE to 900 CE and many of their descendants still live in Central and South America. During the Classic Mayan period, they created a magnificent culture. Their Short Count and Long Count calendars witness their extremely sophisticated level of astronomical knowledge. They had a complex cosmology with signs or glyphs for heavenly bodies, Venus being the one we're sure they made calendar calculations from (see page xi and **Hunab Ku 39/**39). Each month also had its own sign or pebble-shaped glyph. As the Mayans recorded their beliefs, their gods were living and had faces and called themselves *Ahau* (ah-how)—the gods who carry time on their backs. Each day was assigned a "lordly" sign, similar to the image pictured here.

Mayan writing developed in the Formative (300 BCE to 150 CE) and Proto-Classic (150–300 CE) periods. The *Ahau* is one of twenty sacred signs used in the long calendar from the Classic Mayan period: 292–869 CE in Central America. In the Mayan calendar each *katun*, or twenty-year period, is called an *Ahau*, or "lord" of that time period. The *Ahau* pictogram represented the wise and trusted advisor. It combined wisdom and knowledge with the ability to focus. Found on stone pillars, markers, and the walls of temples, the pictogram reminded the Mayan people who could read the stone language that one must be a thinker and be willing to struggle in order to be a teacher. When a priest portraying the *Ahau* climbed to the top of a pyramid, his energy linked the people to all their ancestors, for the *Ahau*, like each Mayan cycle of time, builds on all that has gone before.

PART **V** ~ Blue

Knowledge

Learning is finding out what you already know; doing is demonstrating that you know it; teaching is reminding others that they know just as well as you. You are all learners, doers, teachers.

—Richard Bach, *Illusions*

TEACHER 30

Knowledge can be grouped into two categories: explicit and tacit. Explicit knowledge is what is easily shared in memos and books, numbers, and other forms of hard data like computer codes. People are comfortable with that sort of knowledge. Tacit knowledge is harder to pin down. It's what you know because you've been working with explicit knowledge for a while. It includes mental models and beliefs, something hard to record on a spreadsheet. It is not easy to share tacit knowledge with other people, especially since we all learn differently. Some of us learn best by reading, others by hearing, others by physically working with concepts. Even experts are not always sure of what they are dealing with. Albert Einstein, for instance, said this about laws of mathematics: "As far as they refer to reality, they are not certain and as far as they are certain they do not refer to reality." As our knowledge changes, our sense of reality changes. Since we live in a universe of connected meanings and a collective memory, we turn to others to learn what it is we all know.

The *Ahau* pictured here stares at us with eyes wide, searching our minds, watching our spirit for signs of awakening and growth. Anyone can be our mentor. Anyone who stands beside us, for that is the meaning of *mentor*, can be a partner in a sacred learning relationship. Teacher. Pupil. Pupil. Teacher. Adult. Child. Child. Adult. We reverse roles and learn from each other. But only if our eyes, like the *Ahau*'s, are wide open.

Gandhi once said, "The language of the lips is easily taught, but who can teach the language of the heart?" You can. You can by your willingness to share what you know and who you are, and by being open to learning all you can from everyone you meet. As the Native American saying goes, when you are ready to learn, a teacher will appear.

Hunab Ku

Teachers may come in a form you might miss if you aren't watching for them. Teacher may be a symbol or an image, a color, a word, or a song. Teacher may be a flower, an animal, a person, or a nonphysical being. If our eyes and hearts are open, Teacher's lessons will not be wasted. *A Course in Miracles* claims that any situation enables you to teach others what you are and what they are to you.

Parker Palmer claims the best teachers are those who teach from the heart. In *The Courage to Teach,* Palmer says: We teach who we are. He quotes Rumi: "If you are here unfaithfully with us/you're causing terrible damage." If we are not pure—if we are not faithful to our own inward teacher, and to the great things of this world that our knowledge holds in trust—then we will not be the blessing to those around us we could be. He asks the crucial question: "Who is the self that teaches?"

The fifth chakra, the throat chakra, is called *Visuddha,* which means "purification." This blue chakra is, among other things, the center of sound (see **Sound** 29). This *Ahau's* mouth is open. He may be speaking or singing. By his voice and his breath, he purifies and transforms for he is, in Mayan tradition, the *baktun,* the god of the transformation of matter. Teachers transform minds and attitudes. Teachers assure our basic rights of speaking and being heard.

Teachers can be our adversaries; they challenge us and act as catalysts for our growth. Life events can also be our teachers; watch for and learn from them all. Bathe yourself in blue, for it is the color of wisdom and discoveries, of inventions, innovation, and aspirations. We learn our entire lives, to be teachers. But in early monastic traditions, for instance, people pledged thirty years of their lives: ten to learn, ten to work, and ten to teach. How are you spending your years?

TEACHER
30

Know yourself—and you will know the universe and the gods.

—TEMPLE OF DELPHI INSCRIPTION

PART Y ~ Blue

• *Wooden plaque, traditional, Port Keats, Northern Territory, Australia* •

29

Sound

FOR THE AUSTRALIAN ABORIGINE, GREAT SNAKES LIVE UNDERGROUND OR IN the backwaters called billabongs. These "grandmother snakes" are viewed as powerful manifestations of the rainbow on earth. In Arnhem Land, the Great Mother shares her powers with the rainbow, or what they call the Lightning Snake, who rules the water and impregnates Mother Earth.

The Aborigine represent the dreamtime, the nonphysical world, with dot paintings such as the Rainbow Serpent pictured here from Port Keats in the Northern Territory. Like much Aboriginal art, this one is painted on a board. Many similar intricate works appear on rocks that have been painted and repainted for 40,000 years (see **Serpent 7**). They also create sacred wooden plaques, called *Tjuringa*, which record the ancestors' song lines, but they must not be shown to anyone who is not initiated. If the songs, according to Bruce Chatwin's *Songlines*, are forgotten, the land will die.

PART **V** ~ Blue

Vibration

Nothing rests; Everything moves; Everything vibrates.

—Three Initiates, *The Kybalion, Hermetic Principles*

SOUND 29

In the beginning was the Word. In the beginning was vibration and sound. From it, all things were created. Everything, quite literally, is a vibration. Our senses are designed to interpret only select parts of the wide spectrum of vibrations all around us. Our ears can hear pressure wave vibrations as sound. We can hear everything from slow waves that move 20 times a second, up to waves that move at 20,000 times a second—about ten octaves of sound (two and two-thirds more octaves than a grand piano can produce). In contrast, of all the electromagnetic waves around us, our eyes are designed to see only about one octave's worth: waves with a length of 0.5 microns (blue light) to waves with a length of 0.9 microns (red light). A micron is 0.000001 centimeters long. The highest sound we can hear vibrates at 20,000 hertz, or 20,000 beats per second. The longest radio wave is 1 million hertz, and the longest visible light wave is a billion times faster than that.

We are surrounded by other vibrational realities, which our physical senses simply are not designed to perceive. Some animals hear sounds much higher or lower than we can, and others see different spectra than we do. We use vibrations to heat food in microwaves and to send messages to satellites.

Hans Jenny, a Swiss scientist, captured sound vibrations on film. In the 1960s he discovered that various vibrations produce different shapes. He passed sounds through water, oil, and sand and captured their intricate mandalas on film. Low frequencies produced simple circles; higher frequencies created very complex patterns. Furthermore, tests have shown that regardless of who speaks it, the sound "ohm" creates a predictably intricate pattern. Fritjof Capra said in *The Tao of Physics*, "All things...are aggregations of atoms that dance, and by their movements produce sounds. When the rhythm of the dance changes, the sound it produces also changes. Each atom perpetually sings its song."

Hunab Ku

The Vedic tradition teaches that there are seed sounds or *bijas* that can wake up the body's key energy centers: red, *lam;* orange, *vam;* yellow, *ram;* green, *yam;* blue, *ham;* and indigo, *ohm*. And for the violet crown chakra, a silent ohm. Pick a note and hold it. Try the blue chakra seed sound: haaaahhhhmmmmmmm. Relax and feel the vibrations in your throat, neck, and shoulders as you intensely imagine the color blue at your throat.

The composer Olivier Messiaen listened to water and wind, and said they represented music to him. He created examples of colored music, synaesthesia or the perception of sounds as colors and colors as sound, just as the Australians captured song lines with their rainbow snakes. He said, "In thy Music, we will see music; in Thy Light we will hear light." Blue light vibrates at a higher rate than red because it is less dense. Colors and sounds are just different speeds of vibrating energy.

The numbers two plus nine equal eleven. Eleven, like the numbers three, five, seven, thirteen, seventeen, nineteen, and so forth, have no divisors other than themselves. They are pure and one in themselves, like the wholeness of Sound.

Sound vibrates with pure energy. What melodies might you sing that were handed down from your ancestors? Right now brilliance for you is joined to movement and abundance. Sound brings you beauty and healing; move the vibrations within and around you. Pray into your chakras, for prayer focuses your attention.

SOUND

29

I am the name of the sound and the sound of the name ... and they will find me there, and they will live, and they will not die again.

—The Thunder, Perfect Mind, A GNOSTIC TEXT

PART **V** ~ Blue

• *Gold coin, 100* BCE, *England* •

28

Adult

WORK IS PAID IN COIN. THE GOLD CELTIC COIN OR *STATER* PICTURED HERE IS from the tribe of Bellovaci from around 100 BCE. A classical design style was adopted but changed into recognizably Celtic free-flowing, interwoven curved shapes. This coin was found at Fenny Stratford in Buckinghamshire, England. The coin is reminiscent of Queen Boudicca, who epitomized the Celtic warrior when she sacked the Roman settlements at Colchester, London, and St. Albans. Long-limbed and red-haired, she came from the Iceni tribe, and she is usually shown driving her chariot with her two daughters beside her. She conducted the first battles in Britain at which the Roman suffered defeat. Later the Romans brought in their crack forces to capture the queen and her daughters. All three women took poison to avoid dying at Roman hands.

The female figure on this coin exemplifies Boudicca's vitality, but it may actually be a coin maker's image of Andraste, the Celtic goddess of victory. Other coins from this time are dedicated to Epona, the Celtic horse goddess.

PART V ~ Blue

Work

> Good work is a way of living... it is unifying and healing. It brings us home from pride and despair and places us responsibly within the human estate. It defines us as we are: not too good to work with our bodies, but too good to work poorly or joylessly or selfishly or alone.
>
> —Wendell Berry, *The Unsettling of America*

ADULT 28

Play is what we do until we feel we *must* do a task. Then it becomes work. Fragmenting work into an assembly-line process destroys Wendell Berry's sense of "good work" and leaves us only jingling coins as repayment for our labors. Czech writer Karel Copek coined the word *robot*. It is derived from the Slavic root word for "worker." There is a move afoot to reclaim "good work." Good work never comes from people who are asked to be only robots. Instead, good workers bring their minds and their hearts to their workplace. Progressive, and long-lived, profitable companies empower their workers by giving them a sense of the larger picture and a stake in their combined success.

Much has been said about quality in the workplace. The true goal of all quality work, according to the author Michael Munn, is attained when "every person can achieve personal harmony, harmony with others, and harmony with the seen and unseen universe." Anything less than that tends to make us either bored, stressed out, or cynical at work.

Boudicca calls us to rethink how we treat women and other ignored groups in our workplaces, to not mistreat them the way the Romans did her people. Everyone should receive fair pay, fair benefits, and fair hiring. Fairness and justice are not just ideals, they are necessities if we want to move into a harmonious future.

You may find yourself unemployed right now or underemployed. Or you may find yourself earning more than you ever dreamed you could earn. How do you work? Why do you work? With whom do you ideally work? Do you take full responsibility for all the stakeholders in your work community? Do you work just for the wages and

Hunab Ku

benefits? Does work bring its own reward? John Updike cautioned us to "work steadily, even shyly, in the spirit of those medieval carvers who so fondly sculpted the undersides of choir seats."

At twenty-eight, we are usually in full control of our mental and spiritual worlds, able to move through them with ease and grace, after years of study and thought. We eagerly continue to enjoy the fruits of the physical world. Adult reminds us to "grow up" and assume responsibility for our actions, our investments, our time, our relationships, and above all, our chosen work. The counterpart to this image is **Youth 28**. Look at it again, to contrast where you are now with where you were then. The working world is where we learn about how the universe works and about our place in it. We don't learn by sitting on the sidelines; we don't learn by merely reading words about it. We learn by plunging in.

ADULT

28

Our adult phase covers a great deal of our lifetime. Many coins travel through our hands in our adulthood. Adult appears in our life before we become the **Wise Old One** 17. Earlier stages include **Womb 6, Child 17, Youth 28,** and **Hunab Ku 39/39**. The final door we pass through is **Released Soul** 6.

Some communities use a bartering wage system; in earlier times, salt was the currency, hence our word *salary*. Besides salt, Mayans used cloth and cacao, chocolate beans. Cows still replace money in some cultures. Belgian economist Bernard Lietaer, father of the euro, says we have yin currencies and yang currencies, and like the symbol itself, we need a balance. Yin currencies are egalitarian; they discourage accumulation, lead to decentralization, are always available, and create investments in long-term goods and services. Yang currencies, on the other hand, are based on hierarchies, lead to centralization, are based on scarcity, and create competition.

The Way grows before us—let us begin.

—ZEN INVOCATION

PART **ν** ~ Blue

199

Limestone bas-relief, 1500 BCE, Knossos, Crete

27

Ankh

THE ANKH IS AN OVAL OVER A CROSS—THE SYMBOL FOR VENUS AND FOR woman. Its rounded upper part and vertical handle suggest a hand mirror. The Egyptian word *ankh* does, in fact, mean "life" and "hand mirror." The ankh pictured here appears in a painted limestone bas-relief in a hieroglyphic inscription of Ma'at, daughter of Re of Egypt's 19th dynasty. Ma'at is the goddess of truth and justice who wears a feather on her head, the symbol for truth. She was lawgiver and judge of the dead, weighing their souls for the afterlife.

We did not understand hieroglyphs until after 1799. French soldiers in Egypt restoring a fort near Rosetta in the Nile Delta discovered a black polished basalt slab with the same inscription repeated three times: in hieroglyphic; in a later cursive form of writing called hieratic; and in Greek, the language of the ruling class. The Rosetta Stone, now at the British Museum, dated to 196 BCE, weighs three-quarters of a ton and is about three feet by two and a half feet. Thomas Young, a brilliant British linguist and physicist, had read the Bible twice by the age of four, and knew twelve languages by the time he was twenty. In 1814, he identified six groups of hieroglyphs enclosed in ovals that he thought must relate to the names in the Greek text. Around 1818, a French Egyptologist named Jean-François Champollion made a major breakthrough. The names *Cleopatra* and *Ptolemy*, which appeared in the Greek text, were foreign words in Egyptian, so they would have to be spelled phonetically in hieroglyphics! Champollion then went on to study these oval cartouches of other rulers' names and discovered that phonetic spelling was widespread. Using his understanding of Coptic, which he rightly assumed was directly related to old Egyptian, he was able to finish his translation of the entire stone in 1822.

PART V ~ Blue

Life

Life is what's happening while we're busy making other plans.

—John Lennon

ANKH

27

As far as symbols go, the circle and the cross are big ones. They may actually hold the key to life. In most cultures the circle symbolizes wholeness. It is the sun, our symbol of life that is recognizable all over the planet. When looking at a circle we experience, to varying degrees of course, oneness and unity. Seventeen of our seventy-seven shapes appear in circular forms (**Weaver-Warrior 8**, **Sun 12**, **Twins 24**, **Artist 26**, **Fire 27**, **Wheel 31**, **Constellation 34**, **Healer 37**, **Saturn** 33, **Adult 28**, **Winged Dog** 23, **Moon** 22, **Counselor** 19, **Scarab** 9, **Mystic** 8, **Double Spiral** 5, and **Unicorn** 1).

The plus sign or equidistant cross, according to Angeles Arrien in her book, *Signs of Life*, "symbolizes the process of relationship and integration. This is a coupling, synthesizing, integrating and balancing process. This process carries the need for connection—to a creative project, to a group, to another person, or to oneself. It is the symbol that demonstrates integration and balanced connection." The circle and the cross create what Jung called the *crux ansata*, or the symbol of creation and key of life. He pointed to the oval as an ancient *sistrum*, Isis's musical instrument made of rattling wires that made a sound when it was shaken. The cross symbolizes matter, the earth. The masculine vertical line intersects the feminine horizontal line (see **Cross** 38 and **Water 16**). In Egypt, the ankh was also a symbol of sexual union: the oval at the top was likely colored red and the phallic crosspiece white. The ankh was also called the Key of the Nile because the divine annual sexual union of Isis and Osiris, at the rising of the summer star Sirius, was thought to be the key that released the Nile floods, rejuvenating the crop lands (see **Star 23**).

The Knot of Isis, resembling an ankh, was thought to bring life to the dead, to dead seeds, dead relationships, and dead lives. Egyptian myth tells us Isis carried her son,

Hunab Ku

Horus, in her linen shawl, knotted at her waist. Knotted and braided breads and pretzels are still edible reminders of these sacred knots. As a knotted sign for life, the ankh came from a primitive sign for the goddess, most likely out of the Phoenician culture (see **Water 16**).

Ankh brings you protection and promises to animate something in your life that is dead. The knot will also connect you to health and well-being. The number twenty-seven, whose integers (two and seven) add up to nine, is a number of fulfillment and truth. Nine brings forth fortune and a rich harvest. What are you harvesting or about to harvest?

The ankh represents a human form, with the head above outstretched arms. Ankh calls us to be balanced humans. Blue is often associated with Isis as well as Mary and other feminine divine figures. Blue calls up images of the night sky and stars, of the moon. It connotes compassion, devotion, love, and justice.

Just as Isis carried life in her knotted shawl, we too carry life within us. Ideas and artistic creations come from an inner womb-like place. We give life in many forms. Our task is to enliven those around us rather than contribute to any deadness. What do you see when you hold up a mirror to your face? And what will you see tomorrow?

ANKH
27

O Isis, the Great, God's Mother, Lady of Philae . . .

Who issues orders among the divine ennead

According to whose command one rules.

Princess, great of praise, lady of charm

Whose face enjoys the trickling of fresh myrrh.

—Hymn to Isis, Temple of Philae

PART ע ~ Blue

• *Chalk hill figure, 1400 BCE, Uffington, England* •

26

Magician

THE 365-FOOT-LONG EARTH FIGURE CUT OUT OF CHALK PICTURED HERE HAS been dated much earlier than 100 BCE, as was once thought. The White Horse of Uffington is a product of the early Bronze Age and one of many hill figures in the English Wiltshire district. It races across the northern escarpment of the Berkshire Downs overlooking the little hamlet of Uffington in Oxfordshire. Opinions differ as to what they mean and why these ancient hill figures were created (see **Giant 22**). Like the Cerne Giant, this horse figure is restored and scoured once every seven years.

The white mare may be a tribute to the Celtic horse deity Epona, the Horse Goddess. Iron Age Britons believed her flesh was eucharistic—sacred food. A new Celtic king had to "mate" with a mare in order to rule. That mare, symbolic of the divine Mare, was then sacrificed and boiled. The king not only bathed in the broth, he shared the "goddess" flesh in communion with his people. Most northern people had horse feast days marking times of leadership changes and fertility rites. Today many people do not eat horse flesh, although they may not realize it has been seeded within us in archetypal remembrance of these early sacred rites.

The white horse pictured here was the site of ceremonial games and celebrations. Every seven years great fairs were held high on the hill to celebrate cleaning the chalk lines and restoring the figure. Some researchers suggest even older images are superimposed beneath the present horse. It is lucky, folks say, to stand on the horse's eye. From that vantage point you can easily see the mound below and to the left, known as Dragon's Hill. This is the spot, legends tells us, where St. George killed the dragon.

PART V ~ Blue

Power

Power is the strength and the ability to see yourself through your own eyes and not through the eyes of another. It is being able to place a circle of power at your own feet and not take power from someone else's circle.

—Lynne V. Andrews, *Flight of the Seventh Moon*

MAGICIAN 26

The word *magician* comes from the old Persian for "magus," or *magush*, which meant "one able to hold power." Magicians cast reality in a new light; they use tools to make things happen. Magicians can materialize and transform what is around them. You are a magician. When we team up with the divine energy within us, when we become active partners with God, Goddess, All That Is, we all become magicians. The magician part of you dares to face the dark and bring in the light, dares to harness your own power for good.

Knowledge is power, Francis Bacon said. But wisdom and understanding wake us up to a more complete view of what power can do. "Magic makes it possible to use the limitless power of spirit to reshape the world in accordance with the fondest desires of the soul." These words come from Donald Tyson, a Nova Scotian who brings the best of the East and the West, the past and present together. This is not sleight of hand trickery. This is the real thing. The church did, and still may, frown upon magicians. Only holy people were supposed to have the power to transform and shift. Magician tells you that you have that power as well. Like the galloping white horse, you are filled with high purpose, ready to run sacred races. In *New Millennium Magic*, Tyson says: "In magic, Heaven and Earth are recognized as one all-pervading, timeless unity. No one can flee the world, because the world is a vision created within the mind, and no one can run away from the self. Heaven is not some distant state difficult to attain but is constantly present and enfolds all things.... Humanity creates its own hell on Earth from moment to moment, and can never escape until it stops creating it."

Hunab Ku

Archetypes create fields of power. The horse archetype invites you to transform yourself with grace and ease. Horses, especially white ones, are considered good luck. With the Archangel Gabriel at his side, Mohammed rode his horse, Alborak, from Mecca to heaven. Horses carry us, symbolically, from one world to another.

As a magician, you have the power to transform words to poetry, yeast to bread, clay to pots, breath to song, egg and sperm to child. Magicians can turn pain into health, pollution into purity, fear into love, despair into hope. We can dare to expect the miraculous. Magician encourages you to use your intuitive magic; listen to your deep urgings and be open to how Spirit may direct you.

The integers of twenty-six (two and six) add up to eight. Look at **Weaver-Warrior 8** and **Mystic** 8 to see how both of these archetypal energies create magic. You are dealing with enormous strength and movement here. You are self-reliant and self-sufficient.

Blue can help you. Blue flows and puts you in touch with your perceptions. The blue chakra is expressive and unafraid to stand on a hill for all to see and hear. The color blue is, in itself, a magician, as it can cause your brain to secrete eleven neurotransmitters that can tranquilize, slow your pulse, and deepen your breathing.

MAGICIAN

26

Knowing others is intelligence; knowing yourself is true wisdom.
Mastering others is strength; mastering yourself is true power.

—Tao Te Ching

PART Ⅴ ~ Blue

Rock carving, 1600 BCE, Ostfold, Norway

25

Boat

THE BRONZE AGE ROCK CARVING FROM OSTFOLD, NORWAY, PICTURED HERE was created around 1600 BCE and shows humans with outstretched hands riding in a boat. Around the boats sun disks indicate that the boat is sailing away from the dark, into the light.

The Vikings called themselves Ostmen, men from the east. Both their square-sailed fighting ships and their fatter-bellied merchant cargo ships carried from thirty to sixty men. Ancient Norse used the same word for "boat," "cradle," and "coffin." Early Scandinavian graves were sometimes marked by stones that formed the image of a ship. Their culture saw the crescent moon as a boat, carrying souls to the afterlife.

PART V ~ Blue

Journey

**It is good to have an end to journey towards;
but it is the journey that matters, in the end.**

—Ursula K. Le Guin, *The Left Hand of Darkness*

BOAT 25

Many cultures made the connection between a boat and the womb; therefore, the boat became a symbol of the vehicle that carried the soul to rebirth in the afterlife. Egyptian culture was also saturated with images of the boat as a journey to the next life. An enormous Nile barge was buried next to the Great Pyramid. Small stone boats graced every temple of Isis, who was also called Lunar Mother, Rebirther.

Ceremonial ships can be found engraved on the stones of megalithic tombs throughout Europe. At a time when land transportation was slow and difficult, the boat united Northern Europe into one homogeneous culture. Water connected the worlds.

You have embarked upon a life journey. You plan, prepare, note the markers along the way, and set your goals and final destination. You are the captain and the crew. You watch the stars and chart your course. Are you where you want to be? Your journey goes on from precisely where you are this moment.

Boat may have come to you because you are planning to take an actual trip somewhere. Or perhaps you attracted Boat to you because you're journeying over emotional waters and may be feeling adrift. Perhaps you are contemplating a career move. Make your career an exciting journey.

This image calls up many stories of journeys, including, of course, Odysseus's sailing ventures. Think of all the explorers, pilgrims, and adventurers who have set sail without knowing for certain their final destination. People travel to new places to discover further who they are. Blue water draws you. You sail into the unknown, the unconscious, with intuitive oars and prayerful sails. Contemplation and meditation are easier when you surround yourself with blue light or actual blue items or clothing. Blue stills the mind, like a calm ocean.

Hunab Ku

Boat also symbolizes conquest. Boats made communication and connection possible before the airplane was invented. The dominant culture was the one with the best sea maps. What maps make up your inner cartography? What impels you forward? Inner as well as outer journeys test one's motives. Is it a restless, searching nature that propels you forward?

Carl Jung said water represents your feeling function. How are you feeling about this journey you are on? What do you wish you'd have packed to take with you? Who are the other people on board with you? Are you traveling toward something or away from something?

BOAT 25

I will soar higher than the highest heaven,
I will dive deeper than the depths of the ocean,
I will reach further than the wide horizon,
I will enter within my innermost being.

—HAZRAT INAYAT KHAN, *Gayan*

PART Ⅴ ~ Blue

• *Wood carving, traditional, Maprik, Papua New Guinea* •

24

Pelican

The Melanesian bird woodcarving pictured here combines male and female symbolism—the phallic beak together with the central moon symbol—to create a whole. Together, they form a powerfully integrated bird. These images were traditionally hung on the walls of New Guinean spirit houses.

Carving in wood is an important artistic expression in traditional New Guinean culture. In one of the area's creation myths, a sky being carved a crocodile out of wood, and after he painted its face with sago milk, the creature opened its eyes, came alive, and became the first man. This man asked for companions, some of which turned their backs on their creator, and when these creatures killed animals for food they turned back into half-crocodiles.

When someone died in northwestern New Guinea, a wooden figure called a *korwar* was carved, a human figure with a small body and a large head. Sometimes the statue's head was hollowed out to hold the deceased person's skull, and it was believed that this ancestor could be called on in times of trouble. Someone holding the statue could even communicate with the spirit, whose voice would speak through them.

PART V ~ Blue

Sacrifice

This is the true joy in life. To be used for a purpose recognized by yourself as a mighty one.

—George Bernard Shaw

PELICAN 24

The pelican was a popular medieval symbol for Christ's sacrifice because it was mistakenly thought that the pelican fed its children with blood from self-inflicted wounds to its breast. This Early Christian symbol possibly began with an Egyptian myth: The pelican loved its young, but when the chicks grew they eventually struck out at their parent, seemingly for no reason. The parent bird, as a result, struck back, killed the chicks in anger, and was instantly overcome with grief. On the third day, the mother pelican pecked open the side of her body and restored the chicks to life with her blood. Dante knew about this myth and called Christ "Our Pelican."

All large birds—eagles, vultures, herons, and pelicans—spread their wings and bring food to their young. Their devotion is recorded in early Egyptian and Hebrew ideograms. The birds became known for their devotion, compassion, and sacrifice. The pelican was named the nourisher.

Sacrifice means the act of offering something precious, giving with no thought of return. It's a word that seems out of place in today's culture, for surely we don't kill an animal or person as a gift to a deity anymore. We no longer rip out bloody hearts and place them, steaming, on Aztec temple steps. But we are still called upon to make sacrifices. Something must be given up in order to become something new and different. New parents sacrifice freedom when they have a child; money that might be otherwise spent is sacrificed for the child's care, for the child's education and betterment. Parents are nourishers, just as the pelican was thought to be.

"It is good," Bill Tyson, author of *New Millennium Magic*, says, "to sacrifice the lower for the higher, and evil to sacrifice the higher for the lower." What are the "higher" goods for which you are willing to make a sacrifice? Does true service require sacrifice?

Hunab Ku

See **Water Bearer** 32. Tyson continues: "There is no sacrifice in service to the greater good, only perfect fulfillment.... Personal sacrifice is not necessary for service. Quite the contrary, sacrifice of genuine happiness can never result in either service or destiny, because happiness is the reward built into the human genetic coding for the fulfillment of a life, both on the lower level of the individual ego, and the higher level of the evolution of the universe."

If you are called upon to make a sacrifice and willingly respond, don't let it bloody your breast; put it in loving perspective. Think of your blue chakra expanding, taking wing, in a motherly pelican way, until it is large enough to hold the compassion needed to feed everyone who needs to be fed. Perhaps you are called to feed others with your words. Work with this blue center for freer expression in your writing.

Early builders of sacred sites quarried blue stones in Wales, and transported them, no doubt at great sacrifice, about 140 miles to their final standing places at Stonehenge on the Salisbury plain in Wiltshire, England. The tiles in the Blue Mosque in Istanbul were lovingly created to enhance that special worship place.

We hang onto things, long after they are no longer useful to us. Some things to think about sacrificing: a low self-esteem; negativity in all its forms; being judgmental; being overly critical; spiritual pride; selfish personal ambition; fear; guilt; feeling responsible for words and deeds that are not yours; a neediness to be cared for; sickness; self-pity. You can continue the list from your own storehouse of personal clutter.

PELICAN

24

The man who sacrifices his desires and his works to the Beings from whom the principles of everything stem, and by whom the Universe was formed, through this sacrifice attains perfection.

—*Bhagavad-Gita*

• *Minoan coin, 1400 BCE, Knossos, Crete* •

23

Winged Dog

A FEMALE FIGURE WITH INSECT EYES, FLANKED BY TWO WINGED DOGS, decorates the Minoan seal or coin pictured here from 1400 BCE. This bee goddess image was found in Knossos, Crete, and it is just over an inch in diameter. Two sets of bull horns on her head are topped by a double-axe design representing a butterfly. Both the horns and the insect images are symbols of new life. The butterfly, as in **Released Soul 6**, carries a message of rebirth and transformation.

Like the hunter/protectress of animals, Artemis, who is often portrayed with stags and her dogs, this goddess is dutifully guarded by two stylized hounds barking at the moon, heralding life and regeneration. The skeletal remains of dogs, presumed to have been sacrificed in a funeral rite, have been found, buried with their master or mistress. Even in death, they guard their loved ones. Howling dogs, like the ones pictured here, were harbingers of death in many old European cultures. When dogs, or other canines, howled at the moon, people believed they caused the moon's cycles to change. Leaping and flying dogs often flank tree of life images, indicating their dual cosmic life and death guardian roles.

PART V ~ Blue

Guardian

> **There can be no progress, however, on the path to higher knowledge unless we guard our thoughts and feelings in just the same way we guard our steps in the physical world.**
>
> —Rudolf Steiner, *Knowledge of Higher Worlds and Its Attainment*

WINGED DOG 23

Dogs often accompanied ancient goddess figures, and when the matriarchal culture collapsed and the divine feminine fell into ill repute, the female dog insult began to be used against women, rather than in their honor. The goddess was once called the Great Bitch, and her priestesses were the Hunting Bitches. Sometimes referred to as Moon Dogs, her dogs were thought to travel with the dead to the otherworld. Throughout mythology, dogs travel and guard. The three-headed dog, Cerberus, for instance, guarded the gates of hell. Anubis, the jackal in Egypt, was thought to have come from Sirius, the Dog Star. Medieval Europeans believed moon dogs came and carried away the dead.

Guardians link us to a lighter world. Some people hear them; some see them; some feel their presence in nonphysical ways. They are called angels, or helpers, or watchers. In order to communicate with guardians, however, we must practice inward stillness. Guardians always speak the truth. Why do they often have wings? Thomas Aquinas said that angels don't need bodies for their own sakes, but for ours. Winged guardians sometimes assume human bodies. Their wings probably represent their ability to move around with ease, for they appear here and there with great speed. Hildegard of Bingen said God determined that angels would protect us, so God made angels a part of our human community (see **Angel Guide** 4).

You may wish to keep a dream journal as you work with the *Hunab Ku* images. Images, such as this one of winged dogs, are never still. They're charged by whatever archetype lies behind them. What is the message for you, lying behind Winged Dog?

Hunab Ku

If you want to understand the images on more than just a surface level, you have to be involved with them. Engage them. Interpretation demands your whole intention.

Winged dogs, for instance, guard the road to the underworld, which is really our dream world. Record your dreams and then have a dialogue with the images later. Simply visualize the image you encounter in your dream, and ask it if there is anything else that image wants to tell you; then write down exactly what jumps into your mind without censoring it. It takes a little practice, but it's a gratifying way to explore the dream world further.

The number of this image, twenty-three, is related to **Star 23**, for Isis/Sirius is the Dog Star, Orion's guardian and companion. You'll notice this image also has a star in the background.

WINGED DOG

23

God within me, God without, how shall I ever be in doubt?

There is no place where I may go and not there see God's face, not know I am God's vision and God's ears... I am the sower and the sown,

God's self unfolding and God's own.

—Asmund Karasun, c. 1050 CE, Rune Stone near Västerby, Uppland, Sweden

PART V ~ Blue

Ancient spring, modern cover, 1900 CE, Chalice Well, Glastonbury, England

22

Moon

CHALICE WELL, NESTLED IN THE SHADOW OF THE GLASTONBURY TOR, IS AN ancient site where people once gathered to feel the moon's powers, to drink and bathe in holy water, and to celebrate oneness with the earth and the universe. Wells mark very old gathering places, and the one pictured here in Somerset, England, is no exception.

A reddish-colored water still passes through this ancient spring into Chalice Garden at the rate of twenty-five thousand gallons a day. Flowing from the Black Mountains in Wales on the other side of the Bristol Channel, the water tastes of iron and it looks a bit like blood. Two blood legends exist about the well: one legend says that the well is a holy goddess place where her menstrual waters still flow, restoring life and fertility to the earth; the other, more recent legend tells of a man named Joseph of Aramathea. The tin trade brought him on business from the Mediterranean, and he carried a chalice, the Holy Grail, still bearing Christ's blood. This chalice, legend says, was the very one Jesus and his followers drank from when they broke bread and shared wine before his death. One legend claims the chalice was thrown into this very well. Later, as the story goes, the chalice was rescued and resides somewhere in Glastonbury (see further Grail legends in **Chalice** 14).

Bligh Bond crafted the ironwork cover pictured here for the well in the early 1900s. Bond received automatic writing messages from a source he called the Monks. The Monks told him, among other things, where to find King Edward's Lost Chapel in the ruins of Glastonbury Abbey. The chapel was unearthed exactly where the Monks had suggested.

PART vi ~ Indigo

Dreams

MOON 22

> Dreams are the best evidence that we are not as firmly shut in our skins as we believe.
> —Friedrich Hebbel

Your misty moon-side harbors messages from your unconscious. Honor your dreams, for when they come in the night, they reflect a part of you that is often hidden during the day. The image pictured here invites you to swim through dark waters. It asks you to reflect on the watery images you hold within. The **Winged Dog** 23 invited you to record your dreams and not fear them, since they are your guardians. Now Moon invites you to delve even deeper into the images. The circular image pictured here is a mandala. *Mandala* is a Sanskrit word meaning "circle." But it is not an ordinary circle. Like a snapshot of motion, it spins and whirls, drawing you deeper and deeper inside. The well cover depicts a mandala of our deep, dark unconscious. Tibetan Buddhists call a circular ritual motif a *yantra*. A *yantra*'s purpose is to help you meditate and focus your concentration, rather like a visual mantra. Rabindranath Tagore said, "The center is still and silent in the heart of an eternal dance of circles."

Marti Cain, a New England woman who works with labyrinths, talks about "the spin" one feels while walking a labyrinth (see **Mystic** 8). She says, "The self pulls us inward to our essence which is hidden in the subconscious. It focuses us upon our inner journey and can be understood as a spinning center or 'pole.' The nature of this spinning is that it throws off impurities and only at the center is there any stability." Mandalas, circular sandpaintings, and Aboriginal art all work the same way. They draw our eyes into the center and pull us deeply inside the image.

The moon comes to you in a full, round circle every 29 days, 12 hours, 44 minutes, and 5 seconds. She tugs at our planet's waters; tides and moods follow her call. As she waxes and wanes and remains completely dark for three days before glowing once again, she reminds us of our own cycles and journeys of change. The moon's cycle

Hunab Ku

mirrors women's menstrual cycles. She has long been a feminine image. The Arabic name for "moon" is the feminine *Al-lat*, which was later masculinized to *Allah*.

A halo around the moon is produced when light enters hexagonal ice crystals in our upper atmosphere. The light goes in one face of the crystal and comes out an adjacent face, bending the light exactly twenty-two degrees outward from the central circle. Moon calls up our deep wisdom. The number twenty-two doubles the wisdom found in the **Owl 2** image.

MOON 22

Moon will show you many things in your own dreams that you may have missed before. Don't be afraid to dive deep into your own well waters.

In Bond's well cover at Glastonbury, two circles of bronze intersect, forming a womb or a fish, a *vesica piscis*. Early persecuted Christians used the *vesica* as a secret way of identifying each other. Two circles overlapping represent the joining of heaven and earth, above and below, the Creator and the created, male and female, light and dark. This well is very old and was a sacred gathering place long before Christians came to Glastonbury. The five-sided stones that line the well are similar to stonework in Egypt and at Stonehenge. Although the cover comes from the early twentieth century, its design captures the mystery of this place. The well invites you to listen to the rhythms of your own body and use the moon's powers to imagine your future.

Indigo rays, gathered at the chakra between your eyes, *Anja* chakra, influence your intuitive powers. The center of your forehead is the center for sight and clairvoyance. Indigo assists with your dreams, as well, so use the color for nighttime exploration. Let deep purple help you manifest your dreams.

Hearken, O divine queen, light-bringing and splendid Selene . . .
Shining in the night, like a jewel, you grant fulfillment and favor.

—"TO THE MOON," ORPHIC HYMN

PART *vi* ~ Indigo

Incised stone slab, 700 CE, Burghead, Scotland

21

Bull

THE CELTS' ORAL TRADITION IS LOST TO US, BUT THEIR STONEWORK REMAINS. The bull pictured here, which comes from Burghead, Morayshire, in Scotland, was incised on a stone slab around 700 CE. The curling lines are indicative of the Pictish style. "Pict" was the nickname the Romans gave to northern Britons in 297 CE. The Pictish kingdom, lying well above Hadrian's Wall, existed from 700 BCE into the ninth century CE. *Picti* means "the painted people," for they were heavily tattooed. They used woad, a plant that produced a dark blue dye, for their body art. They also, according to Robert Graves, enjoyed wearing blue faience beads, which were manufactured in Egypt between 1380 and 1350 BCE. The Picts imported the beads.

Graves mentions the Picts' earlier connections to the blue-eyed, blond Thracians, people who lived along the Black Sea coast, who were also skillfully tattooed and who carried long spears and white ox-hide shields. They were a highly cultured nation of male and female warriors and poets (see **Adult 28**).

PART **vi** ~ Indigo

Strength

BULL 21

> *The bull is a mystical life-source, an earthly manifestation of the cosmogenic primordial waters.*
>
> —Marija Gimbutas, *The Language of the Goddess*

Time-honored bull games and dances in the Mediterranean were centered around the bull's sexual power. Bull sacrifice was common in the worship of Attis and Cybele as well as with Mithras, whose worshippers were drenched in the sacrificial bull's blood. El is the Phoenician bull deity. In Sumeria, he was known as Enlil. At the Neolithic Turkish site Çatal Hüyük, bull figures outnumber every other animal in the rooms thus far excavated. One six-foot red bull, encircled by small male figures, covers an entire north wall. Most of the bull images face the Taurus (Bull) Mountains. Many cave images of bulls were painted during the astrological age of Taurus, from 4000 BCE to 2000 BCE. The bullfights in Spain are reminiscent of the ancient sacred games around the sacrifice of bulls. The most famous games may have been the bull dances in Knossos, Crete, where highly trained acrobats wore bull-headed masks of the Minotaur and flung their bodies over the horns. American rodeos carry a faded glimmer of that past glory.

Bull reminds you of your Taurean nature, your earth power. Take a few moments to review the images in the red palette, the earth chakra. Bring your life force, your magnificent bull-like strength to all you undertake. While Bull can be rather lazy at times, Bull also reminds you to take great pleasure in exercise and all physical pleasures. Slow and steady, like mighty indigo rivers, Bull's strength flows over you, flooding you with desires, emotional freedom, and sensual creativity. Claim your Taurus health and vitality. Watch that you are not too stubborn or set in your ways, however. You can usually accomplish most anything by just putting your head down and moving forward.

Strength comes to you in many forms. Like the spiderwebs in the old African proverb, "When spider webs unite they can tie up a lion," uniting with others creates

Hunab Ku

more powerful results than going it alone, although that is Bull's innate nature. Your shoulders may carry many burdens, but your obstinate and possessive nature is balanced by your patience and your perseverance.

Your sixth chakra, the indigo center, is sometimes called the third eye. Activating this energy center increases your intuition and your creative imagination. The actual point of this chakra lies in the middle of your head at brow level. Esoterically the pineal gland has been associated with the third eye. Its principal hormone is melatonin. Watch your light sources. Artificial lights can lead to depression, and dark days may lead to mood alterations.

In her book *Dove in the Stone,* Alice O. Howell says the penalty for the biblical killing of Abel was Cain's loss of his "third eye." He had psychic insight, but it was taken from him. Your active indigo chakra will enhance your creative and intuitive use of the *Hunab Ku* images.

This image's number is twenty-one, and the integers (two and one) add up to three. Three represents Bull's generative force and forward movement. It promises success because the number three has a beginning, a middle, and an end. Like a triangle, it is stable, and so are you. Twenty-one is also a triple seven, the biblical number of abundance and strength. The Pythagoreans esteemed seven because it represented the number of life itself. Seven combines our threefold nature (spirit, mind, and soul) with earth's fourfold nature and first geometric solid. Solidity: the message of Bull.

O Osiris! Thy strength is vigorous . . .

O Osiris! Thy neck is made firm,

O Osiris! Thy heart is glad, Thy speech is made effective . . .

Thou art established the Bull in Amentet.

—PAPYRUS OF ANI (*The Egyptian Book of the Dead*)

PART *vi* ~ Indigo

• *Limestone figurine, 3000 BCE, Cyprus* •

20

Balance

THE SQUATTING FIGURINE PICTURED HERE, CARVED FROM WHITE LIMESTONE, was found in Cyprus. It is 15.5 inches tall and dates from 3000 BCE. The triangle in the center, formed by the vulva-stylized breasts, is a common motif for artifacts of this era. Down-pointing triangles represent femininity, fertility, and completeness. The triangle's three sides embody the three phases of the moon: waxing, full, and waning. The figurine was made in the Chalcolithic or Bronze era when copper tools were available.

PART vi ~ Indigo

Choice

BALANCE 20

> The powers of the Goddess are fully released from
> the underworld in order to create balance with the powers
> of the gods, the patriarchy. Slowly, woman within will awaken
> just in time to prevent ecocide, the suicide of Planet Earth.
>
> —Barbara Hand Clow, *Heart of the Christos*

Elizabeth Cady Stanton, the nineteenth-century New York woman who, with Susan B. Anthony, launched the women's suffrage movement, wrote: "The masculine and feminine elements, exactly equal and balancing each other, are as essential to the maintenance of the equilibrium of the universe as positive and negative electricity, the centripetal and centrifugal forces, the laws of attraction which bind together all we know of this planet whereon we dwell, and of the system in which we revolve."

How do we choose what to believe? "Some beliefs are like blinders, shutting off the power to choose one's own direction," Sophia Fahs said in *It Matters What You Believe*. She said, "Other beliefs are like gateways opening wide vistas for exploration."

The 1980s and 1990s exploded with books and events designed to meet a deep yearning for a God who looks like women, and people seriously began searching for a woman-affirming spirituality. In other words, they wanted a choice, a chance to balance what had for too long been male-dominated religions, with a return to the Great Mother in her many forms. Some people claim this return, this goddess movement, was born out of the ecology movement and a synthesis of many spiritual paths. This alternative to a masculine deity has been called by many names throughout history, for She has been around a *very* long time. In order to balance our understanding of God, we sensed a need to move beyond a masculine language—to move beyond *He*. One goddess handbook claims there have been more than eleven thousand goddess names throughout history.

Hunab Ku

The image pictured here holds out her arms to embrace you and to show her love to all. We don't know her name, but she embodies all the Great Mother's names. Perhaps she is just Ma. The Egyptians called her Ma'at and gave her scales to hold. When people died, Ma'at weighed their lives against her feather of truth. When Justice is depicted in statues or paintings, she is always a woman. Why? Like Libra, those who value balance are sophisticated, refined, and artistic. Justice begs you to balance issues that appear to divide us. Harmony and justice are within your grasp. Just stretch out your arms.

BALANCE
20

What choices are you facing right now? What is being weighed in the balance scales? What needs to be brought back into proportion? What might be tilting you off center?

The third eye's pineal gland has been called the seat of the soul. It is developed by the time we are seven years old and, although we don't understand exactly how, it continues to influence our central nervous system. Because it is affected by light, keeping light and dark in balance seems to equalize our body's chemistry.

The sixth chakra is called the gateway to wisdom; it is the *Anja* chakra, meaning "to perceive" and "to command." You have it within your command to visualize a world much more harmonious and balanced. This image can help. The number twenty will help as well, as it represents a powerful awakening. Ten plus ten balances perfections, body and spirit. When either is neglected, we list, we tilt, we lean. And sometimes we fall over.

The One who gives sight to the blind… the excellent Guardian who protects the one who invokes Her on the day when he faces life or death. Ma'at the Great, Mistress of Sentences for the supplicants, who does what is right for the one who is zealous.

—Hymn in the Temple of Dendera

PART vi ~ Indigo

• *Carved chalk cylinder, 2000 BCE, Folkton, Yorkshire, England* •

19

Counselor

THE CARVED CHALK CYLINDER PICTURED HERE WAS FOUND IN A CHILD'S grave in Folkton, Yorkshire, England, and it dates back to 2000 BCE. Similar drums are as elaborately incised as this one, with motifs repeated in the panels. The eye design is encircled by water wavelets or repeated eyebrows. Neolithic eyes are found inscribed on stones and bones all over Europe. Like the Yorkshire cylinder, many inscribed eyes are surrounded by multiple eyebrows, creating owl eyes that feather outward (see **Wise Old One** 17).

These drums were probably children's toys, and they were often buried with small children. Archaeologists speculate that these toy eyes were placed in the grave to watch over and comfort the child in death.

PART vi ~ Indigo

Nurturing

COUNSELOR 19

What do we live for if not to make the world less difficult for each other?

—George Eliot

What would a world look like if everyone living were nurtured and cared for? What if fourteen million American children did not go to bed hungry every night? What if people sent out, instead of negative thoughts, creative and powerfully loving thoughts? What would a world look like if everyone could develop his or her highest potential? What if there were no more boredom, no more dependency on outside stimulants, no more judgmental thoughts clouding our relationships? What then? We would become our own spiritual masters. And we would sense wholeness on all levels.

The carved rock pictured here is ever watchful. Look into the eyes. Deeply. What do you see? What do you see when you gaze at your own eyes in a mirror for some length of time? Hildegard of Bingen painted elaborate mandalas of universal wonder, and many of them have ever-watching eyes. Archangels, it is said, have eyes on their wings. There are watchers and holy ones close by (see **Angel Guide** 4).

Hunab Ku images invite you to see life differently. To see *through* metaphors and symbols to another side. This image is not simply a carved rock toy, but a watcher. The toy's face is a mandala of swirling lines, inviting you to look inside yourself. Go inside to see what might coincide! William Blake saw a whole world in a grain of sand. Julian of Norwich saw a complete and perfect world in a hazelnut. How do you see the world?

In *Zorba the Greek*, Nikos Kazantzakis says, "Everything in this world has a hidden meaning. Men, animals, trees, stars, they are all hieroglyphics . . . when you see them, you do not understand them. You think they are really men, animals, trees, stars. It is only later that you understand." Later, we may understand that this chalk figure is more than a toy. Later, we realize someone nourished us, when at the time it seemed like anything but. Hindsight is as much of a gift as foresight.

Hunab Ku

This image tells you to look beyond the ordinary. Look for counselors; they are in and around you. Some may be children. Lee Carroll and Jan Tober have written several books about the Indigo children, children who are born with exceptional gifts and psychic abilities. Films and books can now help you explore further these amazing children.

COUNSELOR

19

Royal blue or purple is the color of insight, telepathy, psychic connections, inner visions, and enlightenment. In many early cultures, only those in power were allowed to wear purple. Dr. Max Lüscher developed a comprehensive theory of color psychology in the late 1940s, setting the standards for subsequent color work. Lüscher said dark blue, because it was associated with the night sky, became connected to quietude and passivity, whereas bright yellow, like the daylight, was considered to be filled with hope and activity. In sickness and exhaustion, the need for dark blue increases. By selecting a blue-violet image, Lüscher would say you have a need for understanding and for affectionate give-and-take, and you may be impatient as the need grows. As children, we are impatient because we want speedier results. We easily become restless. Counselor helps the child within you understand how the world works, and how you fit into that larger context. Counselor helps you understand what is *you* and what is *other*, and how we are related to and nourish one another.

The eyes of all look to thee, and thou givest them their food in due season;
Thou openest thy hand, thou satisfiest the desire of every living thing.

—PSALM 145

PART **vi** ~ Indigo

• *Shell and lapis lazuli game board, 2500 BCE, Uruk, Mesopotamia (Iraq)* •

18

Light

THE GAME BOARD PICTURED HERE, TOGETHER WITH ITS STONE MARKERS, was found in Uruk, Mesopotamia (Ur), now in Iraq. It was originally made around 2500 BCE. Its twenty squares are fashioned from red sandstone, shell, and lapis lazuli, a semiprecious azure blue stone. This eight-petaled rose, symbol of the lotus and the goddess Kali, like the eight-pointed star of Ishtar, appears on five of the squares. Other squares are decorated with circles, dots, small squares, and eye designs.

PART vi ~ Indigo

Imagination

LIGHT 18

We are what we imagine.

—Scott Momaday

The first book of the Bible begins: "Let there be light, and there was light." The Koran says: "God is the light of the heavens and the earth." Some legends say earth remained light until Adam and Eve ate the forbidden fruit, and then darkness settled. Others say it remained dark until Jesus came, claiming to be the light of the world. Though light remains a mystery, it unfolds and grows within us. It nurtures our ability to imagine.

Many cultures have light celebrations, reminiscent of early winter solstice bonfires. Several events, like the eight-pointed rose pictured here, are celebrated for eight days, such as Hanukkah's festival of lights and the southern African Swazi's *Incwala* festival. Lighting candles rekindles memories of earlier dark times and brings the sky's light to earth. Craftspeople opened up dark walls in gothic cathedrals to allow light, often colored by glass, into worship spaces. Light enters the ancient temple of Newgrange on winter solstice to illuminate a triple spiral (see **Mother 15**). All light entering sacred spaces stimulates our imaginations and shortens the wavelength we need to communicate with our divine source. For the Jewish people, light is earth's purpose, and each person, being a microcosm of the world, has the responsibility to bring light to every situation.

Zeus means "shower of light." Imagine taking a shower in light! Or imagine your chakras as a Jacob's ladder of light, with angels ascending and descending on steps of color, from red to violet and back to red again.

Imagination calls us to look at all symbols as doorways to higher meaning and greater understanding. The flower in this image, like the lotus, invites endless openings. Rudolf Steiner placed *imagination* in the realm of the etheric, that close aura-like sheath that surrounds our physical body. He tied *inspiration* to the soul's astral realm. In the astral world, he said, colors flow freely, like flames or rainbows, and beings there

Hunab Ku

speak through color. He placed *intuition* the highest of the three, linking it to the realm of the "I" or the spiritual self.

Steiner brings Goethe's color theories into perspective. Goethe argued that white light does *not* contain all colors. There is an inner life of color only our souls understand, Steiner argued in *Colour*. Steiner claimed our senses have been dulled so colors no longer speak to us with integrity. But, he said, we as humans are evolving to a point where colors will be more intense and less "washed out." Goethe believed all colors come from yellow and blue, not from white. He said yellow was highest in purity, and some colors were "yellow plus" colors (such as red and orange). Blue was lowest in purity, closest to darkness. Blue, he said, is a contradiction between excitement and repose.

Light reminds you to give your imagination free rein; let it blossom. This is a time to birth your imaginings into reality by using your magician's power of illumination and transformation (see **Magician** 26). The integers of the number eighteen (one and eight) add up to nine, the number of originality, initiative, courage, and determination. Painters once painted halos or circles of yellow light, the light of glory, around the heads of holy people. It was their way of painting auras. Hildegard of Bingen put it this way: "We are all sparks of the divine flame . . . no creature exists that lacks a radiance, be it greenness or seed, buds or beauty."

LIGHT

18

Which are the mountains not clothed with your beams? Which are the regions not warmed by the brightness of your light? Brightener of gloom, Illuminator of darkness, Dispeller of darkness, Illuminator of the broad earth.

—GREAT HYMN TO SHAMASH, MESOPOTAMIA

PART v̇ı̇ ~ Indigo

• *Carved phalange, 2000 BCE, Almeria, Spain* •

17

Wise Old One

BONES, THE RELICS OF FORMER LIVES, ARE OFTEN HONORED—CAREFULLY arranged and safely kept. Ancient Middle Eastern people, as well as Egyptians, revered the sacrum as the sacred bone from which the rest of the body could be resurrected. It was called "the seed bone."

Surrounding the eyes on the bone pictured here are enigmatic lines and designs like ancient script, triangles, hourglass shapes, and nets. Many carved phalanges found in graves and Neolithic settlements have round owl eyes. The owl can see into the future, it is believed, and often symbolizes death, regeneration, and life beyond this world (see **Owl** 2). This wise old owl bone, and others like it, were found in Almeria, Spain, and are dated to around 2000 BCE (see **Counselor** 19).

PART *vi* ~ Indigo

Rest

WISE OLD ONE 17

Let us learn from this: Wisdom is wisdom, the source cannot matter.

—Paula Underwood

Elders, because of their years of experience, have learned the art of living. They have had more practice. Indigenous elders often share their ceremonies and rituals with others, thus preserving them. Monks served the elder function throughout the Dark Ages in Ireland and preserved manuscripts that would have otherwise been lost. Native American elders have been entrusted with deep earth wisdom. First Peoples around the world keep wisdom alive in songs and stories, in dances and symbols. Egyptian wisdom has been kept alive in the tarot system, preserved by Gypsies. Wise old women kept the lore of herbs and plants alive by healing and by apprenticing younger people.

Wise old ones invite seekers into their space. Wise old ones lend their integrity and grace to meetings. In New Zealand a Maori *comátoa*, a male elder, sits by the door of a meeting, welcoming and then bidding farewell to all who come. He has a deep link with his intuition and healing powers, going back and forth between the ancestors. The *kuia*, the female elder, relates to the land and pays attention to each person's lineage; she has a sense of time and flow. When elders are asked to hold a particular space, to create, by their prayerful and centered attention, a sanctified area, they do so with great equanimity and without judgment.

Elders know about truth as well as life. They have lived with the rhythm of their soul, as John O'Donohue puts it in *Anam Cara*: "Wisdom is the way that you learn to decipher the unknown; and the unknown is our closest companion. So wisdom is the art of being courageous and generous with the unknown, of being able to decipher and recognize its treasures."

We have a wise counselor within us, as close to us as our own bones. It's a quiet inner voice, Meredith Young-Sowers says in *Wisdom Bowls*, that overrides the normal

Hunab Ku

confusion and struggles we feel. Our wise inner counselor helps us see wisdom inherent in life's challenges, suggesting possibilities that we would ordinarily miss.

Most people believe retirement is a time of earned rest. Rest, however, is necessary at all stages of our lives. People who are no longer employed full-time often find rest is not so necessary any longer, and many have energy for more pursuits than ever before. We, as a culture, would do well to ask the advice of our Wise Old Ones, rather than relegating them to separate communities. Wisdom is built upon the gifts of many old bones who have gone before.

WISE OLD ONE
17

Wise Old One encourages you to look after your own bones, or perhaps to pay more attention to how and when you rest. Value the advice you receive from wise older people, whether living friends or the wisdom they have left behind. Rely on the ancient wisdom that lives deep inside yourself, which is always yours for the asking.

In Sanskrit, dark blue is called *nila;* it is the most suitable environment in which to meditate. The German word for this dark-blue mood is *gemüt,* which approximately means "sensitivity of feeling." Dark blue has a depth and an awareness not found in other colors. Indigo indicates that you have attained wisdom. It is a mature, often feminine, color suggesting night. Sometimes it triggers a sense of loss and confusion. It is a manifesting color encouraging you to use your eyes, outer and inner, to visualize your goals and follow through on your dreams. Pair **Child 17** with this image for additional insights. Wise Old One invites you to draw inside yourself for rest and reflection.

One who finds his happiness and joy within himself, and also his wisdom within himself, is one with God. And, mark well, the soul which has found God is freed from rebirth and death, from old age and pain, and drinks the water of Immortality.

—Bhagavad-Gita

PART vi ~ Indigo

Burial chamber interior, 2500 BCE, Orkney, Scotland

16

Square

THE OPENING SQUARE ENTRANCE PICTURED HERE ALLOWS LIGHT TO ENTER A burial chamber in Orkney, Scotland. Of the seventy islands that make up the Orkneys off the northeastern tip of Scotland, at least four of the smaller islands shelter chambered monuments. Even today, the people living in this area have a separate identity, and it was, no doubt, once a society unto itself. Some stone houses in Megalithic village sites were built in 3500 BCE.

This particular chamber dates to 2500 BCE. Megalithic rock structures and chambers are often formed from upright stones covered with a mound of earth, forming a cairn. These upright stones, or dolmens, are found throughout Europe and Britain as well as in parts of New England; many are arranged in circles or in lines, such as the mile-long rows of stones at Carnac in Brittany.

The speculated uses for these rock structures range from tombs to living spaces, from settings for ritual worship to astronomical calendar devices. The people who built them were sailors and navigators, accustomed to watching the stars and interacting with many cultures. Rock carvings of ships, such as the one in **Boat** 25, have been carbon-dated in Malta, Brittany, and Scandinavia as far back as 8000 BCE.

PART **vi** ~ Indigo

Opening

SQUARE 16

> Curiosity is the doorway that stimulates growth, joy and expansion
> and allows you to begin to remember who you are.
>
> —Emmanuel, *The Choice for Love*

A square, according to Carl Jung, symbolizes earthbound matter. It is a body's four-sided boundary. It implies orderliness and trustworthiness, like a town square. A square can represent the four corners of the earth, the four directions, or the four cross quarter days: equinoxes and solstices. Ninety- and 45-degree angles create harmony. Squares express firmness and stability. Like the four seasons, the four directions, and the four elements, squares suggest that we, too, have limits. The square symbolizes earth (see **Earth 5**). The square thrones that Egyptian royalty sat upon firmly anchored them to the earth. Alchemists squared the circle to unite the circle or divinity/heaven with the square or matter/earth. In the hermetic tradition, a squared circle represented salt, which stood for the soul's wisdom.

Mandalas, Eastern magic circles, are often surrounded by a square. Temples are usually enclosed in square spaces, so are castles and theatrical stages. The image of a square calls up the holy of holies, the inner sanctum. Heaven to the Chinese is made of four beams of cosmic force. Gates are openings, which signify that those who pass through them have entered hallowed ground. Eastern Christian churches have sanctuary screens called Gates of Heaven. In the Bolivian Andes, on the roof of the Americas, a huge doorway cut from a single block of stone called the Gateway of the Sun has been excavated. Graceful gateways called *torii* mark the entrances to Shinto shrines (see **Bridge 36**).

This stone gateway image invites you to enter. The inscription hanging over Carl Jung's doorway read: "Called or not called, God will be there." You need not be afraid. Your inner resources will always be with you as you step through a new opening. As

Hunab Ku

Thomas Merton said: "It is by the door of the deep self that we enter into the spiritual knowledge of God."

The image pictured here is of a burial chamber, but it could also represent the doors of your perceptions, as William Blake described them: "If the doors of perception were cleansed everything would appear to be as it is, infinite." Look beyond the confines of this doorway into a timeless reality; enter a place with infinite perspective.

SQUARE
16

Square may have come to you right now because something is actually opening up for you—or will be soon. Change is now evident. Step over the threshold.

The number of this image is sixteen, four times four, a holy space squared. The integers (one and six) add up to seven, the number representing spirituality and mystery. It is the number of healing and of miracles.

Indigo opens up visions beyond your present reality. This color represents higher callings—from royalty to the priesthood. Acknowledge your spiritual powers. The gate you pass through leads to the entire universe. Open to the beauty that lies around you. Ralph Waldo Emerson said, "Never lose an opportunity of seeing anything that is beautiful, for beauty is God's handwriting. The beauty of the stone, the beauty of the light, the beauty of an opening are a message for you."

Elusiveness falls away and the truth becomes evident.

At the threshold is the door. The destination is one. Neither beginning nor end, the arrival departs and soon is one. The understanding is in the meeting, in what is gleaned and explained, in the meaning of understanding.

—HEBREW PRAYER, VAQQAHSHAH TRANSLATION

PART *vi* ~ Indigo

Rock engraving, 13,000 BCE, Les Trois Frères, Ariège, France

15

Shaman

PAINTED IN THE LES TROIS FRÈRES CAVE NEAR ARIÈGE, FRANCE, THE PALEOLITHIC figure pictured here was created sometime around 13,000 BCE. To reach this man with owl eyes and antlered cat body, you must first crawl through a hundred-yard-long lava flume. Suddenly you emerge in a large chamber filled with dancing animal forms. This figure is engraved up on the rock wall over twelve feet above the floor. He appears above an opening to an underground well.

Small shallow cups have been discovered near cave paintings. They perhaps held pigments together with fat or oils with which the artists spread their colors. Most cave art is composed of red, black, and dark brown pigments with some yellows. Vegetable dyes and oils together with red ocher, black manganese oxides, carbon, and animal fats made up their palettes.

Stenciled hands are often seen surrounding cave art. The artist may have signed a piece by blowing paint around a hand pressed against the stone. Most of the hands are left hands, and the relative smallness of some handprints suggests to some archaeologists that women as well as men were involved in this ritual painting process that was taking place in caves all over southern Europe twenty thousand years ago.

Between Marseilles and Cassis in southern France, a cave was discovered in 1991 and named after the man who found it: Henri Coscquer. L. Robert Keck tells us in *Sacred Quest* that this cave was once three hundred feet above sea level and, beginning about 18,500 years ago, cave artists were at work painting images on those cave walls and continued to do so over a span of several thousand years.

PART vi ~ Indigo

Ecstasy

SHAMAN

15

> The soul really does seem to have left the body.... There, an unearthly light is revealed which she could never have imagined had she spent her entire life trying to dream it up. In an instant her mind is alert to so much at once, that the intellect and imagination could never list a tiny part of it all.
>
> —St. Teresa of Avila, *The Interior Castle*

The word *shaman* comes from the Tungus people of Siberia who call a time traveler *šaman*, a noun based on their verb *ša*, "to know." It means "to know." In shamanic cultures, these courageous men and women take journeys outside time and space to do healing work, usually with power animals as protectors. In the Mayan culture, a *h-men* is a "knower." The shaman was the traditional healer or soul doctor of indigenous people. Native healers are often initiated into their healing roles through physical or mental challenges. One Native American named Medicine Grizzlybear Lake described in his book *Native Healer* how traumatic events or accidents can propel a person into shamanic wisdom. "In this kind of school we learn about fear, anger, hate, confusion. We learn about other worlds and how to travel between both. We learn about our strengths and weaknesses, power, love, reality, healing, and life itself. We learn that there are, indeed, two separate but interrelated worlds of existence, the physical and the spiritual."

Ecstasy comes from the Greek *existanai*, a trance that transports you to another place. Shamans enter a trance state by purifying themselves, then fasting, praying, drumming, dancing, ingesting consciousness-altering plants, and so forth, depending upon their culture. The purpose of this ecstatic state or spirit journey is not self-gratification but to heal another. Many times shamans have to go to the otherworld to retrieve a soul that has strayed or to commune with otherworldly sources for information regarding the healing. Telepathy often takes place in this trance state. Sometimes, as with the ancient cave figure pictured here, the dancer wears a mask, perhaps of the bird or animal that helps them transport.

Hunab Ku

SHAMAN
15

In *The Masks of God*, Joseph Campbell speculates about a shaman's alignment with the trickster (**Trickster 30**), someone who ritually enacts beast-like behavior as a visual portrayal of disorder and chaos. We no longer know what this particular image's theatrical behavior is intended to evoke, but we can be sure it was part of a sacred ritual drama and highly valued, considering the care with which the cave engraving was detailed. Cave people hunted for about two months out of the year, and they created beautiful images the rest of the time. Here we are, five hundred generations later, hard pressed to create anything more compelling.

Shaman says, "Come dance with me. Spin your way to another consciousness, another world." The image pictured here has taken on forms of the stag, the lion, and the owl. What do those beings say to you? Do you have or need a lion's strength? An owl's sight? Stag horns helped the dancer to perform regeneration magic. This cave dancer dares the dark, and ecstatic energy lights up his very being. Shamans learn to "die" so they can fly to other places. What is asking to be released from your life now? What must be given up so that *you* can fly?

This image number is fifteen, the number formed in the magic square shown in **Earth 5**. The Chinese called this shamanic square the magic square of three, and they found it validated many natural laws according to ancient Chinese thought. Use the color indigo to stimulate your third eye's shamanic sight as you explore your own shamanic journey.

Eyes cannot see it, speech cannot describe it, nor the mind conceive it. We know not, nor can we imagine how to convey it. For it is different from the known; and beyond the unknown. Thus have we heard from the illumined ones, who have told of it... if realized here, then truth exists; if not realized here, then there is only ignorance.

—Kena Upanishad

PART **vi** ~ Indigo

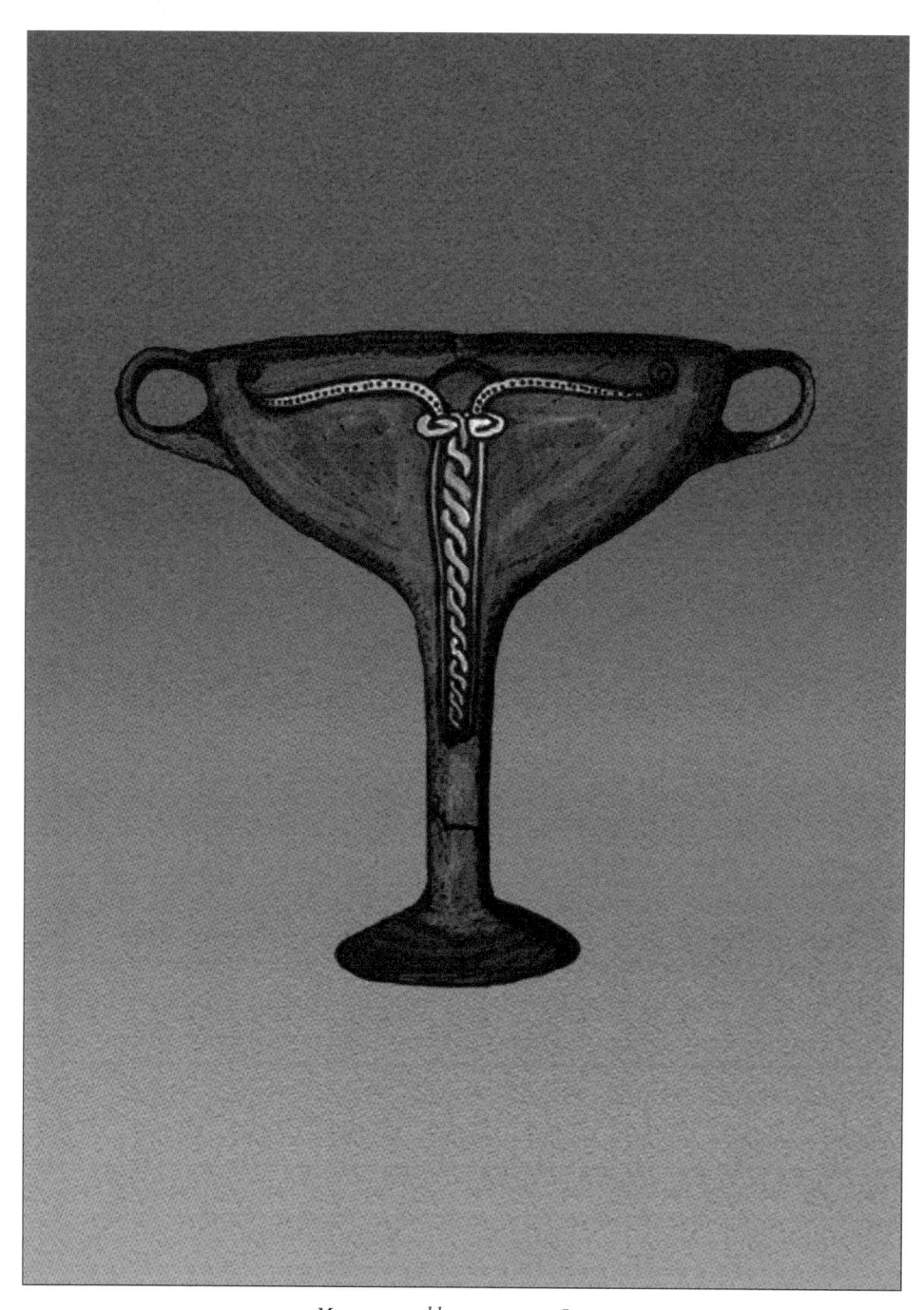

Mycenaean goblet, 1200 BCE, Greece

14

Chalice

THE VESSEL PICTURED HERE IS A MYCENAEAN GOBLET FROM KALYMNOS, Greece. It is terra-cotta and dates from 1200 BCE. The goblet is currently housed in the British Museum in London.

The word *grail* may have come from *graal*, which is Welsh for "pair." It is also related to the Latin word *gradalis*, which means "step by step" and may refer to one's gradual spiritual unfolding. Long before the legend of the Holy Grail, most cultures had stories of sacred vessels: cups, bowls, cauldrons, and goblets. Often these vessels are womb symbols, containers for life. This vessel's decorations have been likened to other ancient depictions of a woman's fallopian tubes and uterus. In Plato, souls who long to experience Matter (life on earth) drink from the *krater* cup; the drink weighs them down so heavily that they come back to earth. They come back to the journey, and begin again the quest of incarnation.

In one Grail legend, the Vedic god Indra drinks from the liquid that is held in the moon, and he renews the barren lands by thrusting a spear into the earth.

Longinus, the story goes, a centurion (Roman military officer), pierced Jesus's side with his spear as Jesus hung on the cross. Joseph of Aramathea, in the Grail legend, had the cup from the Last Supper with him when he prepared Jesus's body for burial, and blood from Jesus's wounds accidentally spilled into the cup. It is this cup that Joseph took to Britain seventy years later, having been given the mystery of the Mass and celebrated the first Communion. In the Arthurian legends, the Fisher King, who was the Grail Keeper, was also wounded with a spear. His land was barren until Parceval, or in some versions Gawain, succeeded in the Grail quest, and the Fisher King was healed. Only then were the crumbling castle, wasted gardens and dried streams restored.

PART vi ~ Indigo

Quest

CHALICE 14

Whom does the Grail serve?... It is a question whose primary purpose is not to elicit data or information but to open up a situation to a new perspective. A Grail question can reveal the sacred in a situation or can bring to light creative possibilities that we otherwise might have missed seeing.

—David Spangler, *A Pilgrim in Aquarius*

John Matthews, an English writer of many Grail tales, calls the Grail "a mixture of alchemical lore and classical myth, of Arabic poetry and Sufi teaching; of Celtic mythology and Christian iconography." In Old French, *san grial* means "sacred dish." This term sounds like *sang real* or "true blood."

In *The Hero's Journey*, mythologist Joseph Campbell describes the hero quest as the night journey "where the individual is going to bring forth in his life something that was never beheld before." Campbell likened the Grail romance to that of "the God in your own true heart. The Christ becomes a metaphor—a symbol for that transcendent power which is the support and being of your own life."

Chalice offers you all that it holds. It is your sacred vessel. Chalice calls you to search, to quest, to yearn for something to fill your emptiness. Like Arthur's knights, you long to be challenged, to be called.

It might be well to ask yourself, what is at the heart of your pilgrimage and your life? Annie Dillard pointed out that "the way we spend our days is the way we spend our lives." How are you spending your days? For what are you questing? Like Galahad, Parceval, and Bors, you are, no doubt, also searching for enlightenment and everlasting life. You're on the big quest. You may think, like Hercules, that you're after the golden fleece, the unattainable. Parceval heals the Fisher King by asking the right question, "Whom does the Grail serve?" Keep searching; the key question is, Who will be served by your finding the Grail? Perhaps it has been within you all along.

Hunab Ku

Indigo dye was already being made by the ancient Harrapans in India four thousand years ago. The Greeks called it *indikon* because it came from India. The indigo energy center in your brow is where you envision possibilities.

The integers of the number fourteen (one and four) add up to five, the number that vibrates with the planet Mercury and symbolizes communication and movement. Rely on your inner wisdom. In his book *Sacred Quest*, L. Robert Keck reminds us that "to quest is to question, and the quality of the sacred quest has more to do with the questions we ask today than with the answers entombed within past dogma." Whom do *you* serve?

	CHALICE 14

Search me, O God, and know my heart!
Try me and know my thoughts!
And see if there be any wicked way in me,
And lead me in the way everlasting!

—PSALMS 139:23–24

PART vi ~ Indigo

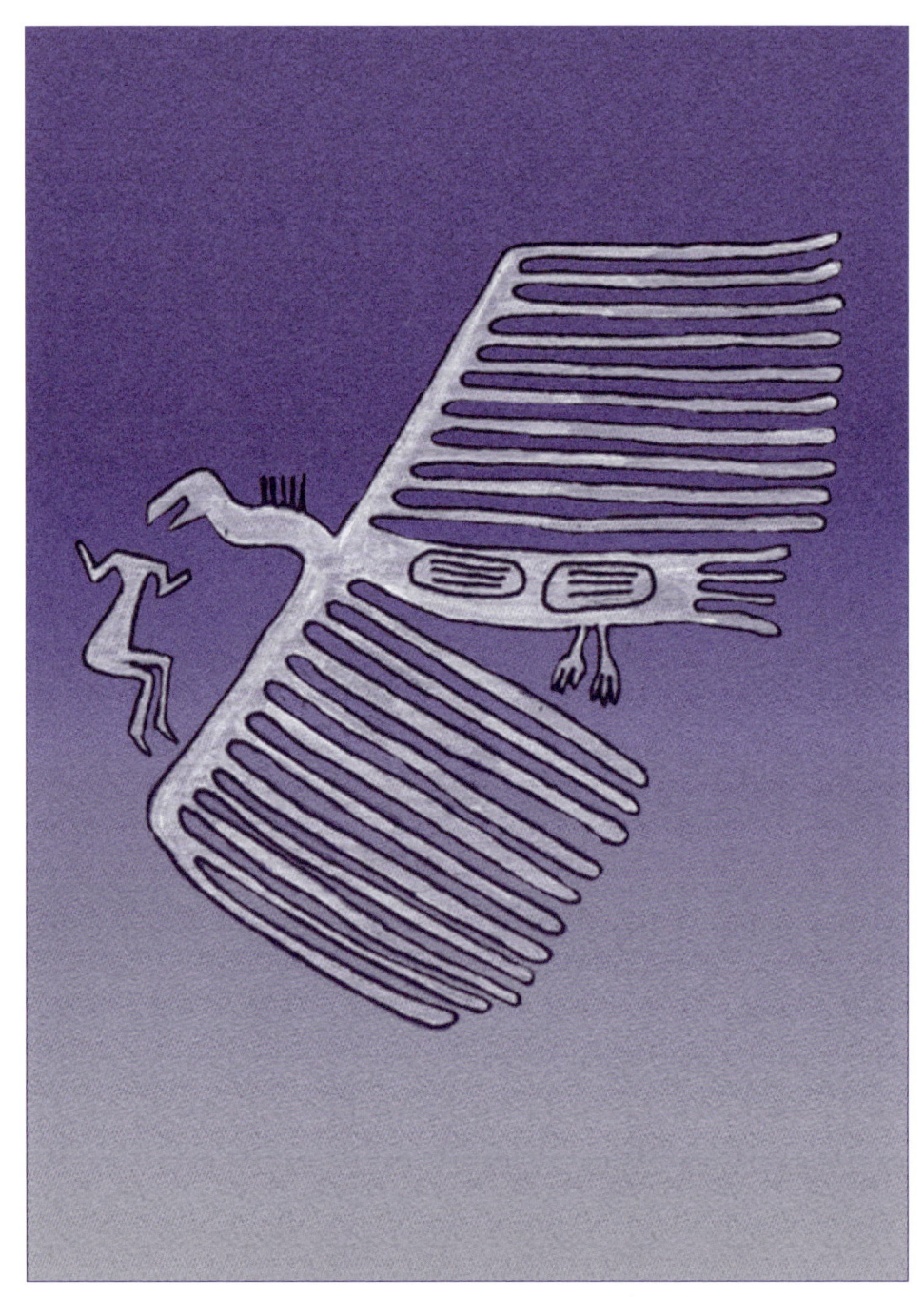

• *Wall mural, 6000 BCE, Çatal Hüyük, Anatolia (Turkey)* •

13

Vulture

AT ÇATAL HÜYÜK IN TURKEY (ANATOLIA), REMAINS HAVE BEEN FOUND OF A city that flourished from 6400 BCE to 5600 BCE. It may have been our first urban center, with perhaps six thousand inhabitants, and evidence abounds that is was a place of peace-keeping people who ate well, did not go to war, and had time for the arts.

The site is a fifty-foot Neolithic mound with twelve different cities built up on top of one another like a pueblo. James Mellaart, who excavated this site in the early 1960s, found 139 rooms, 48 of which seem to be sacred rooms. Several of these shrines are still colorfully decorated with vulture wall murals. In what is called the Vulture Shrine, seven vultures swoop down on six headless humans, as in the image opposite. In another shrine, a vulture with human legs stands beside a decapitated human. Some vultures have wingspans of over nine feet. The gigantic birds are painted in dark red lime against a pink background. Layers of paint indicate this was a much used and much valued space, often repainted and refurbished.

The one vulture's human legs suggest she is the Goddess in disguise. She is the One Who Gives Life and the One Who Takes Away. The vultures seem to symbolize profound links between life and death. One vulture fresco, according to Marija Gimbutas in *The Language of the Goddess*, "is immediately adjacent to one which features a huge bull's head, symbolic of the vital life force, below which rests a human skull. Here is direct assurance that resurrection follows death. At the fateful moment, the vulture Goddess 'snatches the soul,' but the head from the fresco's decapitated body is carefully placed in contact with the regenerative bull." James Mellaart found vulture skulls inside each red breast painted on a wall relief.

PART vi ~ Indigo

Death

VULTURE 13

If we really want to live, we must have the courage to recognize that life is ultimately very short, and that everything we do counts.

—Elizabeth Kübler-Ross, *Death: The Final Stage of Growth*

We tend to think of vultures as carrion birds, nasty creatures with huge flapping wings and beaks capable of tearing flesh. On first glance, it's hard to equate them with a loving mother, yet that is exactly what many ancient cultures did. In Gimbutas's books about early goddess cultures, she said the vulture images at Çatal Hüyük not only represent death, but also rebirth.

The word for vulture among Siberian Yakuts means "mother"; the Egyptian hieroglyph for mother is also a vulture. In early Egypt, the goddess Mut or Nekhbet was called the Vulture Goddess, the Crone of Death. Every day she devours the sun and then the next morning, rebirths it. She fetches souls and carries them off to the otherworld. In Hebrew the word for vulture means something very close to "pity," "compassion," and "womb." Early peoples believed the vultures, like the phoenix, needed no male to assist in conception. They were the virgin mothers holding within them birth *and* death. Kali Ma, in Tantric cosmology, embodies the concept of life and death. She wears blood-dripping skulls around her neck and is the vulture-headed being thought to haunt graveyards. Like the vulture, she chews up all things. But she also gives birth to all that lives. She is called Virgin Mother Maya and offers new life, forever.

In India as well as in Pakistan and Nepal, vultures eat the flesh of dead animals and, in some cases, of dead people. The Parsees, for instance, place their dead in Towers of Silence, where vultures may eat the bodies, hastening their rebirth. They call it Sky Burial. Vultures once roosted on windowsills in Delhi, but now the vultures themselves are dying. They are extremely endangered. In fact environmental researchers claim 95 percent are now gone. Their demise started in the 1980s. After eating livestock that has been injected with antiinflammatory or painkiller drugs, the birds can no longer live.

Hunab Ku

Even tiny doses of drugs like aspirin can kill vultures. What does this mean for the world? When species start dying, like dominoes falling, other lives are always affected.

Vulture offers release and transformation. Remember, Buddha said, "Death is the temporary end of a temporary phenomenon." You may not be facing actual death right now, so don't worry. Perhaps something in your life cries to be resurrected. All things end and give way to new life. It is the way of our planet. Vulture may be encouraging you to let go of your emotional attachments to something or someone. Loss leads to renewal; death brings life.

VULTURE
13

Indigo is like a dark night, a deathwatch color. It's easy to feel guilt and grief; looking at this color for a while can help to dissolve grief. Royal purple suggests a death of red (energy) and a death of blue (what you thought was spirituality), creating a new combination of the two: an energetic spirit life grounded here on earth in your body. Anatolian vulture figures were usually painted in red, the color of blood and life. There is nothing to fear. Fly proudly on strong wings with your eyes already fixed on your new life ahead.

The number thirteen has long been associated with death and betrayal. Our superstitions lead us to skip from floor twelve to fourteen in hotels and to leave thirteen out of flight numbers. Look at **Venus 13**, and you'll be reminded that it is a strong, loving number as well. Twelve completes a cycle, and thirteen starts something new. Welcome thirteen as you invite Vulture into your life. You still have your head, and you have decisive new beginnings at your fringed wingtips.

The power who exists in all beings as Shadow, reverence to Her, reverence to Her, reverence to Her, reverence, reverence.

—HYMN TO DURGA, *Devi Mahatmya*

PART **vi** ~ Indigo

Stone monument, possibly 7000 BCE, Giza, Egypt

12

Sphinx

THE GREAT SPHINX PICTURED HERE, FACING THE RISING SUN ON THE GIZA plateau, is 240 feet long and was supposedly cut from a single stone. It has been resurfaced and weathered and refaced again. Some think Chephren, Khufu's successor, built this huge symbolic animal on its granite hill, but others believe he only restored it. How old is it? Was it built in 3400 BCE during Egypt's 4th dynasty, as the carved hieroglyphic stela says? Or does it go back to 7000 BCE, or even earlier? The Sahara is seven to nine thousand years old. Before the desert sands crept in, before the Delta was formed, the Great Sphinx gazed out at the sea. The core stone has erosion patterns that could only be created by moving water, and seashells have been found around it. A very early temple to Isis may have rested on this spot.

Sphinx is sometimes depicted with the face and breasts of a woman, the body of a lion, and wings. Oedipus, supposedly, answered Sphinx's riddle: What walks on four legs in the morning, two legs at noon, and three legs in the evening? A human who crawls as a baby, walks upright as an adult, and uses a walking stick in old age.

Edgar Cayce, the American psychic from Virginia Beach, claimed the Great Sphinx predated 10,500 BCE, when it was rebuilt on an even more ancient ruin. Its purpose, Cayce said, was to guard the Temple of Records—an underground complex of chambers, tombs, and temples where records from Atlantis were stored. Could the Great Sphinx be covering the true entrance to the nearby Great Pyramid, protecting rolls of papyri and clay tablets? What sort of ancient records detailing our human story here may one day be discovered?

PART vi ~ Indigo

Time

SPHINX 12

*Time like an ever-rolling stream, bears all our years away;
They fly, forgotten, as a dream dies at the opening day.*

—Isaac Watts, hymn

The word *sphinx* is Greek, meaning "to draw or bind together." Time *sphinxes* us. Time binds us together in days and years, and then releases us into the no-time of eternity. If we hadn't created our concepts of time, everything would come at us all at once and our brains would not be able to make sense of it. We would be in constant dreamtime. So we live in increments of seconds and minutes and hours. Still, we know time is relative, for we've all heard Einstein's story of how very short a minute is when a young man is with his girlfriend, and how extremely long a minute is if he's sitting on a hot stove. Time can quantum leap and literally fold over on itself. To a child, time passes slowly, and then, as the sphinx riddle shows, our bodies grow frail, and for the aging time seems to pass very quickly. When we sleep, we withdraw from the normal cycles of time and enter dreamtime once more, where time seems to disappear.

When we use our left brains, we think in timelines going from point A to point B. We think in linear terms. Ancient cultures saw time as spiraling. There is a belief, particularly among indigenous people, that things happen when they are supposed to happen and "white people's time" really means nothing. The Hopi people, for instance, speak a language that has no time references. They use no tenses. Yesterday is the same as tomorrow. The only difference is in *what has already manifested* and *what is becoming*. Hopis structure their words in terms of potential. So, it seems, time is a cultural construct and some of us don't "get" how multidimensional time really is. An American brain surgeon, Karl Pribram, poses: "Maybe in the holographic state—in the frequency domain—4,000 years ago is tomorrow." We've all experienced that feeling of there having been no gap in time when we meet a special friend we haven't seen for years. We pick up right where we left off. The Greeks had several important words for time.

Hunab Ku

Chronos, or formal time, is usually how we live. *Kairos*, the "ah-ha!" time, is the richness for which we all yearn.

The Great Sphinx has been called a stone book containing ancient wisdom. Seek knowledge, then, not for answers but for an increased awareness and a chance to move into your wisdom. You have the resources to solve riddles. Your answers are as good as anyone else's. *Gnosis* means inner knowledge. It is already yours.

The Egyptian sun god, Ra, traveled through the sky for twelve hours before being reborn. In China they use a twelve-unit counting system, rather than a ten-point decimal system. The number twelve in many cultures is connected with time. It is the completion of a cycle. Heracles had to perform twelve labors. Some researchers claim the key to the Great Sphinx, which was built on principles of numerology, lies in the number twelve and its multiples.

SPHINX
12

There is an appointed time for everything, and a time for every affair under the heavens. A time to be born, and a time to die; a time to plant, and a time to uproot the plant; a time to kill, and a time to heal; a time to tear down, and a time to build. A time to weep, and a time to laugh, a time to mourn and a time to dance…

—Ecclesiastes 3:1–4

Memorial stone, 400 BCE, Vallstena, Gotland, Sweden

11

Universe

STONE WHORLS MARK THE MEMORIAL STONE PICTURED HERE, WHICH WAS discovered on an island called "God's Land," or Gotland, in Sweden. It dates from 400 BCE and can now be seen in a Stockholm museum. Deer and hunting images surround the strong, long awaited, vigorous sun and wheeling planets. Norse midwinter festivals called forth the sun to counteract the forces of dark, cold, and silence.

Spirals and coils on ancient stonework seem to describe unfolding energy. They beautifully illuminate cyclical time as well as the pulse of life coming from the sun. Spirals first began appearing on cave walls, with their serpentine squiggles and zigzag shapes. Spiral designs on pottery emerged around 6300 BCE in southeastern Europe, spreading to the Balkans and the Danube basin. Spirals with leaves sprouting from them appear on temple megaliths in Malta from 3000 BCE, about the same time that stone spirals began showing up in Ireland.

PART *vii* ~ Violet

UNIVERSE 11

Consciousness

The whole of the created universe has been breathlessly anticipating your arrival.

—Martin Bell, *Return of the Wolf*

What do we mean when we use the word *universe*? An astronomer's definition includes everything: our planet, our solar system, our galaxy, and at least two hundred billion stars—all the objects and also all the empty space between them. Recently that empty space has gotten a lot less empty. We now know that the universe also includes vast amounts of "dark matter." We only know that this dark matter is there through calculating its gravitational effects on the objects that we can see. The dance of the stars gives away the presence of matter we cannot yet see. This mysterious dark matter may constitute as much as 95 percent of the mass of our universe! The vast majority of our universe is still a total mystery to us. The stars in the universe are spaced rather uniformly, several light-years away from each other. This spacing, however, means that the universe is full of energy and is almost empty of matter, like the human body's atoms and electrons.

Twylah Nitsch, Keeper of the Wolf Clan, one of eight Seneca Iroquois clans, teaches this way of experiencing the universe: "Don't say you are a part of the universe, but rather the universe is a part of you." Rudolf Steiner, a German teacher, lecturer, and writer, said, "humans are the key to grasping the universe." We are here to consciously understand it. We are not just perceivers, but also the embodiment of the universe. We are made up of the same stuff as everything else, so our bodies sense inner rhythms in keeping with the movements of the moon, the planets, even the stars. Because we are all made of pulsing energy, we spiral and move together in similar fields. We know a little about some fields, like gravity; other fields we can only imagine. It's as if we are living in a battery, and everything in it is constantly charging and recharging. Caught up in this cosmic exchange, we begin to remember what we have known for eons.

Hunab Ku

UNIVERSE
11

The image presented here suggests it is time to center yourself and take a leap into consciousness. "It is a state of consciousness in which we experience ourselves as beings alive invisible inaudible beyond definition, dancing and resonating and speaking and forming simultaneously in all the spheres of our substance," says M. C. Richards in *Centering,* her book of pottery and poetry.

Physicist David Bohm called the universe "holographic." He said its galactic core is held in every atom, just as each strand of your DNA holds your entire genetic code. Each of us, then, is filled with dancing star seeds.

Vaclav Havel said, "We may know more about the universe than our ancestors did, and yet it seems they knew something more essential about it than we do." What the ancients knew and how they embedded that knowledge into writings and images continues to challenge us. Kabbalism, a mystical interpretation of Jewish scriptures, for instance, describes the universe as a progression through four worlds, each one denser than the last: the archetypal, the creative, the formative, and the material. In that Hebrew tradition, eleven signifies death and rebirth.

To the Chinese, eleven is a symbol of wholeness; for them, it is one whole decade. Eleven symbolizes the Tao. Jung defined Tao as a conscious way to unite what is separated. "It's a reunion," he said, "with the unconscious laws of our being and the purpose of this reunion is the attainment of conscious life . . . the realization of the Tao."

Consider yourself reunited. You can triumph in all your undertakings. That is the power Universe bestows on you. Things are coming together for you now. Feel the power in your innermost being. This image acknowledges your achievements with a huge medal to mark your worth.

God is in truth the whole universe: what was, what is, and what beyond shall ever be. . . . He is the inmost soul of all, which like a little flame the size of a thumb is hidden in the hearts of men.

—*Svetasvatara Upanishad*

PART *vii* ~ Violet

• *Minoan gold bee pendant, 1700 BCE, Mallia, Crete* •

Honeybee

THE GOLD BEE PENDANT PICTURED HERE, CRAFTED AROUND 1700 BCE, WAS discovered in the royal Minoan cemetery of Mallia. It can be seen in the Heraklion Museum on Crete. On the pendant, two bees are sucking a drop of honey.

Bee forms frequently can be found on early pottery and jewelry, with some figures appearing as early as 6500 BCE. A nearly one-foot-long bee shape with uplifted antennae was carved on a cave wall in late Neolithic times in Sardinia near Bue Mariono, Dorgali. Early Minoan bee seals predate the gold bee pendant pictured here by several hundred years. Anthropomorphized, the bee shape often assumed human proportions, with arms as well as wings. These bee women appeared on many gold plaques and figures from the seventh to the fifth centuries BCE from Rhodes to Thera in the Mediterranean Sea.

Demeter, the Greek earth goddess, was affectionately called the Pure Mother Bee. Predynastic Egyptian kings used the title "One of the Bee" to define their connection to the goddess's power. Early matrilineal cultures considered the world of bees to be a perfectly organized society because it had a queen at its head. Bees became a symbol for the golden age where a land flowing with milk and honey was an archetypal picture of abundance and peace. Artemisian priestesses were called *Melissai,* or "worker bees." A body of priests attached to the Artemis, and later Diana, temples were called essenes or "drones." The honeycomb came to symbolize various goddess figures, especially Aphrodite, and people believed bees were the souls of those who served her. The honeycomb with its perfect hexagons appealed to people steeped in sacred geometry; sixty-degree angles formed cosmic patterns of perfect beauty.

PART vii ~ Violet

HONEY-BEE 10

Emotions

Bees surrender themselves entirely to Venus, unfolding a life of love throughout the whole hive.

—Rudolf Steiner, *Nine Lectures on Bees*

According to recent discoveries, honey can kill harmful bacteria and promote healthy tissue growth. Egyptian papyri, 3,600 years old, document honey's effective healing powers, particularly when used in salves. Honey has been found in Italian tombs 2,500 years old, still sticky and golden. Honey was used long ago to embalm the dead. People were placed in a fetal position, in womb jars, ready to resume birth's journey. When Egyptians died, it was said they fell into the honeypot. Rudolf Steiner, in addition to claiming bees are connected to Venus and love, points out that honey is as important to aging people's health as milk is for children.

Honeybee offers you golden richness. Abundance is yours. Study bees to learn more about community and kinship. Roger Saillant, a modern businessman and beekeeper, says bees teach him to adjust his pace, to follow patterns, and to work smoothly. Over the ages, beekeepers and their bees create a conscious field of energy.

Your field of energy also includes bees right now. Sense their presence and imagine your home as your hive. Some ancient people built hive-shaped structures to honor the goddess's presence. How does your home honor the divine?

This image calls your emotions to the forefront. Like bees, emotions can sometimes sting. Emotions come from your feminine side, but they are natural to every human and must not be denied or hidden. Wrap yourself in this bee's gauzy wings and give yourself a honeymoon. Honey-gold abundance is waiting for you, but just as bees industriously structure their lives, you, too, may have to really work for it.

The honeybee is a traditional matriarchal image for the sign of Cancer. The Cancer constellation is a tight group of about four hundred stars, which are called the beehive. You are balanced, as are bees, between wanting to stay in your protective environment,

Hunab Ku

HONEY-
BEE

10

your hive, and going out to gather pollen and seek adventure. Bees prefer the pale blue of the sky or the white of the moon—perfect "bee-ings" for the violet palette. Beekeepers once were called bee servants. Whether you see yourself as a keeper or a bee, you are serving.

The seventh chakra calls you to *be*, rather than calling you to *do*. Your crown chakra, *Sahasrara*, offers you the consciousness to understand all the energy points in your body. The crown center is the seat of enlightenment. Yogis spend entire lifetimes practicing how to achieve the sweet nectar of freedom and the honeydew of divine wisdom. It does not come to all, but as worker bees, we buzz about, searching, and often find it.

The number ten, composed as it is of one and zero, symbolizes the uniting and balancing of male and female energy. It is a strong and dignified number. When you "receive" the number ten, you are both the bee and the peacock (see **Peacock 10**).

Flowers and bees may be different, but the honey is the same. Systems of faith may be different, but God is One.

—RIG VEDA

PART *vii* ~ Violet

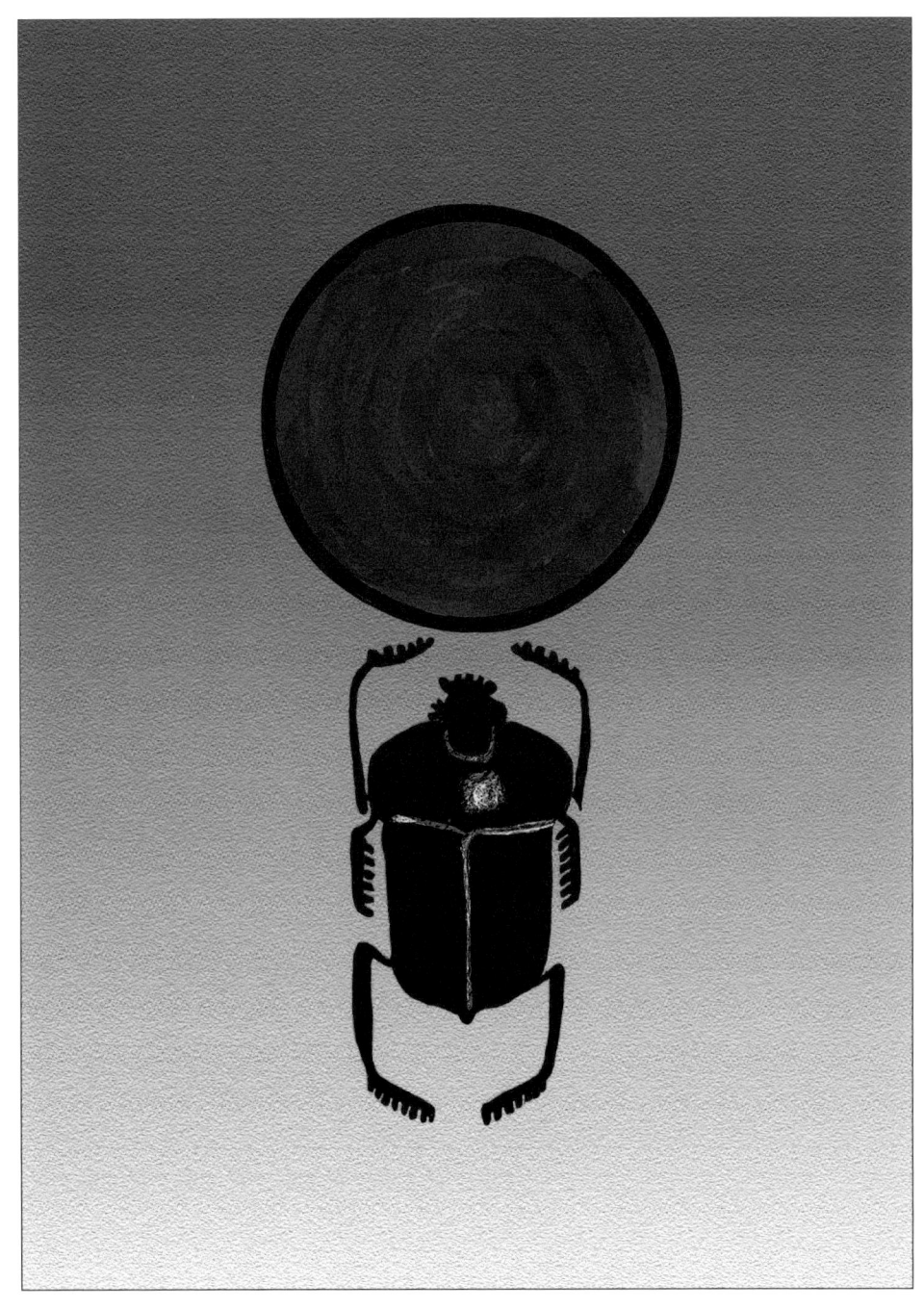

Papyrus painting, 1100 BCE, Egypt

Scarab

THE SCARAB PAPYRUS PAINTING PICTURED HERE, ESTIMATED TO DATE FROM 1100 BCE, comes from *The Egyptian Book of the Dead*, which is housed in the British Museum.

In the Egyptian Zodiac of Dendera, the crab appears as a scarab beetle, sign of the god Kheperi, who was a deity associated with the sun. In the Egyptian papyrus called Ani, the king's companion to Seti II says, "Among the Egyptians, the Scarabeus Beetle is no god, but one of the emblems of the Creator, because it rolls a ball of mud between its feet and sets therein its eggs to hatch. As the Creator rolls the world around, and causes it to produce life."

From an egg warmed by the sun, to a larva uncurling from the sun-cracked dung, to a hard wing-cased insect unfolding its green wings to fly off to meet the dawn, the scarabaeus beetle's life cycle epitomizes transformation.

PART *vii* ~ Violet

SCARAB 9

Manifestation

We live in a cosmos that at its deepest level is made of unfolding relationships ... manifestation is an act of participation. We grow what we wish from within ourselves.

—David Spangler, *Everyday Miracles*

For a time, the scarab was popular with the Egyptian male priesthood because they saw it as a symbol of independent male creation. It was believed that the male scarab beetle could hatch young all by itself out of the ball of dung it rolled in front of it. Then it was discovered that the beetle egg had to rest under the earth for twenty-eight days before it could hatch. It rested for a single complete moon cycle. The moon was a feminine principle in ancient Egypt, so this discovery brought male and female principles together. The priests were called *scarab*, and they placed a jeweled effigy of this winged beetle at the mummified heart of those who had died.

Things that we can see and touch we call manifest. "The Unmanifest is an infinitude of possibility outside of finite time and space ... the whole art of magic is in learning to reach across the veil and bring the fire of the Unmanifest into perceived existence." Donald Tyson described manifestation this way in *New Millennium Magic*. Something can come from nothing. Scarab tells you that you, too, are a magician (see **Magician** 26). You can bring to life what you truly believe in. Expect miracles and your powerful thoughts will create them. You can rebirth yourself, as surely as the scarab rolled the sun-globe up out of the darkened underworld every morning in Egyptian legend. You can become a sun in your own world, lending light and warmth to those around you.

Scarab is enlightenment personified. Your violet crown chakra connects you to the nonlinear world. The color violet helps you tap into a consciousness beyond your ordinary one (see **Universe** 11). Wagner is said to have composed his extraordinary music surrounded, purposefully, by violet draperies. Violet is a magic color that brings together two worlds: the relaxed world of blue and the stimulating world of red. Violet

Hunab Ku

SCARAB 9

assists the pineal gland in restoring rhythm to one's system.

Scarab is number nine. Carl Jung taught that traditionally the number nine means being in the company of the gods. Medieval Christianity used nine to represent the Trinity. Nine mystically combines three times three to create a holy combination of body, mind, and spirit. Nine is a magical manifestation. When you add all the numbers from one through nine together, the result is forty-five, and those integers (four and five) add up to nine once again. Three triangles is a common symbol for the ancients. Some ancients thought there was a ninefold division of the universe.

In Greek, *ennea* means "nine" and the ennead, as three times three,+ was a blessed number. Egyptians believed that they would receive the ennead's blessing if they walked around the granite scarab sculpture at Karnak nine times. The Greeks originally had three Muses, but their ranks later expanded to nine and each of them was assigned a discipline: Calliope, epic poetry; Urania, astronomy; Polyhymnia, sacred poetry; Terpsichore, dance and song; Clio, history; Melpomene, tragedy; Erato, love poetry; Euterpe, lyric poetry; and Thalia, comedy.

Scarab invites you to receive your muses and open up to your "thrice-blessed" vital creativity.

The thought manifests as the word; the word manifests as the deed; the deed develops into habit; and habit hardens into character . . . let it spring from love, born out of concern for all beings.

—BUDDHA

PART **vii** ~ Violet

• *Stone labyrinth, 1200 CE, Chartres, France* •

8

Mystic

ONE OF THE FIRST LABYRINTHS EVER BUILT WAS DISCOVERED AT LAKE MOERIS in Egypt. It was a matrix once filled with deadly crocodiles and whose shape reflected the structure of the cosmos. The meaning of *cosmos* is "whole." Later, Daedalus built a labyrinth in Crete that was said to house the bull-man, Minotaur, and it came to symbolize life and death. They called their seven-circuited maze the House of the Double Axe, named after the labrys, the double crescent moon shape associated with the Goddess. When a labyrinth walker comes down one of the eleven circular paths to one of the ten double axes on the labyrinth, it is time to change direction.

The labyrinth in Chartres Cathedral in France, pictured here, was constructed during the early thirteenth century on the floor under the western rose window. People had to cross it to reach the altar. The outer ring of the labyrinth is a lunar calendar, marking twenty-eight cusps or points in each quadrant. The entire figure measures forty-two feet in diameter, nearly the width of the nave, and features a one-way unicursal path of 276 white limestone slabs marked by blue-black marble dividers that lead to the center and out again. Dr. Lauren Artress, in *Walking a Sacred Path*, claims labyrinths are divine imprints. You can't get lost.

Pilgrims journeyed to Chartres in lieu of actually traveling to the Holy Land. A dance called "The Way to Jerusalem" was timed so that as people spiraled inward from right to left, the leader arrived at the center exactly on the last syllable of the chant. Medieval maps often depict the world as a labyrinthine circle with Jerusalem in the center. A six-petaled brass-and-copper rose now marks the spot in the center of this Chartres labyrinth, which once had a design of three figures: Theseus, Ariadne, and the Minotaur, the three main characters in the Greek labyrinth legend—the seeker, the helper, and the challenger.

PART **vii** ~ Violet

MYSTIC 8

Wonder

The new meaning of soul is creativity with mysticism. These will become the foundation of the new psychological type and with him or her will come the new civilization.

—Otto Rank

Walking a labyrinth, we wonder whether we'll ever find our way to the center. Then we wonder whether we'll ever find our way back out again. What lies in the center? Is it some sort of inner minotaur, waiting to gore and trample us? Will we face something we'd otherwise choose not to see? When we hold big important questions going in, we often find, when we finally rest in the center, that new ideas fill our brains and our bodies with the knowledge that something *big* is happening here. We no longer wonder; rather we are filled with wonder and awe. We experience body prayer. We contemplate our own death and rebirth. The center is a sacred place between the worlds where one pauses to be reborn.

The old Celts called Chartres the sanctuary of sanctuaries. Some claim that, like the Sphinx and so many other sacred places on earth, this cathedral is a mystical spot because of how it is aligned with earth's energy flow; legend says seven streams crisscross deep beneath it. Long before a cathedral stood on this holy ground, it held a Druid university and attracted students of science, math, philosophy, astrology, geometry, and astronomy. Before that, the site was home to a sacred well, a goddess site. A holy well descends as far into the earth below the crypt as the spires ascend into the heavens.

Sanctuaries provide space for inner work. Enter this *temenos*—this holy ground—and you will find Ariadne's thread guiding you. She brings you to your center. Your holy dance is a quest for your grail, the spark of divinity that lies within you. Your task is to seek the right grail question (see **Chalice** 14). Parts of your journey may be dark

Hunab Ku

MYSTIC 8

and convoluted, but you are on a holy path. Lose yourself in the mysteries; live in the wonder. Your center will hold. You are being initiated into something much bigger than yourself (see **Labyrinth 9**).

Leonardo da Vinci said the meditative state can be enhanced ten times under violet light streaming through a stained glass window. The west rose window above the labyrinth at Chartres is precisely the same size as the labyrinth circle—forty-two feet in diameter. When its glassy colors fall on worshipers below, mystical things can happen; violet is the most mystical color of all. It's the color of bliss and enlightenment. Just as transcendent consciousness comes from moving from the edge of the labyrinth to its center, so, too, does activating the crown chakra flood one with wonder. Your inner eye is turned toward your deepest center.

The number eight is a double four, a compounding of the labyrinth's four quadrants. Eight is the infinity symbol (see **Double Spiral 5**). Like the famous Möbius strip, the number eight wondrously wraps you with ongoing stability and wholeness. Eight is a strong symbol of self.

Walk this image with your eyes or your finger. Many cathedrals have wall labyrinths that worshipers trace with their fingers before entering the main body of the church. It stills their minds, places them in a more receptive state, and prepares them for the wonder of entering a holy place. Just as dancers' feet once traced labyrinthine paths, you are invited to follow the labyrinth into a place of *amazement*.

Arise! Watch. Walk on the right path. He who follows the right path has joy in this world, and in the world beyond.

—The Dhammapada

PART **vii** ~ Violet

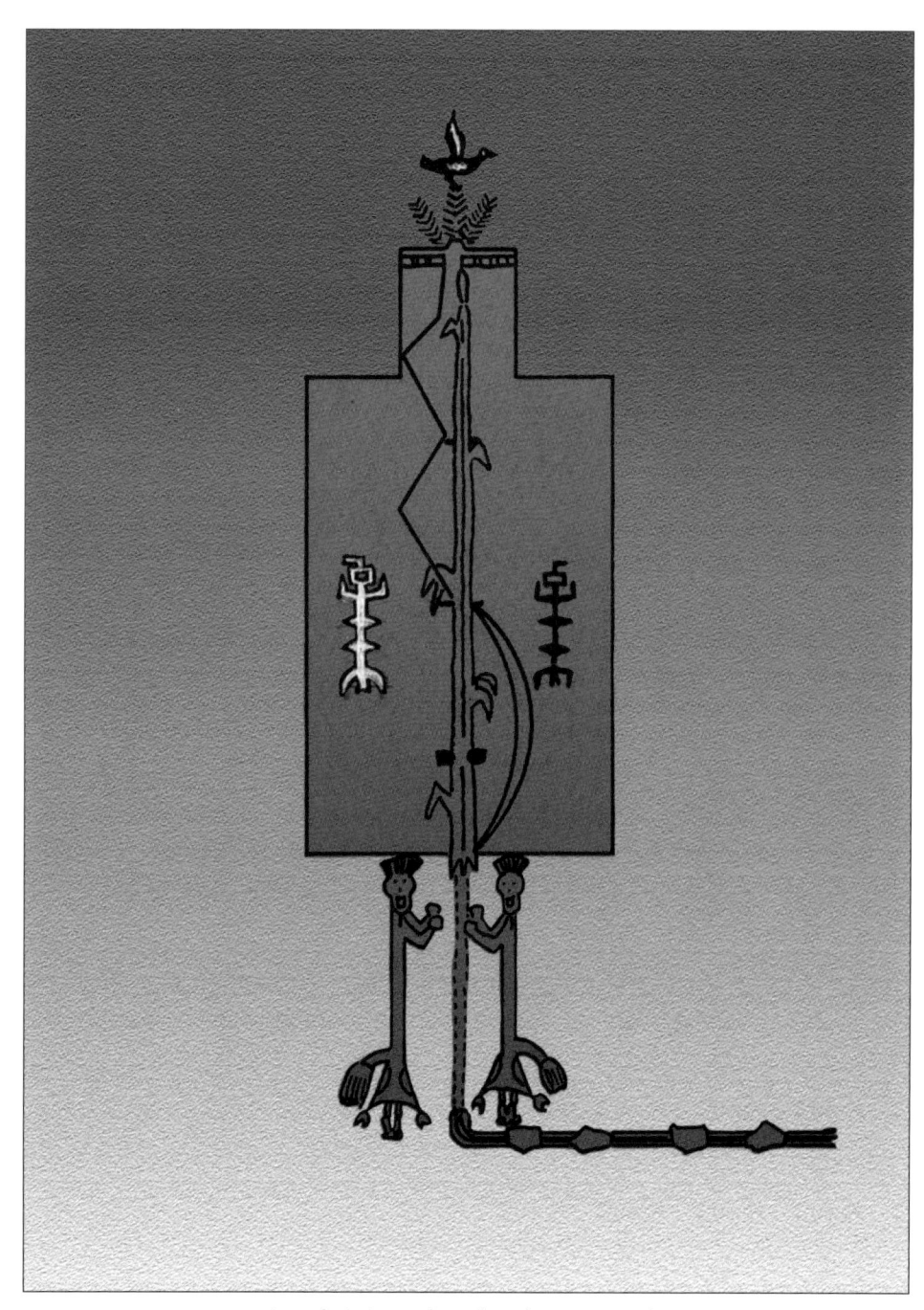

Navajo sandpainting, traditional, southwestern United States

7

Vision

THE NAVAJO SANDPAINTING PICTURED HERE IS CALLED "THE TREE OF LIFE." It is the ladder that ascends from the underworld and pierces heaven. The pollen path or blessing way runs up the center of this tree as a trunk carries sap from its roots to its crown.

Every culture has an *axis mundi*—a world axis or cosmic tree with a vertical pole that holds up the heavens and opens up a pathway of knowledge and understanding. It is the point on which everything turns.

The Mayan world tree is called *Wacah Chan*. It has maize ears for branches and, similar to this Navajo tree, it also has a bird perched at the top, the quetzal with its brilliant plumage. The feathered serpent god, Quetzalcoatl, god of wind and air, will return, it is said, at the end of the current cycle. In Scandinavian mythology, the cock sitting at the top of the giant tree of all life—the ash, Yggdrasil—is called "All Knower." He sits there, ready to crow when the giant serpent's twisting coils start to slip from around the earth, heralding *Ragnarok*—the end times.

The tree of life pictured here is balanced with the masculine zigzag of a lightning bolt on the left and the feminine curve of a rainbow on the right. Like the brain, this sandpainting relates left and right to rational knowledge and intuitive understanding, respectively. At the top of the tree is a bird representing flight, freedom, and total understanding. See **Healer 37** for more insights into Navajo colored sand imagery.

PART **vii** ~ Violet

VISION 7

Understanding

> There is nothing we may do to arrive at understanding, for understanding is an accident. The most we can do is become accident prone.
>
> —Flannery O'Connor

From our three-thousand-year-old redwoods and four-thousand-year-old bristlecone pines, to Tolkien's Ents and the sacred oak groves of ancient goddesses, trees have long stood as doorways to other worlds. Yet their roots, just as our own, are firmly planted in earth. Ancient temples, such as the famous one dedicated to Artemis in Ephesus, Turkey, were surrounded by pillars reaching into the sky. They were marble trees marking a new kind of sacred space. People still come to holy places seeking truth, and *tree* has the same etymological roots as *truth*. The Greek word for truth means "unhiddenness." A tree is definitely unhidden.

James Hillman, the therapist who has written about the world soul, has an "acorn theory." Each person, he says, bears a uniqueness that asks to be lived and that is already present before it can be lived. In other words, each of us has a tree inside us. We can imagine it growing and budding with all the potential within us. We can choose which kind of tree to imagine.

Carl Jung saw the self in the tree form. The tree symbolizes, he said, our fervent goal to attain wholeness. The tree, he claimed, embodies our own rootedness and growth. Our own death and rebirth are mirrored in every tree of life.

All cultures honoring the earth have sacred trees. For the Hindu, it's the banyan; Buddhists revere the bo tree. For Egyptians, it's the sycamore. Greeks couldn't decide on one, choosing laurel, olive, and cypress trees. The Chinese honor the peach. Druids venerate the oak. Early Scandinavians said women came from the elm and men from the ash. The first Celtic woman was the rowan; the first man was the alder, and the birch marks the beginning of the Celtic year.

Hunab Ku

VISION 7

Conservationists tell us 976 tree species are now called "the living dead" because they are so close to dying off. There is, for example, at the time of this writing, *only one* Chinese hornbeam left on our planet. Rain forests in Hawaii, Ecuador, Brazil, Madagascar, the Philippines, India, and Northern California are all in grave danger of leaving us. What then? What will feed us and heal us and shelter us?

The tree of life pictured here offers you vision and, with that, understanding. Just as the bird at the top of the tree is free to fly and return, everyone has the potential to climb the ladder of the soul. **Shaman** 15 shows us how. And like aspens, we are rooted together, so when one of us climbs the tree of life and better understands the universe, others are shown the way. In *Hunab Ku*, we have been ascending our chakras from our red root to our violet crown. Vision brings understanding that life energy flows up and down to places beyond thought, unrestricted and free.

Many ancient "trees" have seven steps. Ziggurats. Menorahs. The Navajo soul tree pictured here has seven cornstalk leaves. The sixteenth-century mystic Jacob Boehme claimed each of us has sevenfold energies: wisdom, understanding, counsel, knowledge, fortitude, piety, and fear of the Lord. Seven is, indeed, a mystical number. Some Native Americans acknowledge seven directions: north, east, west, south, above, below, and within. For Jung, the number seven stood for the highest stage of illumination.

The soul is like the eye: when resting upon that on which truth and being shine, the soul perceives and understands and is radiant with intelligence . . .

—PLATO, *Republic VI*

PART **vii** ~ Violet

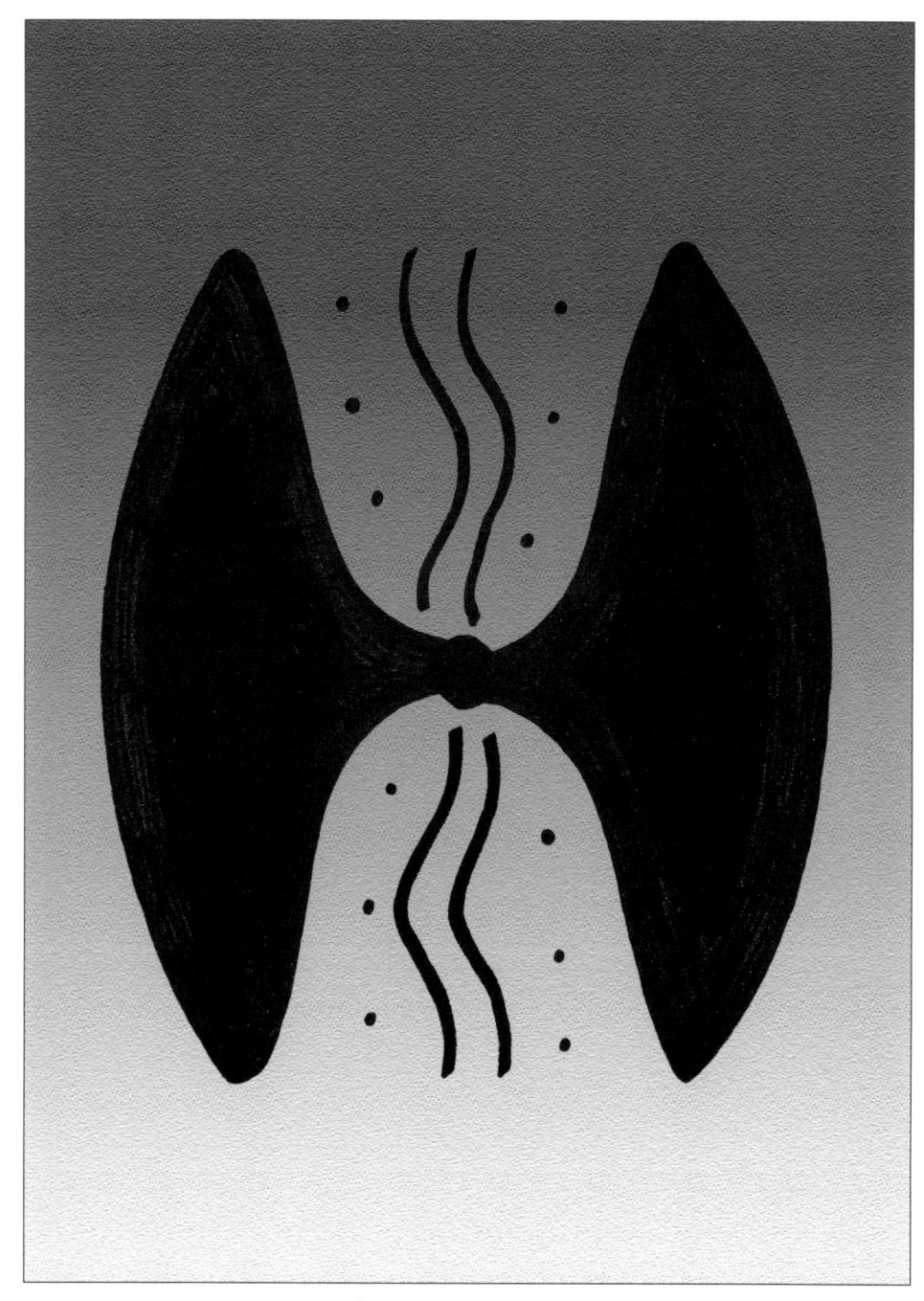

• *Painted vase, 1400 BCE, Mycenae, Greece* •

Released Soul

Butterfly shapes abound in ancient art and many of the wing shapes, such as the ones pictured here, replicate the double axe, the labrys (see **Mystic** 8). This butterfly design appears in much Mycenaean art. This particular vase design was painted dark brown on buff and is called Late Helladic II because the image is more geometrical and abstract, with more parallel lines, than earlier Minoan butterfly designs. Because the butterfly's axe-like wings resemble horns and crescent moons, it was associated with bulls and goddesses, with death and rebirth. According to Gimbutas, "Scenes of regeneration and hymns to rising life are portrayed . . . in [a sarcophagus in western Crete] . . . replicated bull-horn/butterfly motifs. . . . It is a declaration of the triumph of life. . . ."

Part vii ~ Violet

RELEASED SOUL

6

Rebirth

**The Soul is older than the body.
Souls are continuously born again into this life.**

—Plato

The Greeks' word *psyche* was the word for both "butterfly" and "soul." We have incorporated the word into our language to describe the part of us we rationally know is not physical and intuitively know is eternal. The ancients in Greece, the Celtic lands, and China all believed that butterflies were souls flying around between incarnations. These about-to-be-born souls are searching for a new mother. There are many legends of a butterfly landing in a woman's glass and being drunk unseen, and in this way the soul reenters human incarnation. In Cornwall it was believed that spirits of the dead took the form of white butterflies. The Gaelic name for butterfly means "fire of god." The Scandinavians named butterflies after their goddess: Freya's hen. In Mexico, the obsidian butterfly, or Itzapolotl, is called the Source of All Life. And the Cuna people of Central America worship Earth Mother in the form of the brilliant metallic-blue Brazilian morpho butterfly.

Richard Bach said, "What the caterpillar calls the end of the world, the master calls the butterfly." Released Soul enters your world as a powerful symbol of release and resurrection. You are a mature soul now, she says. You've gone through the caterpillar and chrysalis stages. Now you're ready to fly.

The butterfly also symbolizes interconnectivity, as the meteorologist Edward Lorenz pointed out. When testing models of weather prediction, he posed the profound question: "Can a butterfly flapping its wings in Tokyo cause a tornado in Texas?" According to the science of chaos theory, the answer is "Yes." Chaos scientists call this subtle energy "butterfly power." Butterfly power creates what others think impossible. Ask Gandhi. Ask Rosa Parks. Ask yourself.

Hunab Ku

RELEASED SOUL

6

Everyone has ideas of what the soul is. Some use that word interchangeably with *mind*. Since we're speaking of butterflies here, perhaps we could use the larger soul definition: the collective human psyche. Each of us also has an individual psyche, and it lives in that quiet place where our life's purpose and the map for our spiritual journey also rest. At the point of death our soul seems to fly away, leaving the body a quiet, dead mass of tissue and bone. The individual soul then joins up with something beyond the physical "self" that some call Spirit. Hildegard of Bingen believed our souls mirrored the image of angelic spirits. Our souls are filled with light and color, like the butterfly, and when that life force is dampened, a person's eyes appear soulless.

Released Soul doesn't come to imply that you're going to die, any more than the image of **Vulture** 13 suggests that. However, there may be something within or around you that needs to be released. Or you may be flying to new levels of consciousness. Meditation can break open your cocoon and allow your soul greater freedom. Genesis tells us that after six days, God rested. After a lifetime, a soul also rests. The number six represents completion and achievement. Relate this stage of your journey to **Womb 6**. The monarch butterfly migrates thousands of miles; its orange and black wings carry it from its home in the Americas to Hawaii, Indonesia, and Australasia. Souls migrate, too. Released Soul knows the meaning of *cosmos* is "whole"; Released Soul knows its home is infinite.

Great Kunapipi . . . I ask you to care for my spirit soul until my return so that after my passing from this life my two spirits may be reunited in you, before you send me forth again to once more live on earth.

—AUSTRALIAN HYMN TO KUNAPIPI, FIRST MOTHER OF THE ABORIGINES

PART *vii* ~ Violet

Bronze wire brooch, 900 BCE, Greece

Double Spiral

THE DOUBLE SPIRAL INFINITY SYMBOL PICTURED HERE IS PART OF A BRONZE wire brooch dating from 900 BCE in Greece. It is constructed from one line and forms an endless circle. This piece of ancient jewelry is in New York's Metropolitan Museum of Art.

The infinity symbol came west by way of the Arabic numeral system, which originated in India. Like this double spiral brooch, the Indian concept of infinity included a clockwise and a counterclockwise circle, representing male and female, solar and lunar, right and left. The dualities are joined in the center. Two become one in this symbolic sexual union in which we glimpse the infinite.

DOUBLE SPIRAL

5

Infinity

**The pulse of life demands an unending stream
of vital energy to keep it going.**

—Marija Gimbutas, *The Language of the Goddess*

Spirals spin us into eternity. Other images in this book have pointed to this phenomenon. You may wish to look at them now also; some of them may speak even more intently to you than this one. What do these other images say to you? **Serpent 7, Mother 15, Water 16, Fire 27, Healer 37, Bard 37, Sound 29, Counselor 19, Wise Old One 17, and Universe 11**.

All the *Hunab Ku* images with corresponding numbers could be linked to create double spirals. The body numbers, 1 through 39, revolve in one direction, and the spirit numbers, 39 through 1, revolve in the opposite direction. And, just as this bronze brooch forms a whole from two parts, so do you, for spirit permeates matter. Just as physical birth is sparked by the connection of two people, spiritual birth is sparked by the intersection of yin and yang.

You need not feel limited by either time or space. Think of yourself as living in both worlds of now and forever. Like the wires in this image, time circles within eternity.

Meditate on the whirling spirals in the image pictured here, for meditation is the key to going within yourself. And violet is the color palette to best facilitate meditation. Everyone's brain finds it difficult to shut out extraneous thoughts and, in fact, your two brain hemispheres may be sending out different wavelengths. When you relax, your alpha waves increase in amplitude and still your chattering mind, and all parts of your brain resonate together. People who meditate often find a theta state more prevalent. Meditating lowers your blood pressure and relieves stress in your body. There are many suggested meditation techniques, but the main thing is to be comfortable. Some advanced meditation practitioners reach a state the Buddhists call *satori*, which reveals an unfolding world most of us have never seen. Perhaps this is a look at infinity.

Hunab Ku

DOUBLE SPIRAL

5

Buddha taught eighty-four thousand different ways to tame one's emotions. But perhaps the main thing is just to pay attention to your breath as you meditate, quietly going inside yourself. Meditation techniques allow us to be present. Breathe slowly and deliberately. If your thoughts wander, gently bring them back to your breath (see **Air 38**).

Five is a number of wholeness, but with it, expect change. Numbers obviously mean more to some people than to others. The Mayans associated the number five with the swirling serpent. The ruling Aztec deity for five was Tlacolteotl, the goddess of love and childbirth.

Like numbers, images create fields of energy, and the brooch of a double spiral pictured here sets up a powerful field. Pin it on you. Let it be yours.

I am the infinite deep, in whom all the worlds appear to rise. Beyond all form, forever still. Even so am I.

—*Ashtavakra Gita*

PART **vii** ~ Violet

• *Stone decoration, 550 BCE, Pasargadae, Assyria (Iran)* •

4

Angel Guide

THE WINGED BEING PICTURED HERE DECORATED A GATE OF THE PASARGADAE Palace in Assyria. While this carved slab is typical of Assyrian and Hittite construction, it borrows elements, from the Egyptians, particularly the crown, and from Phoenician bronze work.

Pasargadae was Cyrus's capital, built from 559–550 BCE, and by all accounts it was a cosmopolitan city. Cyrus the Great founded the ancient Persian Empire, and he built his capital city near present-day Shiraz in Iran. At the palace's center was a citadel known as throne hill where all the empire's subsequent kings were crowned, even after the capital city moved about twenty-five miles away. The crowning ceremony involved entering the temple of a warrior goddess, putting on Cyrus the Great's own robe, and eating figs and drinking turpentine and sour milk, according to Plutarch of Chaeronea (46–120 CE).

Cyrus the Great's mausoleum still exists. Alexander the Great ordered it to be restored in 324 BCE, and according to his biographer, when Alexander visited the tomb, Cyrus the Great's body still lay there in a gold sarcophagus on a gold bier, with a golden table by its side covered with treasure.

PART vii ~ Violet

ANGEL GUIDE 4

Message

Angels are powerful spirits whom God sends into the world to wish us well. Since we don't expect to see them, we don't.

—Frederick Buechner, *Wishful Thinking: A Theological ABC*

Angels come to earth bearing messages. Perhaps the most dramatic one came from the Archangel Gabriel to Mary: "Do not be afraid, Mary, for you have found favor with God. And behold, you will conceive in your womb and bear a son, and you shall call his name Jesus."

In Greek, their name, *angeloi,* means "messengers" or "emissaries." They have been called watchers, shining holy ones, and birds of god. Ancient texts speak of the descent of luminous beings to earth in disk-shaped ships of fire.

Whatever we call them and however they arrive, they are beings of tireless energy. They help with healing, they swirl around religious events, they hover near at birthing and dying times. They work with creative joy, and in their magnificent way, they keep creation going. When we're awake, we accept their gifts, never sure whose thoughts they were. Don Gilmore, in *Angels, Angels, Everywhere,* says he believes that "angels are forms, images and expressions through which the essences and energy forces of God can be transmitted and that, since there are an infinite number of these forms, the greatest service anyone can pay the angelic host is never consciously to limit the ways angels might appear to us."

Author Terence McKenna points out that "in all times and all places, with the possible exception of Western Europe for the past two hundred years, a social commerce between human beings and various types of discarnate entities, or non-human intelligences, was taken for granted."

The Koran recognizes four Archangels; Christian and Jewish sources claim there are seven. By the sixth century philosophers had divided all the celestial orders of winged beings into nine orders, three groups of three. Closest to God's throne are the

Hunab Ku

ANGEL GUIDE

4

Seraphim, Cherubim, and Thrones, having six wings, four heads, and many eyes. In the second group we find Dominions, Virtues, and Powers. They assume princely duties over planets and generally act as spiritual guides to released souls. Finally there are Principalities, Archangels, and Angels. Some angel experts claim each of us has from twenty-five to forty helpers around us at all times. But those large numbers of angels appear at very rare times; usually there are only three or four that hover close. Angels never interfere with our choices; they encourage us to grow. Sometimes they appear as sound, sometimes as whirlpools of energetic colors.

Thomas Aquinas, the thirteenth-century theologian and writer, was called the Angel Doctor. He said, "The entire corporeal world is governed by God through the angels.... We humans have a dimness of intellectual light in our souls. But this light is at its full strength in an angel who, as Dionysius says, is a pure and brilliant mirror.... Angels do not need bodies for their own sake, but for ours." Anna, in *Mister God, This Is Anna*, puts it more simply. "The difference from a person and an angel is easy: Most of an angel is in the inside and most of the person is on the outside." Angels are within us: in our blood, our brains, our hearts. Every day we choose between listening to the forces of light or the forces of darkness, for we carry it all within us.

The angelic image pictured here has four wings. The number four has a stabilizing effect, as we saw in **Father 4**. Four brings a feeling of calm and peace. Four creates boundaries of protection. We neatly divide our compasses into four or eight parts. We have four limbs. Even our DNA is built on combinations of four. Pythagoreans called the number four the tetrad, the root of all things and the most perfect number. Pythagoras declared the four powers of the soul to be mind, science, opinion, and sense.

Angels and archetypes are the organs of our very souls. They sneak into our consciousness and break down old concepts. The message of archetypes, like this Angel Guide, shatters our rigidity and gives us new wings on which to soar.

Every blade of grass has its Angel that bends over it and whispers, "Grow, grow."

—TALMUD

PART *vii* ~ Violet

Terra-cotta figure, 300 BCE, Ibiza, Spain

Crown

THE HEAD OF A TERRA-COTTA FEMALE FIGURE PICTURED HERE WEARS A magnificent crown and was created around 300 BCE. Although Spanish, the figure reflects a Carthaginian influence. This figure is now housed in the Museo Arqueologico on Ibiza, a Spanish island southwest of Majorca.

The oldest extant "modern" royal European crown belonged to Queen Theolinda of Lombardy, who died in 627 CE. That crown was said to be a reliquary, containing a thorn from the crown of thorns that Jesus wore. The crown was placed on his head in cruel jest and derision, but has, through time, become an archetype of divine suffering and love.

Rulers and those we choose to venerate are often made to look taller. Crowns and elevated thrones accomplish that, and such practices can be traced back to ancient goddess images wearing pyramids of horns or tall headpieces.

PART *vii* ~ Violet

CROWN 3

Reward

> We are midwives to each other. Someday we will
> bring each other into paradise.
>
> —Michael Murphy, *Jacob Atabet*

The crown as a symbol of royal authority developed from many different sources. The royal marriage between a goddess and her chosen consort was recognized by placing a wreath of flowers or leaves on his head. That may have been the very first crown, or perhaps the first crown was a simple circlet of flowers given to a loved one. The traditional Egyptian tall crown is thought to symbolize, in physical form, the upward-expanding energy at the crown chakra when it is fully open. In the Kabbalistic Tree of Life, the uppermost symbol is the crown. It combines male and female divinity—androgynous wisdom. Crowns seem to have been placed on people's heads as a symbol of love, reward, or recognition of some royal aspect of themselves.

When our crown chakra opens, light streams into our body. With it comes wisdom and personal mastery, open-mindedness, and what many now call *enlightenment*. This light teaches us that the gifts we have been given should be passed on to others. In the words of the prayer of St. Francis, "It is in the giving, I receive." Khalil Gibran, in *The Prophet*, puts it this way: "You often say, 'I would give, but only to the deserving.' The trees in your orchard say not so, nor the flocks in your pasture. They give that they may live, for to withhold is to perish."

The inner rewards we receive may seem insignificant to others more attuned to conventional "crowns," but rewards come in all sizes and shapes. In Calcutta, Mother Teresa was often rewarded by little more than a smile or the clasp of a feeble hand. She insisted that she only did small work, albeit with great love.

Many people cling to Christ's words that he spoke to the thief suspended from a nearby cross: "Today you shall be with me in paradise." Certainly that was not a reward for living an exemplary life, but an unconditional gift of grace. Regardless of how much

Hunab Ku

CROWN 3

suffering and pain people must endure here, many believe paradise is their just reward. What if paradise were here and now? What then? Our "just" reward would be getting up to live another day filled with love. Our awakened self is its own reward.

People who have been with their loved ones as they died have often noted a light around the crown chakra, as if the dying person's soul were leaving from the top of their head. It is their crowning moment. The demon associated with this chakra is attachment. People who cannot detach from this life find it very hard to leave gracefully. The pituitary gland, the master gland, may be most connected to this crown chakra. While the pineal gland may be more closely aligned with the sixth chakra, both stimulate growth hormones and both shut down at the moment of our death. The rewards for easing through our last moments are bliss and transcendence. Our reward for living a full life is an ease of passage into the next. This is much better than gold and jewels or terra-cotta masterpieces. They will all turn to dust. Your personal crown is forever.

Crown may be telling you that your achievements finally will be noticed. Many will see your crown, your healthy aura. Keep amethyst nearby to induce meditation and to strengthen your spiritual wisdom. Along with many ancient teachers, it's time for you to realize that three equals completion. You already have glory and riches!

Be content with what you have; rejoice in the way things are. When you realize there is nothing lacking, the whole world belongs to you.

—LAO TZU

PART **vii** ~ Violet

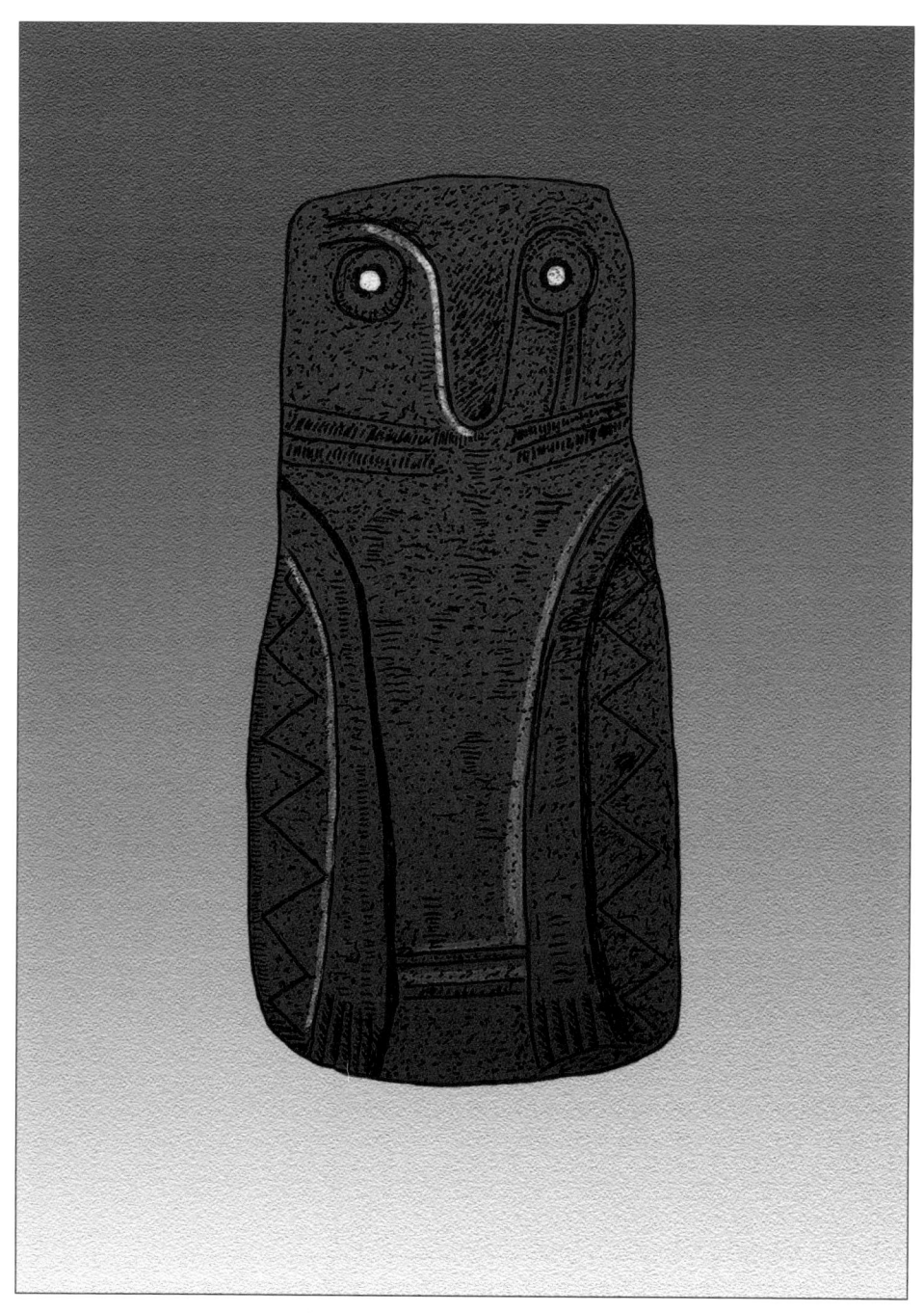

Schist plaque, 3500 BCE, Careres, Portugal

2

Owl

THE CRYSTALLINE ROCK-CARVED OWL FIGURE ON A SCHIST PLAQUE THAT IS pictured here was found in a passage grave in Careres, Portugal. Crafted around 3500 BCE, it is nearly three inches high. Schist is a very hard stone, but because of its parallel-lined structure, it can be easily flaked into arrow and spear points, so it was valued.

The owl, from early prehistoric times to the present, has been a harbinger of otherworldliness. For many cultures, an owl's mournful cry is a death call. The Egyptian hieroglyph for death is an owl. But as also was indicated in **Wise Old One** 17 and **Shaman** 15, an owl's eyes can see through the night. From Neolithic times through the Early Bronze Age, owls have represented the all-seeing goddess. Owls' round eyes and beaks appear again and again all across Europe's early communities.

PART *vii* ~ Violet

OWL 2

Wisdom

Holy wisdom is not clear and thin like water, but thick and dark like blood.

—C. S. Lewis, *Till We Have Faces*

Owl flies into our lives on huge, silent wings. Its unblinking eyes can see as well at night as during the day, reminding us that seeing all sides of an issue is a gift from this wise one. It is a Zen concept to believe that perfect wisdom is inherent in all people, and true wisdom comes to us when we let go of what attaches and binds us to the earth.

Sophia, the early Jewish-Christian name for divine wisdom, is described as brooding over the earth, loving the earth, energizing all she looked at. The Hebrew Book of Wisdom says, "She spans the world in power from end to end and gently orders all things." Sophia—wise, intelligent, and artful—later took on the connotations of the world's soul. Her name is only one for the divine feminine's holy wisdom, wisdom as thick and dark as her birthing blood.

What's the difference between data, information, knowledge, and wisdom? Data might be seen as a set of quantitative facts; information is data with no descriptive words. Knowledge is human-processed information; it has been totally experienced. Knowledge always embodies the concept that one has the ability to learn more. But wisdom is a deeper way of knowing something to be true. Wisdom is about questions and never *tells* answers, but rather encourages each of us to seek our own truth. Wisdom is applied knowledge. While knowledge can be lost or overlooked, wisdom can never be misplaced or forgotten. Knowledge is earth-based civil love; wisdom is universe-based higher love. Amassing knowledge can be an end in itself; wisdom's end is always to benefit others. Wisdom, John O'Donohue says in *Anam Cara*, is "the art of living in rhythm with your soul, your life, and the divine. Wisdom is the way that you learn to decipher the unknown; and the unknown is our closest companion." Wisdom is looking at these images in *Hunab Ku* and knowing the message before reading the words. Owl

Hunab Ku

OWL 2

invites you to go beyond images and words and enter the dark stillness and find, as Bede Griffiths says, "God without form."

With its two eyes and two wings, Owl symbolizes the number two. Two is dark, secretive, romantic, imaginative, and intuitive. Two vibrates in accord with the moon. Two is a perfect number; it embodies polarity and balance. When light is converted into matter, the result is a pair of electron twins, one electron and one positron. Two is an orderly, symmetrical number.

Duality is an archetype. It is the yin-yang motion with which the Chinese describe Earth's rhythms. It is the Hunab Ku, with its balanced dark and light. Owls tend to call in twos: *hoo-hooooo*.

Carl Jung believed the number two was actually the first number because two makes separation, and thus counting and multiplication, possible. Two sets up the understanding that one is separate, different from another. Tension was introduced into creation as soon as Eve opened her eyes (see **Twins 24**). But in her wisdom, Sophia invites us to go further and realize what is beyond our separateness, our "twoness."

Violet endows you with a passion for truth. Your sharp eyes see everything. Approach all problems with deep introspection and a willingness to be silent. Turn your head around, like an owl, to see all sides of an issue. Then look deep inside yourself. Catch a glimpse of your own goodness and your own wisdom.

In Wisdom there is a spirit intelligent and holy, unique in its kind yet made up of many parts, subtle, free-moving, lucid, spotless, clear, neither harmed nor harming, loving what is good, eager, unhampered, beneficent.

—HEBREW BOOK OF WISDOM

PART vii ~ Violet

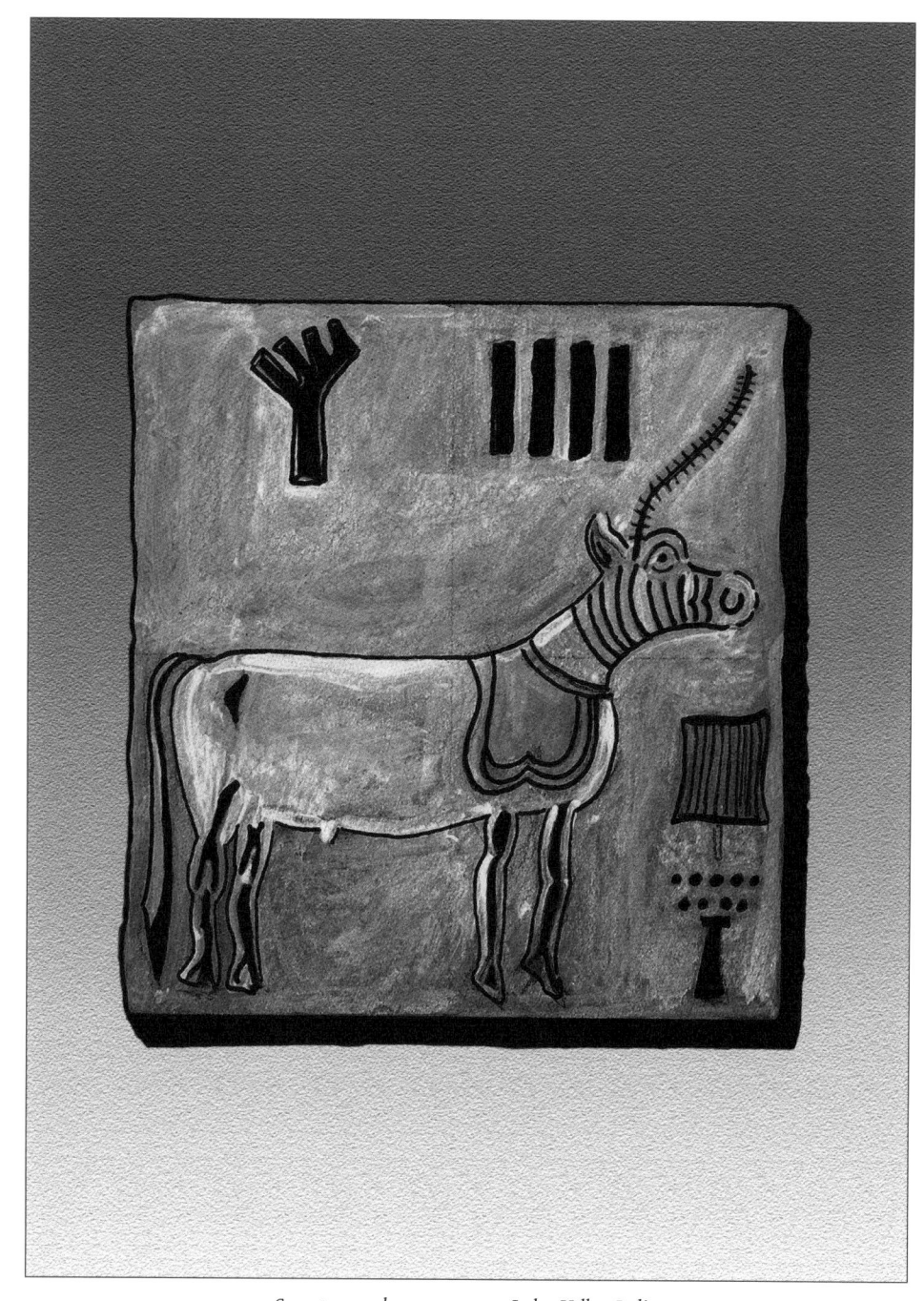

Soapstone seal, c. 2000 BCE, Indus Valley, India

1

Unicorn

An ancient beast with one horn stands and gazes into the future on the steatite seal from India pictured here. This soapstone square, about an inch and a half wide, may have been a business stamp or religious seal used by the Harappans, an advanced people who once lived in cities in the Indus Valley from 2600 to 1900 BCE and then completely disappeared. They apparently had no priest king, and wealth appeared to be evenly distributed. No one can yet read their writing, but it seems to have some elements in common with an even earlier form of writing called Old European Script. This script has 210 identified signs and predates the Harappan writing by several thousand years. Some other signs from this early sacred script, as Gimbutas called these hieroglyphic inscriptions appearing only on religious items, can be found on **Ram 2**, **Weaver-Warrior 8**, **Meander 18**, **Water Bearer** 32, **Goat** 31, **Winged Dog** 23, **Wise Old One** 17, **Released Soul** 6, and **Owl** 2.

Shan M. M. Winn isolated five common elements in early writing, some of which were used in combination: a straight line, two intersecting lines, two lines joined at one end, a dot, and a curved line. The forked "comb" with its varying lines certainly looks like a numbering system. Until the script can be read, we can only speculate about what the writing says. But archaeologists do know that these early script symbols appeared long before people were writing on Crete and Cyprus and about two thousand years before the Babylonians began imprinting their cuneiform alphabets into soft clay.

The unicorn we are most familiar with is the one-horned white horse. But sometimes a unicorn is an ox, a ram, a goat, an antelope, a wild ass, a rhinoceros, a serpent, a scorpion, a fish, or a bull. Whatever the animal, unicorns have a common feature: a single horn.

PART *vii* ~ Violet

UNICORN 1

Unity

"I am not real. And yet in a sense I am that which is the only reality.... You called me, and because there is great need, I am here. As long as there are even a few who belong to the Old Music, you are still our brothers and sisters." The light of the unicorn's horn pulsed. "Before the harmonies were broken, unicorns and winds danced together with joy and no fear."

—Madeleine L'Engle, *A Swiftly Tilting Planet*

Unicorns represent purity and like the Chinese *ki-lin*, they infrequently appear to announce important births. In medieval legends, unicorns were drawn to young women, symbols of purity, and they appear on famous tapestries in quiet, sheltered gardens. The horn, if ground into a healing potion, was believed to prevent convulsions, purify water, and insure virility.

Unicorn tells us we are now at the outer edge of our *Hunab Ku* journey, having circled back to what the early alchemists practicing their Hermetic traditions called the One Thing. Hermes Trismegistus—philosopher, king, and Egyptian prophet—filled *The Emerald Tablet* with alchemical principles. He taught, among other ideas, that as things are above, so they are below. All is one. The universe is replicated within our bodies—macrocosm in the microcosm.

Physicists' new superstring theories now theorize that life is a unified whole. We are held in a "cosmic consciousness." Dr. John Hagelin, the physicist who wrote *The Theory of Everything*, says everything *is* connected in this unified field of incomprehensible complexity. Another physicist, David Bohm, describes unity as an enfolded or implicate order of the whole—that which connects all things.

The physicists have now caught up with the monks, nuns, and mystics who have always known this. One monk, Thomas Merton, put it this way: "Beneath the broken surface of life there is a hidden wholeness." Our task is to recognize our oneness, our hidden wholeness, and cherish it. Unicorn appears in silence, through meditation or

UNICORN 1

prayer. Unicorn, like Great Bear, is a solitary, quiet figure. But the archetypes reflect two very different kinds of silence. Great Bear's hibernation is silent because he is solitary; it is dangerous to approach a sleeping bear! Nature finds ways of protecting us when we choose solitude. On the other hand, Unicorn's silence is magical, and it is a great gift to approach Unicorn. Unicorn invites us near by making our heart as pure as it can be. In the journey toward Unicorn, we approach a mystical experience, glimpsing unity.

We share a common past; together we create our common future. And at the center lies the **Hunab Ku 39/39**, the perfectly balanced matrix of all possibilities, pulsing and vital to everything living. *Hun.* One. *Hun Ahau.* One Lord. Hunab Ku contains all body and spirit images, all numbers, all colors. We are woven into an ancient Loom of Maya. In "The Great Clod Project," poet Gary Snyder wrote: "The cosmic principles go back into silence, non-being, emptiness; a Nothing that will produce the ten thousand things, and the ten thousand things will have that marvelous emptiness still at the center."

Within the encircling arms of the **Hunab Ku 39/39**, we spiral back to where we started, knowing we have just begun to tap into the ancient archetypal images and their multiple layers of wisdom. Like carefully constructed mirrors, each of the seventy-seven images reflects ourselves back to us, our whole selves. We have, Unicorn whispers, a singular purpose: *to love and care for each other and to love and care for ourselves.* Then our unity will be perfect.

Let us be united, Let us speak in harmony, Let our minds apprehend alike.
Common be our prayer . . . Alike be our feelings, Unified be our hearts;
Common be our intentions; Perfect be our unity.

—RIG VEDA

PART vii ~ Violet

1 15 25 30 35 38
14 24 29 34 37 8
2 16 26 31 36
13 23 28 33 7
3 27 32 9
6
17 20
12 10
4 18 22 21 19 5
11 39 11
5 19 21 22 18 4
10 12
20 17
6 32 27 3
9 13
33 23
28
7 36 31 26 16 2
37 34 29 24 14
8
38 35 30 25 15 1

Symbol Readings

The symbols in this book love synchronicity. You may have already flipped to a page that relates to something on your mind. Or you may have selected one image at random, centered, and let the image speak to you. Such serendipitous insights cannot be programmed or controlled, but you can create space that welcomes them. The following symbol readings allow the images to "talk" to one another and offer you random ways to group them into meaningful patterns. As you play with the images, numbers, and colors, you will become more comfortable using them, and you may discover your own ways of reading.

An Insight Reading

First you will need to randomly generate seven numbers between 1 and 39. You might make a set of body and spirit number cards by cutting up paper into seventy-seven small pieces. Then, write spirit numbers 1 through 38 in one color and body numbers 1 through 38 in another color; on the last card, write the number 39 in both colors. Draw seven numbers at random. Synchronicity will always produce the right result. Or you could close your eyes and point to the Hunab Ku illustration on page 308, selecting seven different numbers. Write down your results in a column next to the letters forming the word *insight*, making sure to note whether you pointed to a body or a spirit number.

Example:

I   4 (body)
N   26 (body)
S   13 (spirit)
I   12 (spirit)
G   38 (body)
H   5 (spirit)
T   18 (spirit)

Or you could try something more challenging. For instance, you could jot down a set of numbers that are personal to you, like your name, your age, and your birth date. Your name can be turned into numbers using the following simple code. Keep any number that comes out 39 and under. Add the digits together for numbers over 39.

Hunab Ku

— LETTER VALUES —

A = 1	H = 8	O = 15	V = 22
B = 2	I = 9	P = 16	W = 23
C = 3	J = 10	Q = 17	X = 24
D = 4	K = 11	R = 18	Y = 25
E = 5	L = 12	S = 19	Z = 26
F = 6	M = 13	T = 20	
G = 7	N = 14	U = 21	

Here's an example. John Henry Smith was born on December 9, 1965 and is 39 years old.

John = 10 + 15 + 8 + 14 = 47; 4 + 7 = 11.
Henry = 8 + 5 + 14 + 18 + 25 = 70; 7 + 0 = 7.
Smith = 19 + 13 + 9 + 20 + 8 = 69; 6 + 9 = 15.

Now, by placing these numbers next to the INSIGHT letters, John Henry Smith has this result:

I   11 (John)
N   7 (Henry)
S   15 (Smith)
I   39 (age)
G   9 (birth date)
H   12 (birth month)
T   21 (birth year: 1 + 9 + 6 + 5 = 21)

Now for each number, flip a coin. Decide whether heads is a spirit number and tails a body number, or vice versa.

Turn to the seven chapters discussing the symbols you selected, and note their names. (Later, go back and see what those pages taught you.) Now add the following notations next to your Insight letters; you may wish to record the insights you get here in a journal.

SYMBOL READINGS

I This is your image, your present state, your assessment of your self-image. Ponder this image first.

N This is your negativity image. What is blocking you? What do you wish to work on?

S Your shadow lies here. What in your life is only partly illuminated at this time? What still remains opaque?

I This is your instruction image. Who or what can you look to right now or in the future to help you learn?

G This is your growth image. How might you expect to grow from this helper? In what areas of your life might you need to stretch?

H This is your healing image. How might healing come to you? Where in your body, mind, or spirit do you most yearn to be healed?

T This is your transformation image. This is the place you are moving toward. Dramatic changes are in store; this image helps you understand what you might expect to be changed.

A Work Reading

To focus on work, open the book to **Adult** 28. After spending some time with this image and reading the discussion about it, select five other numbers at random, in whatever way seems right for you. You could select from the illustration on page 308 with your eyes closed. You could write down five words or phrases that come to mind when you think about your job situation, and turn them into numbers using the letter values code on page 311; then flip a coin to see whether they should be body or spirit numbers. (First decide which side of the coin stands for body numbers and which for spirit numbers.) For example, "I am overwhelmed" = 153; 1 + 5 + 3 = 9. Flip a coin. Heads; heads have been selected to be spirit numbers. Look up **Scarab** 9.

Hunab Ku

Jot down the five images in a column with space to write next to them. In descending order, add any thoughts that arise from viewing the images this way:

My first image represents my past, everything that has led me to this point. This is my baggage, what I have hauled around and brought to this work situation. It may represent what I believe to be my professional strengths and talents.

My second image shows me where I find my inner strengths to meet the particular work challenge I am facing.

My third image is my shadow. This is either a person or a situation that makes my life difficult right now. This is someone or something that is fighting me. This is what I fear most on Monday morning.

My fourth image shows me where I am going to get help. This is my helper image. It may show me where I can draw on help from an outside resource, or it may show how I might draw on help from my inner resources.

My fifth image helps me integrate all the others. It is my true work challenge image, and it may not be the one I think I am facing. When I integrate the meanings of all five of these images, using all the hints listed under each image, I may find a solution to this particular work dilemma.

A Rainbow Reading

At random, select one image from each of the seven colors in this book. Do so by generating a number from one to eleven, in whatever way seems right for you, for each color. You could use a pair of dice, and if you roll double sixes you could count 12 as 1 + 2 = 3. This chart will help you quickly find the numbers 1 through 11 in each color by following across from the numbers in the red column. For example, if you roll a seven for yellow, then look up **Triangle 29**; if you roll a nine for violet, then look up **Crown 3**.

SYMBOL READINGS

— COLOR CHART —

Red	Orange	Yellow	Green	Blue	Indigo	Violet
1	12	23	34	33	22	11
2	13	24	35	32	21	10
3	14	25	36	31	20	9
4	15	26	37	30	19	8
5	16	27	38	29	18	7
6	17	28	39/39	28	17	6
7	18	29	38	27	16	5
8	19	30	37	26	15	4
9	20	31	36	25	14	3
10	21	32	35	24	13	2
11	22	33	34	23	12	1

List the images you identify in order by color: red, orange, yellow, green, blue, indigo, and violet. Look at your images in that order, feeling each color and image soaking into your body, into your body's corresponding chakra center. You will get a composite picture of what your body is processing right now. Ponder any blockages. Note any affirmations. Sense heat and pulsations, either moving from your red root chakra and up, or from your violet crown chakra and down your body. Keep in mind, the color green integrates the three chakra centers that are above and below. Your heart knows what is needed to keep you healthy and balanced. Breathe deeply into each new color.

If you practice yoga or any tradition that concentrates on the seven energy centers of your body, you might want to visualize each of your rainbow archetypes deeply as you work in each energy center. Anodea Judith's *Chakra Balancing*, available from Sounds True, is an excellent introduction to yoga's traditional sun salutations, leading you through an exercise for each of the seven chakras that make up the energy system of our bodies.

Hunab Ku

A Courage Reading

Take a good look at **Eagle** 35. Sense its stony strength.

If you care to look closely at any fears you are presently holding, and explore your personal courage, select six other images at random. Write down these six images in a column, in the order you select them, and let each of them help to answer the following six questions:

1. Why am I afraid? Let the image you selected provide you with an answer. Look at all its layers of meaning.

2. Where did I draw my courage as a child?

3. What part of my body should I concentrate on in preparing for this challenge? Think about the color of the image you choose to place third and how it relates to your energy centers.

4. Who can assist me now? Do any of my potential helpers resemble the attributes of this fourth image? Think of the people you know, considering those who are close friends as well as people you know less well.

5. Is there an animal or a part of nature that can give me insights and strength?

6. What will be my courageous outcome? What will I learn?

Symbol Readings

The Bard: Telling Your Story

Focus your attention on **Bard** 37. He is a storyteller; he will help you read the other images and form your own personal story. Now select eleven images at random. Choose them in any fashion you wish, but here's one more idea for generating numbers randomly, using dice. Roll a pair of dice once to decide which color palette to choose from. (We placed eight and nine randomly. For this first roll, the integers of ten, eleven, and twelve can be added together to make one, two, and three. Also, count double sixes as a three.)

Roll the dice a second time to select one of the eleven numbers within that palette. Look down the red column for the 1-11 number and then follow the numbers to the right to identify the image number under your selected color palette. Count double sixes, or twelve, as a three. For example if you roll a six (indigo) and then a ten, look up **Vulture** 13.

— ROLL THE DICE —

ROLL A ONE OR A TEN	ROLL A TWO OR AN ELEVEN	ROLL A THREE OR A TWELVE	ROLL A FOUR	ROLL A FIVE (OR A NINE)	ROLL A SIX (OR AN EIGHT)	ROLL A SEVEN
Red	Orange	Yellow	Green	Blue	Indigo	Violet
1	12	23	34	33	22	11
2	13	24	35	32	21	10
3	14	25	36	31	20	9
4	15	26	37	30	19	8
5	16	27	38	29	18	7
6	17	28	39/39	28	17	6
7	18	29	38	27	16	5
8	19	30	37	26	15	4
9	20	31	36	25	14	3
10	21	32	35	24	13	2
11	22	33	34	23	12	1

Hunab Ku

Write down all eleven images in a column, with space to the right next to them. Now you're ready to create your story. In descending order, add any thoughts that arise from viewing the images this way:

1. Next to the first image, write: "This is my essence—who I am right now."

2. The second image is what gives my story its context, its setting. It tells me what is going on right now.

3. The third image represents the conflict that is entering my story. It is an obstacle standing in my way; it is my central challenge. It needs to be integrated to make my story come out with a happy, whole ending.

4. The fourth image is the root of my problem. It is my unconscious challenge.

5. The fifth image represents my past. I can learn from what this image teaches about what has gone before. It helps me better understand what has happened.

6. The sixth image represents my mind. It is my conscious state and is what fills my thoughts on a daily basis.

7. The seventh image shows me my near future—what is just around the corner. It represents the point I am rapidly moving toward.

8. The eighth image is my self-concept. It is who I think I really am.

9. The ninth image represents my hopes and my fears; it is a double-edged message. I may, without realizing it, project this image out to the world, and it is, therefore, what I am most likely to manifest in my life.

10. The tenth image represents my house. It is where I live, where I am most at home. Who is in this house with me? This is my physical and psychic space, and I share my innermost thoughts with this image.

11. The eleventh image characterizes the final outcome of this story, the denouement. It is how everything gets integrated and resolved.

BIBLIOGRAPHY

Angels/Archetypes/Astrology

Burt, Kathleen. *Archetypes of the Zodiac.* St. Paul, MN: Llewellyn Publications, 1990.

Cobb, Noel. *Archetypal Imagination: Glimpses of the Gods in Life and Art.* Hudson, NY: Lindisfarne Press, 1992.

Eliade, Mircea. *In the Two and the One.* Chicago: University of Chicago Press, 1962.

———. *Symbolism, the Sacred and the Arts.* New York: Crossroads, 1990.

Farrant, Sheila. *Symbols for Women: A Matrilineal Zodiac.* London: Unwin Paperbacks, 1989.

Fox, Matthew, and Rupert Sheldrake. *The Physics of Angels: Exploring the Realm Where Science and Spirit Meet.* San Francisco: HarperSanFrancisco, 1996.

Grasse, Ray. *The Waking Dream: Unlocking the Symbolic Language of Our Lives.* Wheaton, IL: Quest Books, 1996.

Griffin, David Ray, ed. *Archetypal Process: Self and Divine in Whitehead, Jung and Hillman.* Evanston, IL: Northwestern University Press, 1989.

Hanon, Geraldine Hatch. *Sacred Space: A Feminist View of Astrology.* Ithaca, NY: Firebrand Books, 1990.

Henry, Gray. "Regaining the Center." *Parabola* 25, no. 1 (February 2000): 78–80.

Howell, Alice O. *Jungian Symbolism in Astrology.* Wheaton, IL: Quest/Theosophical Publishing House, 1987.

Jung, Carl G. *Jung Collected Works: Psychology and Alchemy*, vol. 14. New York: Pantheon, 1963.

———. *Man and His Symbols.* London: Aldus Books, 1964.

———. *Mandala Symbolism.* Princeton, NJ: Princeton University Press, 1959.

———. *Memories, Dreams, Reflections.* New York: Random House, 1973.

———. "Synchronicity: Timing Is All." *Parabola* 25, no. 4 (November 2000): 56–58.

Lundsted, Betty. *Astrological Insights into Personality.* San Diego: Astro Computing Services, 1980.

Michel, John. *The Dimensions of Paradise.* London: Thames & Hudson, 1988.

———. *Secrets of the Stones: The Story of Astro-archaeology.* New York: Penguin, 1977.

Moolenburgh, H. C. *A Handbook of Angels.* Translated from the Dutch by Amina Marix-Evans. Saffron Walden, Essex, England: The C. W. Daniel Company, 1984.

Murdock, Maureen. *The Heroine's Journey.* Boston: Shambhala, 1990.

Narby, Jeremy. *The Cosmic Serpent: DNA and the Origins of Knowledge.* New York: Jeremy P. Tarcher/Putnam, 1998.

Newhouse, Flower A. *Rediscovering the Angels.* San Diego: The Christward Ministry, 1976.

Nichols, Sallie. *Jung and Tarot: An Archetypal Journey.* York Beach, ME: Samuel Weiser, 1980.

Oken, Alan. *Soul-Centered Astrology.* New York: Bantam Books, 1990.

Peat, F. David. *Synchronicity: The Bridge between Matter and Mind.* New York: Bantam, 1987.

Purce, Jill. *The Mystic Spiral: Journey of the Soul.* New York: Avon Books, 1974.

Sax, Boria. "The Spindle." *Parabola* 25, no. 4 (November 2000): 88–90.

Seward, Barbara. *The Symbolic Rose*. Woodstock, CT: Spring Publications, 1989.

Singer, June. *Androgyny*. New York: Doubleday, 1977.

South, Malcolm, ed. *Mythical and Fabulous Creatures: A Sourcebook and Research Guide*. New York: Peter Bedrick Books, 1988.

Von Franz, Marie-Louise. *Alchemical Active Imagination*. Boston: Shambhala, 1997.

Color Symbolism/Chakras

Birren, Faber. *Color and Human Response*. New York: Van Nostrand Reinhold Company, 1978.

———. *Color Psychology and Color Therapy*. Secaucus, NJ: Citadel Press, 1961.

Gage, John. *Color and Meaning: Art, Science and Symbolism*. Berkeley and Los Angeles, CA: University of California Press, 1999.

Gimbel, Theo. *Healing through Colour*. Essex, England: C. W. Daniel Company, 1980.

Goethe, Johann Wolfgang von. *Theory of Colours*. Cambridge, MA: The M.I.T. Press, 1970, 2002.

Heline, Corinne. *Color and Music in the New Age*. Marina del Rey, CA: DeVorss and Company Publishers, 1964.

Judith, Anodea. *Chakra Balancing*. Boulder, CO: Sounds True, 2003.

———. *Wheels of Life: A User's Guide to the Chakra System*. St. Paul, MN: Llewellyn, 1989.

Lüscher, Max. *The Lüscher Color Test*. Translated and edited by Ian Scott. New York: Random House, 1969.

Stein, Diane. *Stroking the Python: Women's Psychic Lives*. St. Paul, MN: Llewellyn, 1988.

Walker, Morton. *The Power of Color*. Wayne, NJ: Avery Publishing Group, 1989.

Earth Sites/Earth Wisdom/Labyrinths

Artress, Lauren. *Walking a Sacred Path: Rediscovering the Labyrinth as a Spiritual Tool*. New York: Riverhead Books, 1995.

Bahn, Paul G., and Jean Vertut. *Images of the Ice Age*. New York: Facts on File, 1988.

Ceram, C. W. *Gods, Graves, and Scholars: The Story of Archaeology*. New York: Alfred A. Knopf, 1967.

Cousineau, Phil, ed. *The Soul of the World: A Modern Book of Hours*. San Francisco: HarperSanFrancisco, 1993.

Curry, Helen. *The Way of the Labyrinth: A Powerful Meditation for Everyday Life*. New York: Penguin, 2000.

Devereux, Paul. *Re-Visioning the Earth: A Guide to Opening the Healing Channels between Mind and Nature*. New York: Fireside/Simon & Schuster, 1996.

Doob, Penelope Reed. *The Idea of the Labyrinth from Classical Antiquity through the Middle Ages*. Ithaca, NY: Cornell University Press, 1990.

Freeman, Mara. "Ti na Sorcha: Step into the Unearthly Light of Faerie." *Parabola* 26, no. 2 (May 2001): 10–14.

———. "The Wide-Spun Moment: Ecstasy and Madness in Celtic Tradition." *Parabola* 23, no. 2 (May 1998): 29–35.

Grant, Michael. *The Ancient Mediterranean*. New York: Penguin, 1969.

Heselton, Philip. *The Elements of Earth Mysteries.* Rockport, MA: Element, 1991.

Hoffman, Natasha, with Hamilton Hill. *The Standing Stones Speak: Messages from the Archangels Revealed.* Los Angeles: Renaissance Books, 2000.

James, Peter, and Rich Thorpe. *Ancient Mysteries.* New York: Random House, 1997.

Jaskolski, Helmut. *The Labyrinth: Symbol of Fear, Rebirth and Liberation.* Boston: Shambhala, 1997.

Jeanes, Rosemary. "Labyrinths." *Parabola* 4, no. 2 (May 1979): 12–15.

Kern, Hermann. *Through the Labyrinth: Designs and Meanings over 5,000 Years.* New York: Prestel, 2000.

Lawlor, Robert. *Voices of the First Day: Awakening in the Aboriginal Dreamtime.* Rochester, VT: Inner Traditions, 1991.

Lonegren, Sig. *Labyrinths: Ancient Myths and Modern Uses,* 2d ed. Glastonbury, England: Gothic Image Publications, 1996.

Mallam, Clark R. "Ideology from the Earth: Effigy Mounds in the Midwest." *Archeology* (July 1982): 58–64.

Mann, A. T. *Sacred Architecture.* Rockport, MA: Element, 1993.

McLuhan, T. C. *Cathedrals of the Spirit: The Message of Sacred Places.* New York: HarperCollins, 1996.

Michell, John. *Earth Spirit: Its Ways, Shrines, Mysteries.* London: Thames & Hudson, 1989.

———. *The Traveler's Key to Sacred England.* New York: Alfred A. Knopf, 1988.

Miller, Hamish, and Paul Broadhurst. *The Sun and the Serpent.* New York: Pendragon, 1994.

Milner, George R. *The Moundbuilders.* London: Thames & Hudson, 2004.

Molyneaux, Brian Leigh. *The Sacred Earth.* Boston: Little, Brown and Company, 1995.

Noel, Daniel. "Soul and Earth." *Parabola* 23, no. 2 (May 1990): 57–73.

Ó Nualláin, Seán. *Stone Circles in Ireland.* Dublin: Country House, 1995.

Owusu, Heike. *Symbols of Native America.* New York: Sterling Publishing Co., 1999.

Rigaud, Jean-Phillipe. "Art Treasures from the Ice Age, Lascaux Cave." *National Geographic* (October 1988): 482–499.

Rizzoli International Publications and HBJ Press, eds. *Stone Witnesses: The Grand Tour.* New York: HBJ Press, 1980.

Roberts, Elizabeth, and Elias Amidon, eds. *Earth Prayers from around the World.* San Francisco: HarperSanFrancisco, 1991.

Service, Alastair, and Jean Bradbery. *Megaliths and Their Mysteries: A Guide to the Standing Stones of Europe.* New York: Macmillan Publishing Co., 1979.

Simpson, Liz. *The Healing Energies of Earth.* Boston: Journey Editions/Periplus, 2000.

Speerstra, Karen. *The Earthshapers.* Happy Camp, CA: Naturegraph Publishers, 1980.

Swan, James A. *The Power of Place: Sacred Ground in Natural and Human Environments.* Wheaton, IL: Quest Books, 1991.

———. *Sacred Places: How the Living Earth Seeks Our Friendship.* Santa Fe, NM: Bear & Co., 1990.

World Confederation of Organizations of the Teaching Profession. *Man through His Art,* vol. III. New York: Graphic Society, 1965.

Goddess Culture

Ashe, Geoffrey. *Dawn behind the Dawn: A Search for the Earthly Paradise*. New York: Henry Holt, 1992.

Cleary, Thomas, and Sartaz Azziz. *Thoughts from Twilight Goddess: Spiritual Feminism and Feminist Spirituality*. Boston: Shambhala, 2002.

Downing, Christine. *The Goddess: Mythological Images of the Feminine*. New York: Crossroad, 1987.

Gadon, Elinor W. "The Life Cycle of the Goddess." *Woman of Power* (Summer 1989): 6–11.

———. *The Once and Future Goddess: A Symbol for Our Time*. San Francisco: Harper & Row Publishers, 1989.

Getty, Adele. *Goddess: Mother of Living Nature*. London: Thames and Hudson, 1990.

Gimbutas, Marija. *The Civilizations of the Goddess: The World of Old Europe*. San Francisco: HarperSanFrancisco, 1991.

———. *The Language of the Goddess*. San Francisco: HarperSanFrancisco, 1989.

Gleason, Judith. *Oya: In Praise of the Goddess*. Boston: Shambhala, 1987.

Graves, Robert. *The White Goddess: A Historical Grammar of Poetic Myth*. New York: Farrar, Straus and Giroux, 1948.

Gray, William G. *Evoking the Primal Goddess: Discovery of the Eternal Feminine Within*. St. Paul, MN: Llewellyn, 1989.

Hall, Nor. *The Moon and the Virgin: Reflections on the Archetypal Feminine*. New York: Harper & Row Publishers, 1980.

Harvey, Andrew, and Anne Baring. *The Divine Feminine: Exploring the Feminine Face of God around the World*. Berkeley, CA: Conari Press, 1996.

Johnson, Buffie. *Lady of the Beasts*. New York: Harper & Row Publishers, 1988.

Knight, Gareth. *The Rose Cross and the Goddess: The Quest for the Eternal Feminine Principle*. New York: Destiny Books, 1984.

Long, Asphodel P. *In a Chariot Drawn by Lions: The Search for the Female in Deity*. Freedom, CA: The Crossing Press, 1993.

Markale, Jean. *The Great Goddess: Reverence of the Divine Feminine from the Paleolithic to the Present*. Translated by Jody Gladding. Rochester, VT: Inner Traditions, 1997.

Matthews, Caitlin. *Sophia, Goddess of Wisdom*. New York: Harper Collins, 1991.

Mellaart, James. *Çatal Hüyük: A Neolithic Town in Anatolia*. New York: McGraw-Hill, 1967.

Mountainwater, Shekhinah. *Ariadne's Thread: A Workbook of Goddess Magic*. Freedom/Berkeley, CA: The Crossing Press, 1991.

Neumann, Erich. *The Great Mother*. Princeton, NJ: Princeton University Press, 1955.

Noble, Vicki. *Shakti Woman: Feeling Our Fire, Healing Our World*. San Francisco: HarperSanFrancisco, 1991.

Sjöö, Monica. *New Age and Armageddon: The Goddess or the Gurus? Towards a Feminist Vision of the Future*. London: The Women's Press, 1992.

———, and Barbara Mor. *The Great Cosmic Mother: Rediscovering the Religion of the Earth*. San Francisco: Harper & Row Publishers, 1987.

Stone, Merlin. *Ancient Mirrors of Womanhood*. Boston: Beacon Press, 1979.

———. *When God Was a Woman*. New York: Harcourt Brace Jovanovich/Dial Press, 1976.

Von Cles-Reden, Sibylle. *The Realm of the Great Goddess.* Englewood Cliffs, NJ: Prentice Hall, 1962.

Walker, Barbara. *The Woman's Dictionary of Symbols and Sacred Objects.* San Francisco: HarperSanFrancisco, 1988.

———. *The Woman's Encyclopedia of Myths and Secrets.* San Francisco: Harper & Row Publishers, 1983.

Welch, Lynda. *Goddess of the North.* York Beach, ME: Red Wheel/Samuel Weiser, 2001.

Wilde, Lyn Webster. *On the Trail of the Women Warriors: The Amazons in Myth and History.* New York: St. Martin's Press, 1999.

Health and Wholeness

Chia, Mantak. *Taoist Cosmic Healing: Chi Kung Color Healing Principles for Detoxification and Rejuvenation.* Rochester, VT: Destiny Books, 2003.

Groopman, Jerome. *The Anatomy of Hope.* New York: Random House, 2004.

Mariechild, Diane. *Mother Wit: A Guide of Healing and Psychic Development.* Freedom, CA: The Crossing Press, 1981.

Mindell, Arnold. *The Shaman's Body.* San Francisco: HarperSanFrancisco, 1993.

Murphy, Michael. *The Future of the Body: Exploration into the Further Evolution of Human Nature.* New York: Jeremy P. Tarcher/Perigee Books, 1993.

Myss, Caroline. *Anatomy of the Spirit: Seven Stages of Power and Healing.* New York: Harmony Books, 1966.

Osbon, Diane K., ed. *Reflections on the Art of Living: A Joseph Campbell Companion.* New York: HarperCollins, 1991.

Peat, F. David. *Lighting the Seventh Fire: The Spiritual Ways, Healing and Science of the Native American.* Secaucus, NJ: Carol Publishing Group, 1994.

Simpkinson, Charles, and Anne Simpkinson, eds. *Sacred Stories: A Celebration of the Power of Stories to Transform and Heal.* San Francisco: HarperSanFrancisco, 1993.

Mythology and Sacred Wisdom

Alexander, Harley Burr. *The World's Rim: Great Mysteries of the North American Indians.* Lincoln, NE: University of Nebraska Press, 1953.

Argüelles, José. *The Mayan Factor: Path beyond Technology.* Santa Fe, NM: Bear & Co., 1989.

Atwater, P. M. H. *The Magical Language of Runes.* Santa Fe, NM: Bear & Co., 1986.

Barks, Coleman. *The Essential Rumi.* New York: HarperCollins, 1995.

Barnstone, Willis. *The Other Bible: Ancient Alternative Scriptures.* San Francisco: HarperSanFrancisco, 1984.

Battiste, Marie. *Reclaiming Indigenous Voice and Vision.* Vancouver, British Columbia: University of British Columbia Press, 2000.

Bayley, Harold. *The Lost Language of Symbolism: An Inquiry into the Origins of Certain Letters, Words, Names, Fairy-Tales, Folklore and Mythologies.* London: Ernest Benn Limited, 1912.

Bierlein, J. F. *Parallel Myths.* New York: Random House, 1994.

Boorstin, Daniel. *The Creators: A History of Heroes of the Imagination.* New York: Random House, 1992.

Broomfield, John. *Other Ways of Knowing: Recharting Our Future with Ageless Wisdom.* Rochester, VT: Inner Traditions, 1997.

Bulfinch, Thomas. *Bulfinch's Mythology.* New York: Harper & Row, 1970.

Burkert, Walter. *Creation of the Sacred: Tracks of Biology in Early Religions.* Cambridge, MA: Harvard University Press, 1996.

Bushnell, G. H. S. *Ancient Arts of the Americas.* New York: Frederick A. Praeger, 1985.

Calleman, Carl Johan. *The Mayan Calendar and the Transformation of Consciousness.* Rochester, VT: Bear & Co., 2004.

Campbell, Joseph. *The Hero's Journey.* New York: Harper & Row, 1990.

———. *Historical Atlas of World Mythology, vol. 1: The Way of the Animal Powers.* New York: Harper & Row, 1988.

———. *The Masks of God: Primitive Mythology.* New York: Viking Press, 1959.

———. *The Mythic Image.* Princeton, NJ: Princeton University Press, 1974.

———. *Transformation of Myth through Time.* New York: Harper & Row, 1990.

Casson, Lionel, et al. *Mysteries of the Past.* New York: American Heritage Publishing Co., 1977.

Cavendish, Richard, ed. *An Illustrated Encyclopedia of Mythology.* New York: Crescent Books, 1984.

Coe, Michael E. *The Maya.* New York: Praeger Publishers, 1966.

Cooper, Thomas. *A Time before Deception: Truth in Communications, Culture and Ethics.* Santa Fe, NM: Clear Light Publications, 1998.

Drury, Nevill. *The Elements of Shamanism.* Dorset, England: Element, 1989.

Easwaran, Eknath. *Meditation: Commonsense Directions for an Uncommon Life.* Petaluma, CA: Blue Mountain Press, 1978.

Eliade, Mircea. *Rites and Symbols of Initiation.* New York: Harper & Row, 1965.

Elkins, David N. *Beyond Religion.* Wheaton, IL: Quest Books, 1998.

Faivre, Antoine. *The Eternal Hermes.* Grand Rapids, MI: Phanes Press, 1995.

Frazer, James George. *The Golden Bough* (various volumes). London: The MacMillan Press, 1913.

Gebser, Jean. *The Ever-Present Origin.* Translated by Noel Barstad. Athens, OH: Ohio University Press, 1985.

Griffin-Pierce, Trudy. *Earth Is My Mother, Sky Is My Father: Space, Time and Astronomy in Navajo Sandpainting.* Albuquerque, NM: University of New Mexico Press, 1998.

Hall, Manly P. *The Secret Teachings of All Ages.* New York: Jeremy P. Tarcher/Penguin, 2003.

Hamilton, Edith. *Mythology: Timeless Tales of Gods and Heroes.* Boston: Little, Brown and Company, 1942.

Hancock, Graham, and Santha Faiia. *Heaven's Mirror: Quest for the Lost Civilization.* New York: Penguin, 1998.

Hauck, Dennis William. *The Emerald Tablet: Alchemy for Personal Transformation.* New York: Arkana/Penguin, 1999.

Hope, Murry. *Practical Celtic Magic: A Working Guide to the Magical Heritage of the Celtic Races.* Wellingborough, England: Aquarian Press/Thorsons, 1987.

James, E. O. *The Ancient Gods.* New York: G. P. Putnam's Sons, 1960.

Keck, L. Robert. *Sacred Quest: The Evolution and Future of the Human Soul.* West Chester, PA: Chrysalis Books, 2000.

Knight, Gareth. *Tarot and Magic: Images for Rituals and Pathworking.* Rochester, VT: Destiny Books, 1986.

Larson, Cynthia S. "Comes True, Being Hoped For: The Hopi Understanding of How Things Change." *Parabola* 25, no. 1 (February 2000): 84–87.

Lash, John. *The Seeker's Handbook: The Complete Guide to Spiritual Pathfinding.* New York: Harmony Books, 1990.

Leeming, David Adams. *The World of Myth.* New York: Oxford University Press, 1992.

Line, David, and Julia Line. *Fortune Telling by Runes: A Guide to Casting and Interpreting the Ancient European Rune Stones.* Wellingborough, England: The Aquarian Press, 1984.

Logiadou-Platonos, Sosso. *Knossos: The Palace of Minos: A Survey of the Minoan Civilization.* Translated by David Hardy. Athens: I. Mathiouakis & Co., 1986.

Mahdi, Louise Carus, Steven Foster, and Meredith Little, eds. *Betwixt and Between: Patterns of Masculine and Feminine Initiation.* La Salle, IL: Open Court, 1987.

Matthews, John, ed. *At the Table of the Grail.* London: Routledge & Kegan Paul, 1984.

———. *Sources of the Grail: An Anthology.* Hudson, NY: Lindisfarne Press, 1997.

Matthiessen, Peter. *Indian Country.* New York: Viking, 1984.

May, Rollo. *The Cry for Myth.* New York: W. W. Norton and Co., 1991.

McFadden, Steven. *Profiles in Wisdom: Native Elders Speak about the Earth.* Santa Fe, NM: Bear & Co., 1991.

Mitchell, Stephen. *Tao Te Ching.* New York: Harper & Row, 1988.

O'Donohue, John. *Anam Cara: A Book of Celtic Wisdom.* New York: HarperCollins, 1997.

———. *Eternal Echoes: Exploring Our Yearning to Belong.* New York: HarperCollins, 1999.

Pálsson, Hermann, and Paul Edwards. *Egil's Saga.* New York: Penguin, 1976.

Piggott, Stuart. *The Druids.* London: Thames and Hudson, 1968.

Powell, T. G. E. *The Celts.* New York: Thames and Hudson, 1983.

Readers' Digest, eds. *The World's Last Mysteries.* Pleasantville, NY: The Reader's Digest Association, 1976.

Rinpoche, Sogyal. *The Tibetan Book of Living and Dying.* San Francisco: HarperSanFrancisco, 1992.

Santillana, Giorgio de, and Hertha Von Dechend. *Hamlet's Mill: An Essay on Myth and the Frame of Time.* Boston: Gambit, 1969.

Schele, Linda, and David Freidel. *A Forest of Kings: The Untold Story of the Ancient Maya.* New York: William Morrow & Co., 1990.

Sharkey, John. *Celtic Mysteries: The Ancient Religion.* London: Thames and Hudson, 1975.

Sheldrake, Rupert, et al. *Chaos Creativity and Cosmic Consciousness.* Rochester, VT: Park Street Press, 2001.

Singer, June. *Seeing through the Visible World.* New York: Harper & Row, 1990.

Sullivan, William. *The Secret of the Incas.* New York: Three Rivers Press/Random House, 1996.

Suzuki, David, and Peter Knudtson. *Wisdom of the Elders: Sacred Native Stories of Nature.* New York: Bantam Books, 1992.

Temple, Robert K. G. *The Sirius Mystery.* New York: St. Martin's Press, 1976.

Thornkide, Joseph J., Jr., ed. *Discovery of Lost Worlds.* New York: American Heritage Publishing Co., 1979.

Thorsson, Edred. *At the Well of Wyrd: A Handbook of Runic Divination.* York Beach, ME: Samuel Weiser, 1988.

Thunderhorse, Iron, and Donn LeVie, Jr. *Return of the Thunderbeings.* Santa Fe, NM: Bear & Co., 1990.

Vogel, Virgel J. *This Country Was Ours.* New York: Harper & Row, 1972.

Von List, Guido. Edited, introduced, and translated by Stephen E. Flowers. *The Secret of the Runes.* Rochester, VT: Destiny Books, 1988.

Weigle, Marta. *Spiders and Spinsters: Women and Mythology.* Albuquerque, NM: University of New Mexico Press, 1982.

Number Symbolism and Sacred Geometry

Arrien, Angeles. *Signs of Life: The Five Universal Shapes and How to Use Them.* Sonoma, CA: Arcus Publishing Company, 1992.

Conty, Patrick. "The Geometry of the Labyrinth." *Parabola* 17, no. 2 (May 1992): 4–14.

Howell, Alice O. *The Dove in the Stone.* Wheaton, IL: Quest Books, 1988.

———. *The Web in the Sea: Jung, Sophia and the Geometry of the Soul.* Wheaton, IL: Quest Books, 1993.

Lawlor, Robert. *Sacred Geometry: Philosophy and Practice.* London: Thames and Hudson, 1982.

Tyson, Donald. *New Millennium Magic: A Complete System of Self-Realization.* St. Paul, MN: Llewellyn Publications, 1996.

Von Franz, Marie-Louise. *Number and Time: Reflections Leading toward a Unification of Depth Psychology and Physics.* Translated by Andrea Dykes. Evanston, IL: Northwestern University Press, 1974.

Wright, Craig. *The Maze and the Warrior: Symbols in Architecture, Theology, and Music.* Cambridge, MA: Harvard University Press, 2001.

INDEX

A

action, 138–139
addiction, 142–143
adult, 196–199
Ahau pictogram, 188–190
air, 148–151
Alaca Hüyük, Turkey, 181
alchemy, 38–39
Anahata chakra, 135.
  See also green
androgyny, 94–95
angel guardians, 218–219
angel guide, 292–295
Anja chakra, 223, 231
ankh, 200–203
Apollo, 109
Aquarius, age of, 182
archetypes, xiii–xv
Aries, 6
Artemis, 109
artist, 100–103
awakening, 26–27

B

balance, 228–231
bard, 160–163, 316–317
bear, xxii, 1–3
bee, honeybee, 268–271
beliefs, 230
birth, 66–67
blockage, 178–179
blue
  adult, 196–199
  ankh, 200–203
  boat, 208–211
  goat, 184–187
  magician, 204–207

pelican, 212–215
Saturn, 176–179
sound, 192–195
teacher, 188–191
water bearer, 180–183
winged dog, 216–219
boat, 208–211
bones, 240–243
Book of Changes
  (*I Ching*), 42
breathing
  air, 150–151
  dolphins and, 142
  meditation and, 291
bridge, 164–167
bull, 224–227
butterfly, 284–287

C

calendar, xi–xii, 189
Cancer, 270–271
Capricorn, 186–187
Catal Hüyük, Turkey,
  256–257
cave art, 52–53, 248–249
centaur, 136–139
chakras
  blue, 176–219
  green, 132–175
  indigo, 220–263
  orange, 44–87
  red, 1–43
  violet, 264–301
  yellow, 88–131
chalice, 252–255
Chalice Well, England,
  220–221
change, 122–123

Chartres' Cathedral, France,
  276–279
child, 64–67
choice, 230–231
Churchill, Winston, 59
circle, 46, 202
coin, 196–197
color, 239
colored lights, 187
community, 134–135
conflict, 10–11
confusion, 118–119
connection, 158–159
consciousness, 266–267
constellation, 132–135
control, 86–87
counselor, 232–235
courage, 170–171
courage reading, 315
coyote, 116–117, 119
creativity, 102–103
cross, 156–159, 202
crown, 296–299
crown chakra. *See* violet

D

dark matter, 266
death, 258–259
Dogon, 20–21, 23, 89
dog, winged, 216–219
dolphin, 140–143
double spiral, 288–291
dove, 124–127
dragon, 128–131
dreams, 218–219, 222–223
dreamtime, 262
duality, 303

Hunab Ku

326

E

eagle, 168–171
earth, xiii–xiv, 16–19
ecstasy, 250–251
egg, 20–23, 25
eight, 29–31, 277–279
eighteen, 69–71, 237–239
elders, 240–243
eleven, 41–43, 265–267
emerald, 171
emotions, 270–271
energy, 82–83, 106–107
explicit knowledge, 190–191
eyes, 233, 234

F

father, 12–15
fear, 130–131
female, 48–51
feng shui, 62, 130
fertility, 50–51
fifteen, 57–59, 249–251
fifth chakra, 191.
   See also blue
fire, 104–107
first chakra. *See* red
five
   double spiral, 289–291
   earth, 17–19
   protector and, 55
four, 13–15, 293–295
fourteen, 53–55, 253–255
fourth chakra. *See* green
full spectrum lighting, 187
Futami Rocks, Japan, 165–166

G

gates, 246–247
Gemini, 94–95
geomancy, 62, 130
gestation, 22–23
giant, 84–87
goat, 184–187
Goddess
   as balance, 228–231
   crown of, 297, 298
   dog guardians for, 217, 218
   honeybee and, 269
   meander and, 70
   Mother, 57–59
   triangle and, 114
   Venus, 48–51
   Virgo and, 98
   water and, 60–63
grail, 221, 252–255
Great Bear, xxii, 1–3
Great Mother. *See* Goddess
Great Serpent Mound, United States, 24–27
green
   air, 148–151
   bard, 160–163
   bridge, 164–167
   centaur, 136–139
   constellation, 132–135
   cross, 156–159
   dolphin, 140–143
   dragon and, 131
   eagle, 168–171
   healer, 144–147
   Hunab Ku, 152–155
   phoenix, 172–175
growth, 110–111
guardian, 218–219
guide, angel, 292–295

H

Hanged Man, 71
harmony, 114–115
healer, 144–147
Hercules, 85, 86
hermaphrodite, 93–95
Holy Grail, 221, 253–255
homes, xiv–xv
honeybee, 268–271
hope, 174–175
horse, 204–207
hummingbird, 80–83
Hunab Ku, xii–xiii, 152–155, 307

I

I Ching (Book of Changes), 42
ideograms, 61
imagination, 238–239
indigo
   balance, 228–231
   bull, 224–227
   chalice, 252–255
   counselor, 232–235
   light, 236–239
   moon, 220–223
   shaman, 248–251
   sphinx, 260–263
   square, 244–247
   vulture, 256–259
   wise old one, 240–243
infinity, 288–291
initiation, 34–35
insight, 38–39
insight reading, 310–312
inspiration, 90–91
intuition, 58–59
intuitives, 58–59
Isis, 89, 90, 202–203

J

jade, 171
Jesus Christ
    angel and, 294
    cross symbol and, 157, 158
    Holy Grail and, 221, 253
    reward and, 298
journey, 210–211

K

Kabbalism, 267
kiva, 32–35
knotwork, 112–113
knowledge, 190–191, 302
Kokopelli, 160–163

L

labyrinth
    mystic and, 276–279
    spin and, 222
    symbol of, 32–35
lead, 178
Leo, 54–55
life, 202–203
light, 187, 236–239
lioness, 52–55
logic, 14–15
lover/relationships, 154–155

M

magician, 204–207
mandala, 222
manifestation, 274–275
Manipura chakra, 91. *See also* yellow
Mary, Virgin, 98, 294
mattang, 12–13, 14–15
matter, 18–19
Mayan people
    Ahau pictogram, 188–189
    calendar of, xi–xii, 49
    culture of, x–xi
    eagle and, 168–169, 170
    Hunab Ku of, xii–xiii, 152–155
meander, 68–71
meditation, 290–291
menstruation, 49, 223
message, 294–295
moon, 220–223
Mother. *See also* Goddess
    earth as, 18–19
    spirals as, 57–59
    vulture as, 258
    water and, 62–63
Mother Earth, 73
mountain, 76–79
movement, 62–63
Muladhara chakra, 3. *See also* red
music, 160–163, 194–195
mystic, 276–279

N

Nazca Lines, Peru, 80–81
nine, 33–35, 273–275
nineteen, 73–75, 233–235
nurturing, 234–235

O

old one, wise, 240–243
omphalos, 76–79
one
    bear, 1–3
    supreme primal number, 39
    unicorn, 305–307
opening, 246–247
orange
    child, 64–67
    giant, 84–87
    hummingbird, 80–83
    lioness, 52–55
    meander, 68–71
    mother, 56–59
    mountain, 76–79
    player, 72–75
    sun, 44–47
    Venus, 48–51
    water, 60–63
Osiris, 89, 90, 202
ouroboros, 40–43
owl, 240–241, 300–303

P

passage, 166–167
peace, 125, 126–127
peacock, 36–39
pelican, 212–215
perfectionism, 98–99
phoenix, 172–175
Picts, 225
pig, 72–75
pineal gland, 227, 231
Pisces, 142–143
pituitary gland, 299
player, 72–75
power, 206–207
practicality, 186–187

Q

quest, 254–255

Hunab Ku

R

rainbow reading, 313–315
ram, 4–7
readings, symbol, 310–317
rebirth, 286–287
red
  bear, xxii, 1–3
  earth, 16–19
  father, 12–15
  labyrinth, 32–35
  ouroboros, 40–43
  peacock, 36–39
  ram, 4–7
  scorpion, 8–11
  serpent, 24–27
  weaver-warrior, 28–31
  womb, 20–23
reed ideogram, 60–61
relationships/lover, 154–155
released soul, 284–287
rest, 242–243
revelation, 78–79
reversal, 70–71
reward, 298–299
risk, 6–7
Rosetta Stone, 201

S

sacred places, xiii–xiv
sacrifice, 214–215
Sagittarius, 138–139
sandpaintings, 144–147
Saturn, 176–179
scarab, 272–275
scorpion, 8–11
second chakra. *See* orange
sensates, 58
sensuality, 74–75
serpent, 24–27, 146. *See also* snake
service, 182–183
seven, 25–27, 281–283
seventeen, 65–67, 241–243
seventh chakra, 271.
  See also violet
shadows, 178–179
shaman, 248–251
Sirius, 21, 88–91
six, 21–23, 285–287
sixteen, 61–63, 245–247
sixth chakra, 223, 227.
  See also indigo
snake. *See also* serpent
  ouroboros, 40–43
  peacock and, 39
  sound and, 192–193
solar disk, 44–45
solitude, 2–3
song, 162–163
soul, released, 284–287
sound, 192–195
sphinx, 260–263
spider, 100–103
spin, 21, 222
spirals
  double spiral, 288–291
  as mother, 57–59
  universe symbol, 264–265, 266
  World Egg and, 21, 23
square, 244–247
star, 88–91, 132–135
stones, 120–121, 264–265
strength, 226–227
success, 46–47
sun, 44–47
survival, 30–31
Svadhisthana chakra, 51.
  See also orange
swirls, 177
symbol readings, 310–317
synchronicity, xvii, 42

T

tacit knowledge, 190–191
Tao, 267
Tarot cards, 71
Taurus, 224–227
ten, 37–39, 269–271
third chakra. *See* yellow
third eye, 227, 231
thirteen
  beliefs about, xviii
  Venus, 49–51
  vulture, 257–259
thirty, 117–119
thirty-eight, 149–151, 157–159
thirty-five, 137–139, 169–171
thirty-four, 133–135, 173–175
thirty-nine, 153–155
thirty-one, 121–123, 185–187
thirty-seven, 145–147, 161–163
thirty-six, 141–143, 165–167
thirty-three, 129–131, 177–179
thirty-two, 125–127, 181–183
three
  crown and, 297–299
  hummingbird and, 82
  scorpion and, 9–11
  triple spiral, 58, 59
throat chakra. *See* fifth chakra
time, 262–263
tortoise, 17–19
tree of life, 280–283
triangle, 112–115, 228–229
trickster, 116–119, 251
turtle, 17–19
twelve, 45–47, 261–263
twenty, 77–79, 229–231
twenty-eight, 109–111, 197–199
twenty-five, 97–99, 209–211

INDEX

twenty-four, 93–95, 213–215
twenty-nine, 112–115, 193–195
twenty-one, 81–83, 225–227
twenty-seven, 105–107, 201–203
twenty-six, 101–103, 205–207
twenty-three, 89–91, 217–219
twenty-two, 85–87, 221–223
twins, 92–95, 109
two, 5–7, 301–303

U

unconsciousness, 42–43
understanding, 282–283
unicorn, 304–307
unity, 306–307
universe, 264–267

V

Venus, xi, 48–51, 201
vibration, 194–195
violet
    angel guide, 292–295
    crown, 296–299
    double spiral, 288–291
    honeybee, 268–271
    mystic, 276–279
    owl, 300–303
    released soul, 284–287
    scarab, 272–275
    unicorn, 304–307
    universe, 264–267
    vision, 280–283
virgin, 96–99
Virgin Mary, 98, 294
Virgo, 98–99

vision, 280–283
Visuddha chakra, 177. *See also* blue
vitality, 82–83
vulture, 256–259

W

warrior-weaver, 28–31
water, 60–63, 68–71
water bearer, 180–183
waves, 194
weaver-warrior, 28–31
wheel, 120–123
White Horse of Uffington, 204–205
wholeness, 146–147
winged dog, 216–219
wisdom
    owl and, 302–303
    peacock and, 37
    snake and, 26, 27
wise old one, 240–243
womb, 20–23
wonder, 278–279
work, 198–199
work reading, 312–313
world navels, 76–79

Y

yantra, 222
yellow
    artist, 100–103
    dove, 124–127
    dragon, 128–131
    fire, 104–107
    star, 88–91
    triangle, 112–115
    trickster, 116–119
    twins, 92–95

virgin, 96–99
wheel, 120–123
youth, 108–111
youth, 108–111

Hunab Ku